THROUGH THE YEAR WITH PADRE PIO

Through the Year With Padre Pio

365 Daily Readings

PATRICIA TREECE

CHARIS

SERVANT PUBLICATIONS
ANN ARBOR, MICHIGAN

Charis Books is an imprint of Servant Publications especially designed to serve Roman Catholics.

Scripture verses not otherwise noted are taken from the Revised Standard Version of the Bible, copyrighted 1946, 1952, 1971 by the Division of Christian Education of the National Council of Churches of Christ in the USA. Used by permission. Verses marked JB are taken from the *Jerusalem Bible*. Quotes from Douay-Rheims and Challoner-Rheims are indicated.

Padre Pio's Letters Vols. I, II, III, and IV, *The Voice of Padre Pio*, *"Consigli-Esortazioni di Padre Pio Pietrelcina," "Have a Good Day,"* and archival materials are all quoted with the permission of The Capuchin Friars of Our Lady of Grace Friary, San Giovanni, Rotondo, Italy.

Published by Servant Publications
P.O. Box 8617
Ann Arbor, Michigan 48107
www.servantpub.com

Cover design: Alan Furst Inc., Minneapolis, Minn.

03 04 05 06 10 9 8 7 6 5 4 3 2 1

Printed in the United States of America
ISBN 1-56955-277-0

Library of Congress Cataloging-in-Publication Data
Pio, of Pietrelcina, Saint, 1887-1968.
  [Correspondence. English. Selections]
  Through the year with Padre Pio : 365 daily readings / [compiled by]
Patricia Treece.
    p. cm.
Includes bibliographical references.
  ISBN 1-56955-277-0 (alk. paper)
  1. Pio, of Pietrelcina, Saint, 1887-1968--Correspondence. 2.
Capuchins--Italy--Correspondence. 3. Catholic
Church--Italy--Clergy--Correspondence. 4. Devotional calendars. I.
Treece, Patricia. II. Title.
  BX2350.3.P56213 2003
  242'.2--dc21
                                                                2003014547

For
my friends of many years,
Alice Williams and Sister Mary Veronica, o.c.d.
in love and gratitude
for all you mean to me and
for the blessings your steadfast prayers
have obtained for me and mine

And

For

Francis and Mary Levy
Alex and Mia Lipski
Don and Sherry Panec
With loving thanks
for your friendship,
your help, especially your prayers,
and above all, your example
of joy and holiness in marriages that make God smile

About This Book

While this book provides 365 days, a full year's worth, of readings from Scripture and Padre Pio, I have tied these pages to neither the calendar nor the liturgical year, in order that one may begin their use at any point in the year.

What are the sources for Padre Pio's readings? Unlike many important saints, Padre Pio was not a diarist, nor did he write an autobiography. Upon occasion, at the request of his spiritual directors, he did write down details of certain incidents, such as his reception in 1918 of the stigmata. Fortunately he wrote thousands of letters. Most of the excerpts in this book are taken from his four volumes of correspondence.

Volume one, the reader may be interested to note, is the young Pio's correspondence with his two spiritual directors, Padre Agostino and Padre Benedetto, during his seminarian years and the earliest years of his priesthood. We have these letters due to Pio's terrible health, which forced him to pass roughly seven years, from May 1909 to February 1916, outside the friary at his parental home in his native Pietrelcina.

Volume two is composed of letters of spiritual direction to Rafaella Cerase and her responses. Padre Pio led this Italian noblewoman to holiness, though he met her in person only on her deathbed. The huge volume three [I have used the first edition which has just been superseded by a second] contains spiritual direction for a number of people, primarily women who became Pio's spiritual daughters from roughly the World War I era to 1922.

After that Pio's life was so harried that he could rarely write to anyone. I have quoted very little from volume four, letters to various sorts of people, because this volume is at present available only in Italian. The others you may purchase in English through the friary of Padre Pio or through the Padre Pio shrine in Barto, Pennsylvania, which is affiliated with the friary. See page 320 for the address and phone number.

Other readings are reminiscences by friars who lived with the saint. There are also a few from those who were his spiritual children or whose lives were changed by visiting or by simply seeing him. All non-letter materials are either from the archives of the friary, authored by his confreres or published in the friary's English-language publication, *The Voice of Padre Pio*, sources which provide us with the utmost authenticity. Anything written by myself is also based on these first-person accounts.

For those who are inspired to read more about Padre Pio, I suggest *Padre Pio of Pietrelcina: Everybody's Cyrenean,* a biography by Pio's confrere Alessandro of Ripabottoni, published by Pio's friary. Of the complete biographies readily available in the U.S. from American publishers, Bernard Ruffin's *Padre Pio* (OSV) is felt by the friary to be pretty accurate. *Meet Padre Pio,* (Servant) which I wrote with the cooperation of the friary, is a shorter introduction to his life.

Those who wish to read about the mystical phenomena associated with Padre Pio's life—bilocation, the odor of sanctity, his near inedia, and his stigmata—will find this in context in my *The Sanctified Body,* while my books *Nothing Short of a Miracle* and *Apparitions of Modern Saints* contain chapters on inexplicable cures attributed to Pio's intercession since his death. Finally, if this book whets your appetite for another devotional featuring Padre Pio, there is my *Quiet Moments With Padre Pio* (Servant). All these books are listed with publisher information in the "Further Reading" section at the back of this book.

Introduction

A Spiritual Model for Our Times

Any person trying to live a spiritual life as the twenty-first century unfolds is doing so under siege by an unspiritual culture. While his great holiness would make St. Padre Pio a powerful person to have at one's side on life's spiritual journey in any era, the fact that Christian life is particularly embattled today makes Pio an invaluable spiritual guide for this moment.

Padre Pio died September 23, 1968, and was canonized in May 2001. Like a surprising number of saints who lived in the last 150 years, the thrust of his life and spirituality were determined by a guiding vision Pio had as he teetered between childhood and adolescence. Pio's guiding vision is unique, however.

Most visions of this type are beautiful, but the boy Francis Forgione, of a tiny southern Italian farm town called Pietrelcina, had a terrifying vision that featured Satan and Christ. Young Francis confronted a giant figure with whom he was forced, in fear and completely against his wishes, to do battle. At his side, urging him on, was Christ. When the boy, to his own surprise, emerged victorious, Christ let him know that battling Satan in a contest for his own soul and those of others would be his life's work.

Shortly thereafter Francis Forgione entered the Capuchin Franciscan Order (the branch of Franciscans whose robes have the pointed hoods called cowls). There he was renamed Pio, and after years of study he became a priest.

During his eighty-one years Padre Pio gave consummate guidance in the spiritual life to a vast number of people. He heard roughly a million confessions, wrote thousands of letters, and gave occasional conferences to small groups of spiritual seekers. He led a surprising number of these people to spiritual heights.

Padre Pio certainly attained these heights himself—always, however, in struggle and in darkness regarding how he stood with God. His struggles with himself and with darkness also makes him a figure for our time.

There are other aspects of Padre Pio's life that most of us certainly cannot identify with: his stigmata, bilocations, odor of sanctity, levitation, ability to replace by prayer most of the food and sleep normal people require, and mental gifts of prophecy and reading hearts. But these charisms, which helped him carry out God's work, are irrelevant to his journey to sanctity and his role as a model for others. As Padre Aurelio and other friars who lived with Pio have said, his holiness was not what drew them to him: It was his humanity, his sense of humor, his kindness, his sympathetic understanding, and his great-hearted tolerance for others.

I hope you will see all these traits in these pages of Padre Pio's spiritual wisdom and guidance for your soul and mine. If you find here something that encourages you, that clears up some misunderstanding or in any other way makes a difference in your life, Padre Pio, who is still very busy about God's work even after his death, will certainly be pleased.

~ . The Door of the Heart ~

Give glory to the Lord of lords: for his mercy endureth for ever.
PSALM 135:1, DOUAY-RHEIMS

Before the Lord abandons us, we should have to abandon him. In a word, we should first have to close the door of our heart to him, and even then, how many times does he not stretch out his hand to us to arrest our headlong dash toward the precipice! How many times, when we had abandoned him, has he not readmitted us to his loving embrace! How good our God is!

... Open your soul more and more to divine hope, have more trust in the divine mercy.

Letters, Vol. 2, 153

Lord, may the door of my heart always remain open to you.

~ 2. The Humility of a Saint ~

"So you also, when you have done all that is commanded you, say, 'We are unworthy servants; we have only done what was our duty.'"
LUKE 17:10

I pray for ... [the Cerase sisters, his spiritual daughters] more than I pray for myself. The Lord knows that I am telling the truth. The reason why I pray less for myself has no reference to virtue, my dear Father [his spiritual director], but rather to my unworthiness, which prevents me [from] asking for more graces, since I am becoming more and more undeserving of the increase of heavenly favors.

Letters, Vol. 3, 26

Lord, your saint Padre Pio sees clearly his unworthiness to receive great graces. I, on the other hand, tend to be complacent about my spiritual state and take almost for granted your goodness to me. If I can't equal Padre Pio in humility, let me be ever increasingly grateful for all you do for me.

∽ 3. Of the Bitter and the Sweet ∽

Blessed be the God and Father of our Lord Jesus Christ, a gentle Father and the God of all consolation, who comforts us in all our sorrows, so that we can offer others, in their sorrows, the consolation that we have received from God ourselves. Indeed, as the sufferings of Christ overflow to us, so, through Christ, does our consolation overflow. When we are made to suffer, it is for your consolation and salvation. When, instead, we are comforted, this should be a consolation to you, supporting you in patiently bearing the same sufferings as we bear. And our hope for you is confident, since we know that, sharing our sufferings, you will also share our consolations.

2 CORINTHIANS 1:3-7, JB

Firstly I want to tell you that Jesus needs those who groan with him at human sinfulness, and for this reason, he is leading you along paths filled with suffering, about which you tell me in your letter. But may his charity always be blessed—that charity which knows how to mix the sweet with the bitter and convert the transitory sufferings of life to eternal reward.

Letters, Vol. 3, 417

Lord, keep me sweet, not bitter, when I have to suffer, so that I may encourage others going down the same path.

∼ 4. He Who Has Helped You Will Continue ∼

If, because of one man's trespass, death reigned through that one man, much more will those who receive the abundance of grace and the free gift of righteousness reign in life through the one man Jesus Christ.

ROMANS 5:17

As regards your spiritual state, I recommend that you never fear, but on the contrary, I exhort you to confide more in divine mercy, humbling yourself before the mercy of our God, and thanking him for all the favors he wants to grant you. By doing this you will defy and overcome all the anger of hell. Do not fear, my dear daughter. He who has helped you up to now will continue his work of salvation. Without divine grace would you have been able to overcome so many crises and wars to which your soul was subjected? Therefore the same grace will do the rest.

Letters, Vol. 3, 668–69

Thank you, Lord, for all the graces of each day, from food to eat and sleep at night, to my family and friends. Thank you for being with me in hard times and joyous ones. May I always trust in your mercy and love.

∼ 5. Our Natural Materialistic Inclinations ∼

And he said to them, "Take heed, and beware of all covetousness; for a man's life does not consist in the abundance of his possessions."
LUKE 12:15

Just as the bees sometimes fly great distances without hesitation to reach fields where they have a favorite flowerbed and then, tired but satisfied and laden with pollen, return to the honeycomb to complete the fertile and silent work of transforming the nectar of flowers into nectar of life, so must you, after having gathered it, meditate on it with attention, examine its elements, and search for the hidden meaning. It will then appear to you in all its splendor; it will acquire the power of doing away with your natural materialistic inclinations; it will have the virtue of transforming them into pure and sublime ascensions of the spirit, which will bring together ever more closely your heart with the divine heart of your Lord.

Tra I misteri della scienza e le luci della fede,
Giorgio Festa, 172

Father, how easy it is to get caught up in materialism by so many kinds of greed: the greed for beauty in surroundings and clothes; the greed for security, whether in bank and brokerage accounts or money in a sock; the greed for fine foods. Help me to keep my eye on the true meaning of life, so that every kind of materialism may always lessen in me and my spiritual strength may increase.

～ 6. Modesty ～

Let your modesty be known to all men. The Lord is nigh.
PHILIPPIANS 4:5, Douay-Rheims

Once you are outside the church, be as every follower of the Nazarene should be. Above all, be extremely modest in everything, as this is the virtue which, more than any other, reveals the affections of the heart. Nothing represents an object more faithfully ... than a mirror. In the same way, nothing more widely represents the good or bad qualities of a soul than the greater or lesser regulation of the exterior, as when one appears more or less modest.

You must be modest in speech, modest in laughter, modest in your bearing, modest in walking. All this must be practiced, not out of vanity, in order to display one's self, nor out of hypocrisy in order to appear to be good in the eyes of others, but rather for the internal virtue of modesty, which regulates the eternal workings of the body.

Letters, Vol. 3, 90

Lord, in a society where the very word seems laughable, help me to be modest anyway because I am your child, not the world's.

～ 7. Educate the Mind and the Heart ～

Whoever receives one ... child in my name receives me; but who ever causes one of these little ones who believe in me to sin, it would be better for him to have a great millstone fastened round his neck and to be drowned in the depth of the sea.
MATTHEW 18:5-6

[Writing a widow whose husband committed suicide, leaving her with three children:]

These little children will be, for you, by their behavior, of comfort and consolation throughout the course of your life. Always be diligent as regards their education, more as regards their moral education than scientific education. And may all this be dear to you like the pupil of your eye.

See that the education of the mind through good study is always coupled with the education of the heart and of our holy religion. The one without the other, my good lady, causes a mortal wound to the human heart.

Letters, Vol. 3, 131

Lord, help all us who are parents today to educate our children for true wholeness: holiness and health in body, intellect, emotions, and soul. And help today's children who have been given no formal spiritual training to find you, the Way, the Truth, and the Life.

∽ 8. Trying to Love God ∽

[Jesus said,] "You shall love the Lord your God with all your heart, and with all your soul, and with all your mind. This is the great and first commandment."

MATTHEW 22:37-38

You complain and doubt your love for Jesus. But tell me, whoever was it that told you [that] you do not love our most sweet Savior?

Ah, I know you would like to love God as much as he deserves. But you know, also, that all this is not possible for us creatures. God commands us to love him not as much and as he deserves, because he knows our limitations and therefore he does not ask us to do what we cannot, but rather, he commands us to love him in accordance with our strength; with all our soul, all our mind, and all our heart.

Well, then, don't you make every effort to do this? And even if you don't succeed, why do you complain? Why do you worry? God understands very well our intention, which is upright and holy before him. God knows very well the reason why many good desires are not realized except after having worked a great deal, and some are never realized at all. But not even in this is there a reason to uselessly afflict yourself, because there is always profit ... for the soul. Because if nothing but mortification for the soul were gained from this, it would still be a marvelous thing.

Letters, Vol. 3, 927

Lord, you know how much I want to love you and how feeble my love seems to me. Help me, as Padre Pio says, not to uselessly afflict myself over this, while always praying that your Holy Spirit give me more love for you—the real kind that bears fruit and is not useless words or sentiments.

~ 9. Patiently Bear Imperfections ~

You will always have your trials but, when they come, try to treat them as a happy privilege; you understand that your faith is only put to the test to make you patient, but patience too is to have its practical results so that you will become fully-developed, complete, with nothing missing.

JAMES 1:2-4, JB

Be patient, my daughter, in bearing your imperfections, if you hold your ... [being perfected] dear. Remember that this is a very important matter for the building of the spiritual structure. If we want this structure to be masterly and erected quickly, let us try to patiently bear our imperfections. When you are unable to take big steps on the paths to which the Lord leads you, be content with small steps and patiently wait until you have the legs to run.

Letters, Vol. 3, 116

Lord, it is hard for me to see some trials as "a happy privilege," and I certainly find it difficult to be patient. But I am more patient than I used to be, so I cling to the thought that you are working in me and that one day my spiritual structure will be radiant with your beauty.

～ 10. Fight the Good Fight ～

Therefore let us also ... put away every encumbrance and the sin entangling us, and run with patience to the fight set before us.
HEBREWS 12:1, Challoner-Rheims

My daughter, we will never acquire perfect sweetness and charity, if it is not exercised in repugnance, aversions, and disgust.... Always keep Jesus present in your mind. He did not come to rest or in order to have comfort, either spiritual or temporal, but to fight, humble himself, and die. Hold this divine Model tightly to your heart, so that your soul, already pierced with heavenly love, can breathe the sacred words of the loving soul: My Beloved is mine and I am His [Song of Songs 2:16].

Letters, Vol. 3, 750

Help me, Lord, to practice real charity by praying for those whom I find repugnant and, if I can do so without entangling myself unwisely, expressing my charity in deeds as well. May I never give up fighting my human tendency to anger and resentment toward those who hurt me or others. Help me keep my eyes fixed on you.

～ 11. To Desire to Love IS Love ～

As a doe longs for running streams, so longs my soul for you, my God.... In the daytime may Jahweh command his love to come, and by night may his song be on my lips.

PSALM 42:1, JB

You become sad at the love you feel for God. It seems to you that it is little more than nothing. But, my good daughter, don't you yourself feel this love in your soul? What is ... that ardent desire that you yourself express to me?

Well, you should know, my dear daughter, that *in divino* the desire to love is love. Who placed this yearning to love the Lord in your heart? Don't holy desires come from above? Are we perhaps capable of arousing in ourselves one single desire of that kind without the grace of God which sweetly works within us? If there ... [is] nothing but the desire to love God in a soul, everything is present already; God himself is there, because God is not, nor can he be, anywhere except where there is a desire for his love.

Letters, Vol. 3, 669

Holy Spirit, I surrender to you who are the love of the eternal Father and the Christ, his Son. Plant the flag of divine love and mercy in my heart, and rule over my soul.

~ 12. Temptations ~

For the rest, brethren, be strengthened in the Lord and in the might of his power. Put on the armor of God, that you may be able to stand against the wiles of the devil. For our wrestling is not against flesh and blood, but against the Principalities and the Powers, against the world-rulers of this darkness, against the spiritual forces of wickedness on high. Therefore take up the armor of God that you may be able to resist in the evil day, and stand in all things perfect.

EPHESIANS 6:10-13, Challoner-Rheims

My dearest daughter, you cannot believe that temptations against holy purity come from God. Much darkness, weakness, great abandonment, lack of energy, much disturbance in your spiritual stomach, interior bitterness which renders the sweetest wine in the world bitter, may come from God; but diabolical suggestions, infidelity, and incredulity, ah! These cannot come from God. His heart is too pure to conceive such horrible things.

Do you know what God does in such cases? He permits the evil trickster to present us with such things, in order to sell them to us so that we, through our despising him, can show our affection for divine matters. Why, therefore, my good daughter, should we become anxious and distressed for this? Dear God, no! It is the devil who wanders around our spirit, rummaging about and causing confusion, trying to find an open door if he can. He did the same to Job, to the great apostle of the people Paul, to St. Anthony, St. Catherine of Siena, and a number of good souls (it even happened to my own, which is not worth much) whom I know and whom I don't.

But, my dearest daughter, should we become saddened for all this? By all means let Satan show himself to be what he is. Keep all the entrances well closed. Protest before God that you seek nothing except him and what leads you to him. Satan will tire, and if he doesn't, God will make him remove his siege.

Letters, Vol. 3, 634–35

Lord, help me to see every temptation clearly and to turn immediately to you.

～ 13. I Am Not Alone ～

Know that I am with you always; yes, to the end of time.

MATTHEW 28:20, JB

Don't let difficulties you encounter stop you from doing good. Jesus is with you, and you have nothing to fear. My spirit is always close to you. Therefore do not fear.

Letters, Vol. 3, 1055

When life is difficult, help me to remember that you are with me, Lord, and that your friends, the saints, in their union with you, are with me, too. I do not walk alone.

～ 14. Be Joyful! ～

I will greatly rejoice in the Lord, and my soul shall be joyful in my God.

ISAIAH 61:10, Douay-Rheims

21

Padre Pio was not one who usually counseled rejoicing and joy in his spiritual directives, but he certainly lived it, as the friars who shared his life have attested. Even as an unusually prayerful novice, he enjoyed playing pranks. And all his life he liked to tell little jokes, including those at his own expense. His speech was salted with witticisms, never unkind but truly funny. At recreation, whether with other friars or with his many lay friends, Padre Pio was a joyous man.

Patricia Treece

Lord, you called Padre Pio to do spiritual battle from the time he was a teenager until almost his last hour, helping you snatch souls from darkness and death. Yet he kept a joyful spirit, laughed often, and brought this joy and laughter to his friends and confreres. May I, too, laugh much and carry your joy with me wherever I go.

∼ 15. The Truest Help Is in God Alone ∼

Unload your burden on to Yahweh, and he will support you.... For my part, I put my trust in you.

PSALM 55:22-23, JB

Blessed be the fear you have of yourself [that she may turn away from God]. As long as you have this fear in the depths of your heart, you needn't worry. However, moderate this fear with the greatest and most unlimited trust in Jesus, from whom alone you should expect fruits and blessings for yourself. After the abandonment and surrender of your entire self to Jesus, always remember that you are no longer yours but that you belong to him. He will take care of sustaining and helping you. Often renew your abnegation, relying on him for everything, obeying the desires he manifests to your heart.

Letters, Vol. 3, 461

Help me, Lord, to constantly say in my heart, "Jesus, I trust in you!"

～ 16. The Foundation of True Virtue ～

For if any one thinks he is something, when he is nothing, he deceives himself.

GALATIANS 6:3

The knowledge of your interior unworthiness and sinfulness is an extremely pure divine light by which your very being and your ability to commit any sin, without the help of grace, is placed before your consideration. That light is due to the great mercy of God and was granted to the greatest saints because it positions their souls in a place sheltered from all feelings of vanity or pride, thus consolidating humility, which is the foundation of true virtue and Christian perfection....

[However,] this knowledge of possible unworthiness, which consists in our being aware of what we would and could commit when left without the assistance of grace,... must not be confused with *real* unworthiness. The former renders the creature acceptable in the presence of the Most High, and the latter ... is a reflection of the iniquity present in the soul.... In the shadows in which, more often than not, you find yourselves, you confuse the one with the other.

Letters, Vol. 3, 548

Lord, help me to have true humility—that is, to see myself as both nothing before your divine perfection and as your beloved child, held to your heart and carried where the way is hard.

~ 17. Root and Ground Yourself in Love ~

For this reason I bow my knees before the Father, from whom every family in heaven and on earth is named, that according to the riches of his glory he may grant you to be strengthened with might through his Spirit in the inner man, and that Christ may dwell in your hearts through faith; that you, being rooted and grounded in love, may have power to comprehend with all the saints what is the breadth and length and height and depth, and to know the love of Christ which surpasses knowledge, that you may be filled with all the fulness of God.

EPHESIANS 3:14-19

Draw very close, my daughter, to the heart of this divine Model so that, with your soul already pierced with heavenly love, you can breathe those holy words of the loving soul: "My beloved is mine and I am his, he pastures his flock among the lilies" [Song of Songs 2:16]. My most beloved daughter, let this divine Love of our hearts always be on our breasts, in order to inflame and consume us with its grace.

Letters, Vol. 3, 334

Divine Love, root and ground me in yourself, and let me carry that love, a living flame to warm others, everywhere I go.

~ 18. Expect Blessings! ~

But let all who take refuge in thee rejoice, let them ever sing for joy; and do thou defend them, that those who love thy name may exult in thee. For thou dost bless the righteous, O Lord; thou dost cover him with favor as with a shield.

PSALM 5:11-12

Be cheerful and tranquilly rest in the arms of Jesus and mitigate your fears with the greatest confidence in Jesus, as it is from him alone that you should expect many blessings.

Letters, Vol. 3, 389

Dear Lord, it is to you and you alone that I look for deliverance from all my trials and troubles.

～ 19. The Project: To Love God and Neighbor ～

"You shall love the Lord your God with all your heart, and with all your soul, and with all your mind, and with all your strength...." [And] *"You shall love your neighbor as yourself." There is no other commandment greater than these.*

MARK 12:30-31

It is now time to confess it: We are miserable creatures. We are only capable of doing a little good. But God, in his goodness, has pity on us, is content with very little, and accepts the preparation of our hearts.

But what is this preparation of our hearts? According to the divine Word, God is infinitely greater than our heart, and this overcomes the whole world when, leaving aside its entire self, in meditation it prepares the service it must render God: that is, when it establishes the project to serve God, to love him, love his neighbor, to observe the mortification of the internal and external senses along with other good propositions.

Letters, Vol. 3, 685

Lord, you know I want to love you with all my being, and I want, for love of you, to love everyone no matter what. You know also I can do neither without your grace. So help me, Lord.

∼ 20. Moved With Compassion ∼

As he landed he saw a great throng, and he had compassion on them.
MARK 6:34

[Jesus] continues to love me and to draw me closer to himself. He has forgotten my sins, and I would say that he remembers only his own mercy.... Each morning he comes into my heart and pours out all the effusions of his goodness.

Letters, Vol. 1, 299–300

Jesus, help me to plumb the depths of your mercy. If I know nothing else, let me know mercy so I may become mercy in an often merciless world. In spite of my frailties and sins, may your mercy always, in the words of Gerard Manley Hopkins, "wind me round and round."

~ 21. Laughing at Myself ~

A cheerful heart is a good medicine.

PROVERBS 17:22

While he endured constant pain from his stigmata and, in his latter years, other ailments, Padre Pio was known for enjoying a hearty laugh, for pranks and witticisms. Besides his true spiritual children, there were "followers" of Padre Pio who let superstition creep into devotion to him. While he found this annoying and sometimes even got angry when it went too far, in general he maintained a healthy, humorous perspective.

An example: Some of these devotees would call out as he passed, "Padre Pio, my mother had cancer, and I put your picture on her chest, and it disappeared." "Padre Pio, my child was very sick, and I put your picture on him, and he got immediately well." Padre Pio heard so much of the efficacy of his picture and was pretty tired of what he considered rank superstition.

One night, praying alone very late in the choir of the church, he heard footsteps back and forth in the silence of the night. Eventually this disturbed his prayer. He got up and looked out the window. He saw a sinister-looking figure in a cape with something in his hand that might [have been] a grenade or bomb.

This was a time of great political unrest, and Padre Alessio Parente later recalled Pio's telling the other friars, "At first I was so scared he would throw the bomb at me. But then I said to myself, 'Oh, don't worry; I think I've got a picture of Padre Pio somewhere.'"

Kathleen Stauffer, "They Knew Padre Pio,"
Catholic Digest, December 1991
and *The Voice of Padre Pio,* Vol. 20, No. 4, 1990, 7

Lord, help me to always laugh and, above all, laugh at myself in situations where pretentiousness or pride could arise.

∼ 22. Persevere ∼

For a righteous man falls seven times, and rises again; but the wicked are overthrown by calamity.

PROVERBS 24:16

Don't let these little imperfections discourage you. Try to be always watchful in order to avoid sin, but when you see that you fail in some way, don't become lost in useless complaining, but bend your knees before God; be embarrassed at your scarce fidelity; humble yourself greatly; ask our Lord's pardon; propose to be more watchful in the future; and then get up immediately and carry on....

Convince yourselves ... that failings and little flights of the passions are inevitable as long as we are in this life.... Self-love never dies before we do, but it will accompany us to the tomb.... We must always feel the sensitive assaults of the passions....

But what of it? Should we perhaps become discouraged and renounce the life of heaven? No,... let us take heart. It is sufficient for us not to consent with our deliberate will.

Letters, Vol. 3, 510–11

Lord, you know it can be discouraging when one wants to avoid a failing only to fall into it again. Help me not to give in to discouragement or, worse, to self-hate over past mistakes. Instead may I picture myself as a spiritual toddler who must expect falls but has a strong Father ready to pick me up at all times.

∼ 23. Die to Live ∼

Then Jesus told his disciples, "If any man would come after me, let him deny himself and take up his cross and follow me. For whoever would save his life will lose it, and whoever loses his life for my sake will find it."

MATTHEW 16:24-25

The miraculous and great St. Paul, in a very timely manner, awakens us in a loud voice, exclaiming to the ears of my heart and yours: "Lord, what do you want me to do?" [Acts 9:6]. Oh, my dearest daughter, when will it be that we, totally dead before God, will return to live that new life where we will no longer want to do anything, but rather we will let God will all that is necessary for us to do.

Letters, Vol. 3, 335

Lord, as Padre Pio said, how hard it is to die to all within me that would cry, "Me first!" or, "Do it my way!" Yet I glimpse in your saints that only there—beyond the death of what we call the ego—will I achieve the true life where my self, made in God's image, can flourish and fulfill its full potential by freely doing your will.

∼ 24. Rest in Mercy ∼

May the God of hope fill you with all joy and peace in believing, so that by the power of the Holy Spirit you may abound in hope.

ROMANS 15:13

Be cheerful and rest trustingly ... in the arms of divine mercy, and do not fear.

Letters, Vol. 3, 907

Lord, may your holy Spirit keep me in that peace that casts out fear and lets joy and hope flourish. Jesus, I trust in you!

∼ 25. Turn to Prayer in Weakness ∼

The spirit indeed is willing, but the flesh is weak.

MATTHEW 26:41

I exhort you to approach [God] with filial trust and selfless love. He loves you, and you return this love as best you can. He desires nothing else, and you must confide in him, pray, hope, and love him always. Do not be disheartened by ... physical and moral suffering.

It is true that sometimes the spirit is ready to do the will of God whereas the flesh is weak, but console yourself because Jesus wants the spirit and not the flesh. In fact, in his fully accepted agony in the Garden, the humanity of Jesus also felt human nature's repugnance for suffering, so that he prayed to the heavenly Father to remove the chalice, if it were possible; and if this repugnance was overcome, it was due to prayer.

Letters, Vol. 3, 81–82

Thank you, Lord, for Padre Pio's reminder that I cannot avoid fear and repugnance for what faces me at times, but I can always find a way through it if I keep praying.

～ 26. Trust Is Vital ～

Yahweh is my light and my salvation, whom need I fear? Yahweh is the fortress of my life, of whom should I be afraid?

PSALM 27:1, JB

Recommend to those two people to remain quite calm and tranquil and to place unlimited trust in the heavenly Father, for everything will turn out for the greater good of their souls.

They are not to worry about this matter, because this would invariably be harmful to their souls; the intrusion of worry to a greater or lesser degree diminishes charity of heart and trust in God. This must not be considered a small matter, because it prevents the Holy Spirit from acting freely in people's hearts.

Letters, Vol. 1, 486

Lord, it sometimes seems as if my whole life has been a series of exercises aimed to teach me to trust you in every situation and to overcome that anxiety that puts up a barrier to your wonderful work in my life. I have come a long way, but I have much further to go. Lead me on, dear Lord; lead me on.

～ 27. To Be Good Servants ～

But be doers of the word, and not hearers only, deceiving yourselves. For if any one is a hearer of the word and not a doer, he is like a man who observes his natural face in a mirror; for he observes himself and goes away and at once forgets what he was like. But he who looks into the perfect law, the law of liberty, and perseveres, being no hearer that forgets but a doer that acts, he shall be blessed in his doing.

JAMES 1:22-25

Live tranquilly for charity's sake, and don't fear divine work.... In order to be good servants of God, we must be charitable toward our neighbor; have an inviolable determination to do the will of God in the upper part of the spirit; have profound humility and simplicity in order to confide in God, picking ourselves up again many times when we fall and tranquilly bearing [with] others in their imperfections.

Letters, Vol. 3, 932

I thank you for the grace you have given me to pray sincerely for people I don't like and to wish them well. But you know I have no tranquility at all around some people. Bless them, Lord, and forgive me that, far from tranquilly bearing their imperfections, I stay away from them as much as possible.

∼ 28. The Little Things ∼

For you have need of endurance, so that you may do the will of God and receive what is promised.

HEBREWS 10:36

My dearest daughter, make a particular effort to practice sweetness and submission to the will of God, not only in extraordinary matters but even in the little things that occur daily. Make these acts not only in the morning but also during the day and in the evening, with a tranquil and joyful spirit. And if you should fail in this, humble yourself, make a new proposition, get up, and continue on your way.

Letters, Vol. 3, 708

Lord, I accept everything you permit to happen today. Let me listen to your voice so that my deeds, thoughts, and speech may be in sweet accordance with your will.

～ 29. How to Love God More ～

We love, because he first loved us.

1 JOHN 4:19

I implore you by the meekness of our divine Master not to let yourself be overcome by that fear which is apparent to me from your letter—that is, the fear of not loving God....

I know, my dearest daughter, that no soul can worthily love God. But when this soul does everything possible and trusts in divine mercy, why should Jesus reject it? Doesn't he ... command us to love God in accordance with our strength, and not as he deserves? Therefore, if you have given and consecrated everything to God, why do you fear? Perhaps because you can do no more? But Jesus doesn't ask that of you....

On the other hand, tell our good God to do himself what you cannot do. Say to Jesus: Do you want more love from me? I have no more! Give me some more, and I'll offer it to you!

Do not doubt. Jesus will accept the offer.

Letters, Vol. 3, 726

Lord, you know I want to love you with my whole soul, my whole mind, and my whole heart. Lord, you also know I can't do this unless you provide the love and the grace! Help me!

~ 30. I Am God's Child ~

Jesus said, "Let the children come to me, and do not hinder them; for to such belongs the kingdom of heaven."

MATTHEW 19:14

It is an excellent thing to aspire to extreme perfection in the Christian life. But it is not necessary to philosophize, in particular, except on one's ... progress in daily events, leaving the results of your desires to God's providence. Abandon yourself in his paternal arms like a child, who in order to grow, eats what his father prepares every day, hoping he will not let him go without food in proportion to his appetite and needs.

Letters, Vol. 3, 708

Today, Lord, may I truly live in the present moment as children do—and live it in your arms.

~ 31. About Prayer for Health ~

So we do not lose heart. Though our outer nature is wasting away, our inner nature is being renewed every day. For this slight momentary affliction is preparing for us an eternal weight of glory beyond all comparison, because we look not to the things that are seen but to the things that are unseen; for the things that are seen are transient, but the things that are unseen are eternal.

2 CORINTHIANS 4:16-18

I ... always bring pressure to bear on the heart of the heavenly Father for [your sister] Giovina's health, and also for your own.... However, I must tell you for your own comfort that a complete cure of the disease from which poor Giovina is suffering would not be for God's glory, for the salvation of her soul, and [for] the edification of those who live according to the spirit of Jesus Christ. Hence I cannot insist, I cannot demand from the divine Heart to grant her this favor. I will certainly pray and never forget it, since this is the Lord's will, wherever I am and no matter in what state I may be, that the Lord may be pleased to grant her constantly at least the degree of holiness necessary for the fulfillment of her duties. Does this satisfy you?

I am confident that the Lord God, who is so good to his creatures, will not refuse the poor prayer of his servant. In fact, I hope he will grant more grace ... than I dare to ask.

The other reason why I refrain from asking [for] a complete cure for Giovina is because this illness is, for her, a most powerful means of practicing many virtues. I cannot deprive this generous soul, who is so dear to Jesus, of such great treasures through a mistaken sense of pity and affection for you.

Letters, Vol. 2, 261

Lord, it is always right to pray for health, as Padre Pio says he did for Giovina Cerase. Yet we must leave to you the form that health is to take, whether that of becoming more mature in the practice of virtue or a return to physical vigor, which Giovina later experienced. Give me health too, Lord, so I may praise your holy name. But above all, fit me for "the eternal weight of glory."

～ 32. Let God Bury Our Sins ～

Come let us adore and fall down: and weep before the Lord that made us.

PSALM 95:6

During the rioting of the passions and adverse events, keep in mind the dear hope of his unlimited mercy. Let us run with confidence to the tribunal of penance, where he waits for you at all times with the anxiety of a father; and although we are conscious of our debt towards him, let us not doubt the solemn pardon of our sins. Let us bury them as our Lord had done.

Consigli-Esortazioni di Padre Pio da Pietrelcina, 18

Lord, thank you for the sacrament of penance and for forgiving my sins.

～ 33. Place All Your Trust in Him ～

I know the plans I have in mind for you—it is Jahweh who speaks—plans for peace, not disaster, reserving a future full of hope for you.

JEREMIAH 29:11, JB

36

Courage. Suffice it for us to know that Jesus loves us greatly.

Letters, Vol. 4, 1005

Lord, in today's trials I trust you will work things out to my eternal good, and I thank you ahead of time for all your love and care in every situation.

～ 34. Let Hope Be Stronger Than Fear ～

Draw near to God and he will draw near to you. Cleanse your hands, you sinners, and purify your hearts, you ... of double mind.

JAMES 4:8

I have your letter ... in which you describe your imperfection[s] ... [and] desire to obtain some remedy from me with which to extirpate those imperfections from your heart.... [Actually] ... the majority of what you tell me needs no other remedy except the passage of time and the practice of the Rule by which you live [in your religious order].

... Self-love, self-esteem [that is, an inflated self-importance], false freedom of spirit, are all roots which cannot easily be extirpated from the human heart; only the production of their fruits, which are sins, can be impeded. Because their first buds—that is, their first movements—cannot be impeded at all while we are in this mortal life, though their quality and strength can be moderated and diminished through the practice of the opposing virtues, particularly that of love of God.

Therefore we must be patient when getting rid of bad habits, dominating aversions, and overcoming our own inclinations and humors when necessary. Because ... this life is a continual struggle, and nobody can say: "I am not assailed." Calm is reserved for heaven.... On earth we must always fight amid hope and fear, on condition, however, that hope is always stronger ... [because of] the omnipotence of he who comes to our aid.

Letters, Vol. 3, 739–40

Lord, I get nowhere thinking about my imperfections. I make progress when I keep my eyes on you instead. Increase my love for you, so you, your Father, and Spirit may, as a burning bush in my soul, turn all that is dross to ashes.

∼ 35. Let Jesus Handle It ∼

Cast all your anxieties on him, for he cares about you.

1 PETER 5:7

Be cheerful. Jesus will take care of everything. Let us pay no attention to people who do not know what they are saying. Let us trust in Jesus and our heavenly Mother, and everything will work out well.

Letters, Vol. 4, 1005

Jesus, I unload all my troubles and worries at your feet. Free of care, I come to do your will.

∽ 36. Pride—"A Wretched Vice" ∽

In any case,... what do you have that was not given to you? And if it was given, how can you boast as though it were not?

1 CORINTHIANS 4:7, JB

To refuse to submit one's own judgment to that of others, especially to those who are quite expert in the field in question, is a sign that we possess very little docility and an all too obvious sign of secret pride. You know this yourself and you agree with me. Well, then, take heart and avoid falling into this fault again. Keep your eyes wide open for this wretched vice, knowing how much it displeases Jesus, for it is written that *God opposes the proud, but gives grace to the humble.*

Letters, Vol. 2, 260

Pride, Lord, is a tricky thing. I can see that some major accomplishment is your gift to me, then preen myself over some small thing I have done. Most laughable is my pride at being humble!

Bear with me, Lord. After all, my imperfections are part of your design for human beings. And far be it from me, Lord, to suggest you might have done things differently! But some days I wish you could simply make me pride-free instead of letting me struggle.

∽ 37. Steadfast Love ∽

But I will sing of thy might; I will sing aloud of thy steadfast love in the morning. For thou hast been to me a fortress and a refuge in the day of my distress. O my Strength, I will sing praises to thee, for thou, O God, art my fortress, the God who shows me steadfast love.

PSALM 59:16-17

... This most tender Mother has been [in spite of his failings] ... pouring so many and such great graces into my heart that when I am in her presence and that of Jesus, I am ... all aflame.... Here you have a feeble description of what happens to me when I am with Jesus and Mary.... An immense gladness fills my whole heart and makes me blissful and content.

Letters, Vol. 1, 402

Lord, today I am joyful. My heart rejoices in your gifts. And in my soul I sing your praise.

～ 38. Setting the Heart Straight ～

Beloved, we are God's children now; it does not yet appear what we shall be, but we know that when he appears we shall be like him, for we shall see him as he is. And every one who thus hopes in him purifies himself as he is pure.

1 JOHN 3:2-3

Know, my daughter, that charity is made up of three things: love for God, affection for ourselves, and love for our neighbor. And may my poor instructions put you on the path to practice this.

a) Throughout the day, often place your heart, thoughts, and soul in God with great confidence, and say to him, with the royal prophet [David]: "I am thine, save me." Do not spend too much time dwelling on the type of prayer God grants you, but simply and humbly follow his grace in the affection you must have for yourself.

b) Keep your eyes well open for bad inclinations without tiring yourself excessively, in order to uproot them. Do not let [their] sight ... frighten you; think of your heart with a great desire to perfect it. Have an untiring desire to set it straight in a sweet and charitable manner when it stumbles.

Letters, Vol. 3, 740–41

That's it, Lord: I have an untiring desire to set my heart straight so it goes like an arrow directly to you. In only rare instances does this desire win over my weaknesses. But I will keep projecting my little arrows of love and trusting your strength where mine is lacking."

～ 39. Of Birds and Souls ～

Thou openest thy hand, and fillest with blessing every living creature.

PSALM 144:16, Douay-Rheims

Even the sparrow finds a home, and the swallow a nest for herself; where she may lay her young, at thy altars, O Lord of hosts, my King and my God.

PSALM 84:3

Listen to what I am thinking: I consider what writers say about the kingfisher, little birds who build their nests on the beach near the sea. They build it in a circular form and so tightly compressed that the seawater cannot penetrate it. Above it is an opening from which they receive air. Here these graceful little birds place their young ones, so that when the sea comes upon them by surprise, they can swim with confidence and float on the waves without being filled with water or submerging. And the air they breathe through that opening serves as a counterbalance so that those little balls of fluff are not overturned.

My daughter, may Jesus deign to make you understand the meaning of this example of mine. I want your heart to be like this: well compact and closed on all sides, so that if the worries and storms of the world, the evil spirit, and the flesh come up on it, it will not be penetrated. Leave but one opening to your heart that is toward heaven....

How I love and am enraptured by those little birds.... They swim like fish and sing like birds. But what amazes me most of all is that the anchor is cast above them and not below, in order to strengthen them against the waves.

May this poor writing of mine raise your exceedingly downcast spirit and make it ascend to he who is the source of all consolation.

Letters, Vol. 3, 111–12

Lord, this man-made world of books, cars, freeways, and appointments screens your natural world. I forget to look at the squirrel on my fence, the bulbs breaking through the still cold soil. I forget to bless the trees and bow down before the beauty of your sunsets. Let me see past the man-made world, Lord, to your world in all its intricate and incredible beauty. And give me again a child's eye, "looking up filled with wonder like a cup." For when I truly see your world, I see you.

∼ 40. Weaving My Designs ∼

Be patient, therefore, brethren, until the coming of the Lord. Behold, the farmer waits for the precious fruit of the earth, being patient over it until it receives the early and the late rain. You also be patient.

JAMES 5:7-8

Proverbs praises the strong woman: "Her hands hold the spindle" [Prv 31:19]. I willingly tell you something on this point. Your distaff is the multitude of your desires. Little by little every day you weave your designs until it is finished and you will come out on top. But beware of haste because you would knot the yarn and entangle the spindle.

Letters, Vol. 3, 291

Little by little every day, my life is weaving a design. I find that scary, Lord. I would hate to "wake up" to eternity and find my design was full of to-do lists of trivial getting-and-spending activities, instead of laughter, love, courage, adventure, and other things that I really desire and that really matter. Please help me not waste this moment—the only one I can be sure of—on trivia. And since much of life is inescapably mundane, help me offer even small tasks for the kingdom, doing them joyfully and for you. Rain on my soil, Lord, so something beautiful can grow there.

～ 41. Gaining Ground ～

To the present hour we hunger and thirst, we are ill-clad and buffeted and homeless, and we labor, working with our own hands. When reviled, we bless; when persecuted, we endure; when slandered, we try to conciliate; we have become, and are now, as the refuse of the world, the offscouring of all things.

1 CORINTHIANS 4:11-13

Do not have a great desire to be freed from the trial: A soldier must gain a great deal in war before he wants it to end.... True peace does not consist in fighting but in winning. Those who have been beaten no longer fight, but just the same they have no true peace.

Come on, we must humble ourselves greatly, seeing that we are not masters of ourselves to any great extent and greatly love comfort and rest.

Letters, Vol. 3, 750

Lord, I do "greatly love comfort and rest," as Padre Pio says. My being shrinks from the thought of battling, of trials, of being "the world's rubbish," as St. Paul put it. Couldn't you find another way to help us grow?

～ 42. His Mercy ～

"Who has given a gift to him that he might be repaid?" For from him and through him and to him are all things. To him be glory for ever. Amen.

ROMANS 11:35-36

Not one of us deserves anything in this world; it is the Lord who is benevolent toward us, and it is his infinite mercy that bestows everything because he forgives everything.

Have a Good Day: A Thought for Each Day of the Year,
Fr. Alessio Parente, ed., 122, #10

Needing forgiveness of sin is not a popular concept, Lord. I don't like to confront the fact that I can want to do evil: maliciously want to hurt someone, to steal, to lie, to commit adultery, to do so many things I know in my heart are wrong. Sin hurts my beautiful soul made in your image. It hurts others, spreading out often from them to hurt still others. It hurt you, heavenly Father, so you sent Jesus, whose love would make up for all the sins of the world.

In Jesus' powerful love I accept your forgiveness, Father. With a contrite heart I renounce sin. When I am tempted to seek revenge or tell someone off, I will try to give the forgiveness and mercy you give me instead.

∽ 43. The Past: Lost in God's Forgiveness ∽

For you did not receive the spirit of slavery to fall back into fear, but you have received the spirit of sonship.... We cry, "Abba! Father!"

ROMANS 8:15

When you are assailed by fears for the past, think of it as [being] lost in the ocean of heavenly goodness, then turn your mind to the present, in which Jesus is with you and loves you; think of the future, when Jesus will reward your faithfulness and resignation—or rather all the graces he has poured out on you and which you *certainly* have not deliberately abused. Hence, I would ask you in the sweet Lord to cast aside all fears as far as possible—for no one is asked to do what is impossible—and always have confidence, faith, and love.

Letters, Vol. 3, 151

Confidence! Lord, let that be my watchword. May I be always confident in your provision for each moment of my life. In every difficulty, from traffic jams to relationship problems, may my motto be "Jesus, I trust in you."

∽ 44. Exhaustion ∽

For we do not want you to be ignorant, brethren, of the affliction we experienced in Asia; for we were so utterly, unbearably crushed that we despaired of life itself.

2 CORINTHIANS 1:8

You ask me to reply to you at length, and I would like to please you, but, dear God, up to now I have been working indefatigably for twenty hours, and one o'clock in the morning has already struck while I write you this letter. At this stage I am exhausted, and I cannot go on much longer.... Do not let the brevity of my letter cause you to doubt my concern for you. My arms are tired from continually raising them to heaven in order to tear graces from the Lord for you.

Letters, Vol. 1, 777–78

Lord, help me to remember that life, even the life of a saint, often means day after day of hard work and fatigue. Let my work and my fatigue, as well as my joys and delights, serve you.

∼ 45. The Divine Child ∼

Whoever does not receive the kingdom of God like a child shall not enter it.

LUKE 18:17

May the Heavenly Child always be at the center of your heart; may he govern it, enlighten it, vivify it, and transform it to his eternal love.

Letters, Vol. 1, 490

Jesus, I want nothing more than to be your child and to see you, the Divine Child, in all your playfulness and beauty, fill every cranny of my soul.

～ 46. He Who Trusts God Will Never Be Confounded ～

But as for me, I will look to the Lord, I will wait for the God of my salvation; my God will hear me.

MICAH 7:7

I give infinite thanks for you to the Lord, who is so good to all his creatures, especially to those who do their utmost to love him. He never ceases to visit them in time of trial and to send down a heavenly charism into their souls, which must serve them as armor and a shield to ward off the blows of the enemy and further misfortunes. Praise be for ever to Jesus, and may the divine mercy and providence be praised for ever!

But if ever there was a human being in whom the divine goodness and providence shines forth more clearly, it is precisely yourself. This is how things are, Raffaelina. Humble yourself continually before the Lord, keep yourself always in the last place, and never give in to yourself. Have boundless trust in God, even when misfortune and the deceitful prompting of the enemy trouble you. He who abandons himself in God and trusts in him will never be confounded.

Letters, Vol. 2, 398–99

I praise you, Lord, for your mercy and providence. Jesus, I trust in you.

～ 47. The House of the Lord ～

Who has the right to climb the mountain of Yahweh, who the right to stand in his holy place? He whose hands are clean, whose heart is pure, whose soul does not pay homage to worthless things.

PSALM 24:3-4, JB

Enter the church in silence and with great respect, considering your-self unworthy to appear before the Lord's Majesty.... Remember that our soul is the temple of God, and as such we must keep it pure and spotless before God and his angels. Let us blush for having given access to the devil and his snares many times (with his enticements to the world, his pomp, his calling to the flesh) by not being able to keep our hearts pure and our bodies chaste; for having allowed our enemies to insinuate themselves into our hearts, thus desecrating the temple of God, which we became through holy baptism. Then take holy water and make the sign of the cross carefully and slowly.

As soon as you are before God in the Blessed Sacrament, devoutly genuflect. Once you have found your place, kneel down and render the tribute of your presence and devotion to Jesus in the Blessed Sacrament. Confide all your needs to him, along with those of others. Speak to him in filial abandonment, give free rein to your heart, and give him complete freedom to work in you as he thinks best.

Letters, Vol. 3, 89

I love your sanctuaries, Lord, with the sweet emanation of your presence from the tabernacle and the thick patina of prayer. But how often I enter preoccupied and blind to the glory about me. Open my eyes, Lord!

∼ 48. Jesus, My Food! ∼

Approach me, you who desire me, and take your fill of my fruits, for memories of me are sweeter than honey,... They who eat me will hunger for more, they who drink me will thirst for more.

ECCLESIASTICUS 24:19-20, JB

[On receiving Communion:] How happy Jesus makes me! How sweet is his spirit! I ... can do nothing but weep and repeat: "Jesus, my food!"

Letters, Vol. 1, 299

Bread of Life, cup of salvation, in receiving you—the greatest gift—may I be filled with your Spirit and become a gift to others.

∼ 49. Loving the Dear God ∼

I know a man in Christ who fourteen years ago was caught up to the third heaven—whether in the body or out of the body I do not know, God knows. And I know that this man was caught up into Paradise—whether in the body or out of the body I do not know, God knows—and he heard things that cannot be told, which man may not utter.

2 CORINTHIANS 12:2-4

Words are lacking by which to give even a feeble description of what passes between my soul and God.... The things which are taking place at present are so secret and private that anyone who has not himself experienced them could never, never form even a faint idea of them.

What my soul receives in this state is received in a very different manner from previously. It is now God himself who acts and operates directly in the depths of my soul, without the ministry of the senses, either interior or exterior. This is, in a word, such a sublime, secret, and sweet operation that it is concealed from all human creatures and even from the intelligence of the rebellious angels.

In this state my soul is happy, for it feels it loves its dear God and at the same time experiences his love in a very delicate way. All I can say of this ... is that my soul has no concern for anything but God. I feel my whole being concentrated and recollected in God.

Letters, Vol. 1, 509

Dear Lord, thank you for the gift of your saints Paul and Pio, who chart for us the spiritual heights. Mired in the lowlands as I am, it does my spirit good to lift up my eyes and contemplate those ecstatic moments you have shared with your best friends in the midst of all their trials and sufferings. Such moments say to me, "Paradise exists, and all who love God are headed there!"

∼ 50. Live Together in Peace ∼

Mend your ways, heed my appeal, agree with one another, live in peace, and the God of love and peace will be with you.

2 CORINTHIANS 13:11

Be like little spiritual bees, bringing nothing into their hives but honey and wax. May your homes be full of sweetness, peace, agreement, humility, and piety as regards conversation.

Letters, Vol. 3, 567

Make me an encourager, Lord; let me give heart to others and rain on no one's parade. I want to grow into one of those sweet old ladies whose laps are places of comfort for little children and whose conversation is sought by weary adults because it is full of eternal light and divine good humor. Above all, let me bring these traits to my family hearth!

～ 51. On Worldly Preoccupations ～

But a man named Ananias with his wife Sapphira sold a piece of property, and with his wife's knowledge he kept back some of the proceeds, and brought only a part and laid it at the apostles' feet. But Peter said, "Ananias, why has Satan filled your heart to lie to the Holy Spirit and to keep back part of the proceeds of the land? While it remained unsold, did it not remain your own? And after it was sold, was it not at your disposal? How is it that you have contrived this deed in your heart? You have not lied to men but to God." When Ananias heard these words, he fell down and died.

ACTS 5:1-5

Those souls who throw themselves into the whirlpool of worldly preoccupations are poor and unfortunate. The more they love the world, the more their passions multiply; the more their desires are lit, the more they find themselves incapable of carrying out their projects, and thus they are uneasy, impatient, affected by that shock that breaks their hearts—those hearts which do not beat with charity and holy love. Let us pray for these unfortunate and miserable souls, that Jesus may forgive them and draw them to himself in his infinite mercy.

Letters, Vol. 3, 1105

How often I have been an Ananias—wanting to have the riches of the kingdom of God and earthly riches and luxuries too. Keep weaning me, Lord, from all the false gods that make me a hypocrite and liar.

～ 52. Love, Love, Love ～

If I speak in the tongues of men and of angels, but have not love, I am a noisy gong or a clanging cymbal. And if I have prophetic powers, and understand all mysteries and all knowledge, and if I have all faith, so as to remove mountains, but have not love, I am nothing. If I give away all I have, and if I deliver my body to be burned, but have not love, I gain nothing.

1 CORINTHIANS 13:1-3

Charity is the queen of virtues. As pearls are held together by a string, so are the virtues held by charity. And just as the pearls fall if the string breaks, so are the virtues lost if charity fails.

Consigli-Esortazioni di Padre Pio da Pietrelcina, 11

Lord, I desire so much to love you, to love others, and to love your world and all its creatures. When I find my ego getting in the way, love urges me to continue my walk with you. Send your Spirit to help me conquer myself. When my feeble love proves inadequate, give me your love to pass on.

～ 53. Leave Life in God's Hands ～

Come now, you who say, "Today or tomorrow we will go into such and such a town and spend a year there and trade and get gain"; whereas you do not know about tomorrow. What is your life? For you are a mist that appears for a little time and then vanishes. Instead you ought to say, "If the Lord wills, we shall live and we shall do this or that."

JAMES 4:13-15

Be tranquil as far as your soul is concerned. Confide totally, more and more, in Jesus. Make an effort to unite yourself always and in everything to divine will, both in happy and sad events, and don't worry about the future.

Letters, Vol. 3, 459

I know your sense of humor well, Lord. I can almost hear you chuckle as you overturn my plans. It must be like training a puppy for you. But I'm getting the picture. May your will be done, Lord!

～ 54. Give Fearlessly ～

God loves a cheerful giver.

2 CORINTHIANS 9:7

Make Christian use of your money and savings, and then so much misery will disappear and so many suffering bodies and afflicted beings will find relief and comfort.

Consigli-Esortazioni di Padre Pio da Pietrelcina, 61

Lord, over and over I have experienced your supply as endless. Your providence always permits my giving something, and what is given always returns "pressed down and running over." Material things may be destroyed by earthquake, flood, or fire. Stocks may fall and bank accounts hit zero, but the riches of the Lord never run out. Praise to our awesome God!

∼ 55. To Burn With Love ∼

For the whole law is fulfilled in one word, "You shall love your neighbor as yourself."

GALATIANS 5:14

The soul who has chosen divine love cannot remain selfish in the heart of Jesus, but feels itself burn also with love for its brothers and sisters, which often causes the soul to suffer agonies.

But how can all this take place? My daughter, it is not difficult to understand this, because given that the soul no longer lives its own life but lives in Jesus, who lives within the soul, it must feel, want, and live of the same sentiments and wishes of he who lives within it. And you know, my most beloved daughter, even if you learned this at a late stage, of the sentiments and desires which animate the Heart of this divine Master, for God and humanity.

Letters, Vol. 3, 971–72

Lord, I thank you that you have given me the grace to wish everyone well. But I would like to go further than that. It is simple to love people who are clear as rain; it is hard to love others who are dark as mud and go about doing evil. Teach me to see your image, however broken and distorted, in everyone and to respond with something of your own motherly tenderness. May my prayer become that of St. Maximilian Kolbe: "to love WITH-OUT LIMITS."

∼ 56. Of Spirit and Truth ∼

Salvation is from the Jews. But the hour is coming, and now is, when the true worshipers will worship the Father in spirit and truth, for such the Father seeks to worship him. God is spirit, and those who worship him must worship in spirit and truth.

JOHN 4:22-24

May the divine Spirit always fill your heart with all the grace it can contain; may it fortify you, sanctify you always more and more for his glory, your salvation, and that of others!

Letters, Vol. 3, 255

Heavenly Father, I recall the words of St. Edith Stein: Those who seek truth are seeking God whether they know it or not. Help my life be the good example that keeps truth seekers from turning away from your Son, Jesus. And help me to answer questions about my faith with charity, wisdom, and the humility that recognizes that many have your Holy Spirit without knowing you. Or as Edith said, your friends go far beyond the boundaries of the visible Church.

∼ 57. Human Weakness and God's Grace ∼

I love thee, O Lord, my strength. The Lord is my rock, and my fortress, and my deliverer.... He delivered me from my strong enemy, and from those who hated me; for they were too mighty for me.... He delivered me, because he delighted in me.

PSALM 18:1-2, 17, 19

I felt the two forces within me, who were struggling amongst themselves and lacerating my heart: the world that wanted me for itself, and God who was calling me to a new life. Dear God! Who could explain that interior martyrdom that was taking place within me? The very thought of that interior struggle ... makes the blood freeze in my veins, and twenty years have passed now....

I heard the voice of duty to obey you, oh true and good God; but your enemies and mine oppressed me, dislocated my bones, scoffed at me, and tortured my heart! Oh my God, my Spouse, I wanted to obey you. This was always the feeling which stood out in my mind and heart, but where could I gather such strength in order that I might first of all tread on those false enticements with a sure and determined foot, and then on the tyranny of the world, which does not belong to you?!

You know, O Lord, of the warm tears I shed before you during those extremely doleful times! You know, oh God of my soul, of the groanings of my heart.... But you, Lord, who made this son of yours experience all the effects of true abandonment, arose in the end; you held out your powerful hand to me and led me there, to where you had first called me. O my God, may infinite praise and thanks be rendered to you.

Letters, Vol. 3, 1016–17

Lord, your saints are not born. Like Sts. Paul and Pio, they are made by choosing you when it is hard to choose you. Only your grace fortifies them. Paul you had to literally throw down and strike blind.

I want to always choose you. But your Holy Spirit must be my strength. For I see, time and again, how fainthearted are my resolutions to put you first.

~ 58. Sanctify Yourself and Others ~

I am he who searches mind and heart, and I will give to each of you as your works deserve.

REVELATION 2:23

You [the Lord God] had confided a very great mission to your son, a mission which is known to you and me alone. Dear God! My Father! How have I corresponded to that mission?! I don't know. I only know that perhaps I should have done more, and [this] is the reason for my present uneasiness of heart—an uneasiness which I feel increasing constantly within me during these days of spiritual retreat.

Therefore, arise once again, O Lord, and free me first and foremost from myself; do not allow he whom you called with so much care and tore from the world that is not yours to be lost. Therefore, arise once more, O Lord, and confirm in your grace those whom you confided to me, and don't permit any of them to be lost....

O God! O God!... Don't allow your inheritance to be lost. O God! Let yourself always be heard more and more by my poor heart, and accomplish in me the work you have begun. I hear an interior voice which assiduously says to me: Sanctify yourself and others.... I want to do this, but I don't know where to begin.

Letters, Vol. 3, 1017–18

Lord, for all his gifts of reading hearts and minds, Padre Pio was always in the dark as to where he stood with you. Regarding my own soul, Jesus, I beg you to reveal to me those things that you wish changed in me. As for eternity, since I long to be with you, God of tender mercies, I believe I shall.

∼ 59. True Love ∼

If anyone says, "I love God," and hates his brother, he is a liar; for he who does not love his brother whom he has seen, cannot love God whom he has not seen. And this commandment we have from him, that he who loves God should love his brother also.

1 JOHN 4:20-21

Holiness means loving our neighbor as ourselves for love of God. In this connection holiness means loving those who curse us, who hate and persecute us, and even doing good to them. Holiness means living humbly, being disinterested, prudent, just, patient, kind, chaste, meek, diligent; carrying out one's duties for no other reason than that of pleasing God; and receiving from him alone the reward we deserve.

Letters, Vol. 2, 563

I see, Lord, that you are a God of relationships. You invite me to the deepest intimacy with you; and in that intimacy I, one with you, am to offer Jesus to the world, "that they might have life and have it to the full."

How empty I must become to make room for you! My will is willing; my flesh clings to all its little idols and is too weak. But, Lord, I count on you to do what I cannot! For nothing is impossible to you, my God!

∼ 60. Trusting God ∼

Have confidence in the Lord with all thy heart, and lean not upon thy own prudence. In all thy ways think on him, and he will direct thy steps.

PROVERBS 3:5-6, Douay-Rheims

THROUGH THE YEAR WITH PADRE PIO

How happy are those souls who live by faith; who adore the holy plan
of God in everything.

Letters, Vol. 3, 815

Place all your cares in him alone, because he has very great care of you.

Letters, Vol. 3, 131

Lord, today I will make frequent acts of trust in you.

∼ 61. How Great Thou Art! ∼

*How rich are the depths of God—how deep his wisdom and knowl-
edge—and how impossible to penetrate his motives or understand
his methods! Who could ever know the mind of the Lord.*

ROMANS 11:33-34, JB

Be tranquil as regards your spirit, and be certain that my spirit follows
you and goes before you everywhere. Jesus is and will always be yours,
and nobody can take him from you.

Letters, Vol. 3, 906

*Lord, how great is your cosmos. In the material world it stretches from
microbes to nebulae, but even vaster are the reaches of your spiritual realm.
Freed from the shackles that bind most of us, Padre Pio was able to remain
in the friary and visit people far away as your messenger, sometimes carrying your miracles of healing, sometimes watching over his spiritual children as in the letter above. I am comforted, Lord, by reflecting on how
much more there is than what can be seen. My spirit cries, "How great
thou art!"*

~ 62. Love Your Neighbor ~

Love one another with brotherly affection; outdo one another in showing honor.... Rejoice with those who rejoice, weep with those who weep.

ROMANS 12:10, 15

Treat your neighbor well and don't get angry. When necessary, say these words of the divine Master: "I love my neighbors, O Eternal Father, because you love them (Jn 14:21; 16:27). You gave them to me as brothers, and you want me to love them as you do."

[He writes to a teacher:] In a particular way love children, your disciples, to whom the very hand of divine providence accompanied you and united you with a heavenly binding. And don't be surprised at those little attacks of impatience, because there is no guilt in this except when preceded by reflex will—that is, being aware of it without doing your best to calm yourself.

Letters, Vol. 3, 741–42

Help me, Lord, to be a good neighbor to all those you permit to be part of my life—those you put next door, on my block, at my children's school, and in organizations I belong to, including my parish. Let me offer at least a smile and a prayer when I can do no more.

~ 63. Light: Armor and Loving Affliction ~

Let us then cast off the works of darkness and put on the armor of light.

ROMANS 13:12

Once again I exhort you to banish from your soul, with divine help always, even the slightest affliction and to serve the Lord with a joyful spirit. It is true that divine grace often strikes us with an afflicting light, manifesting our unworthiness and divine mercy, but it is always the light of a Father who loves and saves.

Letters, Vol. 3, 78

You, Lord, are the Light of the World. And you are my rock, my fortress, and my armor. To know you and your love is to be impregnably protected from all the lures and assaults of exterior darkness. Your light shines on the dark spots in my soul, only that, being manifest, they may be burned away by your divine mercy. Lord, I surrender these dark spots to you. Rule over my soul!

～ 64. Try to Take the Eternal View ～

I am the Lord your God, who brought you out of the land of Egypt, out of the house of bondage. You shall have no other gods before me.
EXODUS 20:2-3

The children of Israel were in the desert for forty years before they reached the Promised Land, even though six weeks were more than sufficient for this journey. Nonetheless it was not right to question why God led them along winding and bitter paths, and all those who did so died before they arrived there. Even Moses, a great friend of God, died on the border of the Promised Land, which he saw from a distance without being able to enjoy it [Dt 34].

Don't pay too much attention to the path on which you are walking. Keep your eyes always fixed on he who guides you and on the heavenly homeland to which he is leading you. Does it matter whether you get there by way of the desert or through fields, as long as God is with you, and that you finally possess blessed eternity?

Letters, Vol. 3, 836–37

What a thought, Lord! That it does not matter much whether life goes smoothly or with many twists and turns, so long as you are with us and we are headed to heaven. In the light of eternity that seems so true; but in the day by day, it is hard to keep such a supernatural perspective and such detachment. I see what peace such a view brings. Help me, Lord, just for this moment, to hold that thought.

⌒ 65. The Saints, Imitators of Christ and Models for Us ⌒

Be imitators of me, as I am of Christ.

1 CORINTHIANS 11:1

Let us earnestly hope that this new pope [Benedict XV] may be a truly worthy successor of the great Pope Pius X, a truly ... holy soul whose equal has never been seen by Rome. Born of lowly people, he never belied his humility. He was indeed the supremely good shepherd, the extremely peaceable ruler, the tender and meek Jesus on earth. Oh, we shall remember this good pope as an intercessor with the Most High.

Letters, Vol. 1, 554

Today, Lord, is the feast day of one of my favorite saints. But every day is the feast day of someone like the now canonized St. Pius X who has heroically followed Jesus Christ and inspired others like Pio. How rich I am as a member of such a vast family of all the known and unknown saints! As St. Paul and St. Francis, two of his favorites, beckoned Pio on, the whole cloud of witnesses calls me forward. I see the faces of my beloved family saints and my beloved saints of the Church, calling me to imitate them all the way to Heaven. And then, Lord, your banquet!

∼ 66. The Satisfactions of Spiritual Parenthood ∼

I have no greater grace than this, to hear that my children walk in truth.

2 JOHN 1:4, Douay-Rheims

As regards your spiritual state, I exhort you in the most sweet Lord to live tranquilly. I have a great reason to praise the Lord, for having enlightened your spirit somewhat.

Letters, Vol. 3, 682

Knowing that you are always resigned to the will of heaven fills my soul with superlative joy.

Letters, Vol. 3, 96

Padre Pio, those who lived with him testify, year after year lived in aridity and darkness, a warrior battling unceasingly for souls, while never sure whether he himself was pleasing God. At the same time he received great satisfaction, even joy, from the spiritual progress of his spiritual children—a joy that itself was purely supernatural, not an overflow of a constant state of mirth and contentment.

Patricia Treece

Lord, give me the great grace of spiritual parenthood and give me the joy of your saints, which is not dependent upon things "going well" but can coexist with the most difficult circumstances and emotions. Help me especially to release your power by rejoicing and praising you, not only for others' spiritual progress but when times are tough as well.

~ 67. Angels to Guard You ~

"He will give his angels charge of you," and "On their hands they will bear you up, lest you strike your foot against a stone."
MATTHEW 4:6

May your good guardian angel always watch over you; may he be your guide on the bitter paths of life. May he always keep you in the grace of Jesus and sustain you with his hands, so that you may not stumble on a stone. May he protect you under his wings from all the snares of the world, the devil, and the flesh.

Have great devotion ... to this good angel; how consoling it is to know that near us is a spirit who, from the cradle to the tomb, does not leave us even for an instant, not even when we dare to sin. And this heavenly spirit guides and protects us like a friend, a brother.

... It is extremely consoling to know that this angel prays without ceasing for us and offers to God all our good actions, our thoughts, our desires, if they are pure. For pity's sake, don't forget this invisible companion, always present, always ready to listen to us, and even more ready to console us. O delightful intimacy, O blessed company! If we could only understand it!

Always keep him present to your mind's eye. Often remember the presence of this angel; thank him, pray to him, always keep him good company. Open up yourself to him, and confide your suffering to him. Have a constant fear of offending the purity of his gaze. Know this and keep it well imprinted on your mind. He is so delicate, so sensitive. Turn to him in times of supreme anxiety, and you will experience his beneficial help.

Letters, Vol. 3, 84–85

Lord, you know I have always had trouble believing in angels. That Padre Pio saw his angel and had an intimate relationship with him helps. So do the experiences of my friend Eva Ensholm, who saw her angel first as a child and several times as an adult, once when she was in the company of a companion who was healed. Lord, I want to believe; help my unbelief!

∾ 68. Add Patience, Subtract Worry ∾

By your patience, you will win your souls.
LUKE 21:19, Challoner-Rheims

Wait patiently, avoiding any little worry or uneasiness which impedes the effects of patience.... It is through this that we will possess our souls. And to the degree to which it is perfect, the possession of our souls will be entire and excellent. Patience is most perfect when it is less mixed up with anxiety and worry. I hope God will free you from these two inconveniences.

Letters, Vol. 3, 836

We both know, Lord, that I was not born patient. And we both know that from the age of two, when my mother died, I was riddled with anxiety. Yet now I am fairly patient, and anxious much less. It is good to look back,

Lord, and see that over many years you are working a slow transformation within me. I thank and praise you, Lord.

∼ 69. When Prayer Is Hard ∼

We do not know how to pray as we ought.

ROMANS 8:26

You tell me that on account of your sleepy, distracted, fickle, and most wretched soul, frequently with the addition of physical complaints, you cannot bear to remain in church for [very long after Mass to pray]. Don't worry on this account. Make an effort to overcome vexation and boredom, and don't weary your mind excessively with very long and continued prayers when your heart and mind are not so inclined.

... When possible,... in the silence of your heart and in solitude, offer your praises, your blessings, your contrite and humble heart, and your entire self to the heavenly Father.

Letters, Vol. 2, 189

How I relate, Lord, to Padre Pio's spiritual daughter, whose efforts to pray are sandbagged by her sleepiness, her distractions, her physical problems, and so on! Accept my poor plodding prayers, Lord. And send me your Spirit, Lord, to pray in me at depths I cannot consciously reach.

∼ 70. The Humility of Mary ∼

And Mary said, "Behold, I am the handmaid of the Lord; let it be to me according to your word." And the angel departed from her.

LUKE 1:38

Reflect upon the great humility of the Mother of God, our mother. The more she was filled with heavenly gifts, the more deeply did she humble herself, so that she was able to say when overshadowed by the Holy Spirit, who made her the Mother of God's Son: *Behold the handmaid of the Lord.*

Letters, Vol. 2, 436–37

Lord, through all the ages your mother, given to us from the cross, humbly says—as she did at Cana—"Do what my Son tells you." Lord, unlike Mary, who was conceived without sin to be a fitting mother for you and has no will but yours, I am only an earthen vessel. Still, may you so overshadow my sins and weaknesses that I too may birth you into my little world. May those who see me see you and receive your salvation with joy.

∼ 71. Being Less Than I Desire ∼

I do not understand my own actions. For I do not do what I want, but I do the very thing I hate.

ROMANS 7:15

I have had the audacity, Father, to accuse others, while I myself am the worst of all! Now, indeed, do I recognize myself as the most unworthy of all wretched creatures....

My confessor assures me that at most I have committed a venial sin [by telling, Pio says elsewhere, a lie], but what does this matter when in any event I have made Jesus weep?... I tell Jesus that I do not intend to sin anymore, but if he does not sustain me in my weakness, at the first chance I shall show myself to be the same as ever.... Poor Jesus, offended by me once again! My heart is so hard that it is not moved as it ought to be at the thought of the offences I have committed against him. But I want to repent as far as I can for these sins....

When I consider Jesus' love on the one hand and my own ingratitude on the other, my dear Father, I should like to tell him that if I cannot correspond to his love he should stop loving me... But if Jesus does not love me, what is to become of me?... This is too terrifying a thing for me, and hence it makes me invariably pray Jesus to continue to love me and to help me himself if I do not succeed in loving him as much as he deserves.

Letters, Vol. 1, 266–67

It helps, Lord, to know that saints like St. Paul and Pio sometimes "lost it" and that even Pio could not achieve the gratitude he desired. Help me tread that fine line between being complacent about my faults, and thus no longer trying to improve, and morbidly pondering my sins in a way that paralyzes me.

∼ 72. Transformed But Not Perfect ∼

And we all, with unveiled face, beholding the glory of the Lord, are being changed into his likeness from one degree of glory to another; for this comes from the Lord who is the Spirit.

2 CORINTHIANS 3:18

But we have this treasure in earthen vessels, to show that the transcendent power belongs to God and not to us.

2 CORINTHIANS 4:7

I believe you should take a little rest and carefully consider the inconstancy of the human spirit and how easily it becomes embarrassed and agitated. I believe that all the spiritual agitation you suffered in the past was caused by nothing but a great desire to arrive quickly at an imaginary perfection, made with excessive haste.

Let me explain further: Your imagination was intent on reaching a total perfection to which your will wished to lead you. But more often than not it is terrified by the great difficulty and impossibility of reaching this.

Letters, Vol. 3, 684

Dear Lord, how true it is that reaching perfection in this life is humanly impossible. But since nothing is impossible with you, Lord, and it is your will that I become like you, then bring me, even in this life, to spiritual maturity, to wholeness, to holiness—things better, I know, than perfection.

～ 73. The Necessity of Spiritual Winter ～

Someone who has never had his trials knows little.
ECCLESIASTICUS 34:10, JB

I see all the seasons of the year in your heart. Sometimes you feel the winter of great sterility, distractions, restlessness, and boredom; sometimes the dew of the month of May with the perfume of little flowers;... sometimes the warmth of the desire to please our good God. There only remains, then, autumn when you do not see much fruit; but it often happens that when the grain is threshed and the grapes crushed, a greater harvest results than expected from the harvesting.

You would like it to be always spring and summer, but no, my dearest daughter, these vicissitudes are necessary internally as they are externally. In heaven only, everything will always be spring as far as beauty is concerned, everything autumn as far as enjoyment is concerned, everything summer as far as love is concerned. There will be no winter; but here winter is necessary to exercise self-denial and a thousand other little but beautiful virtues, which are practiced in times of sterility.

Always walk in this manner in the ways of love, and don't be upset if it sometimes seems to you that you move rather slowly; as long as you have good and determined intention, you cannot but make progress.

Letters, Vol. 3, 861–62

Lord, I prefer those periods in my life when joy abounds, but I admit that my times of trial have been seasons of growth. Be with me, Lord, in whatever you send today, keeping me, as Padre Pio advises, walking "in the ways of love."

∼ 74. Peace: A Sign of True Christian Life ∼

For he is our peace.... And he came and preached peace to you who were far off, and peace to those who were near.
EPHESIANS 2:14, 17

Jesus stood in their midst, and said to them, "Peace to you!"
LUKE 24:36, Challoner-Rheims

Before anything else, we should try to live in tranquility of spirit. Not because tranquility is the mother of Christian content, but because it is the daughter of love of God and of the resignation of our own will. We can have occasion to practice this daily, because contradictions are never lacking, and when there is nothing that causes this, we form it ourselves.

Letters, Vol. 3, 928

Peace, Lord, is your gift. How often, as Pio says, I create "contradictions" to your peace internally when there are none externally. Rule over my soul, Lord. Bring your peace so deep into my heart that my restless soul will rest in you.

～ 75. Hearts Open Wide ～

Corinthians, our heart is wide.

2 CORINTHIANS 6:11

To see suffering makes me very unhappy! I would gladly stab myself in the heart to take away suffering from someone! Yes, this would be easier for me!

Padre Pio da Pietrelcina: Testimonianze
Vincenzo da Casacalenda, 121

Lord Jesus, your saints Paul and Pio emptied their hearts of all that was not you. Then, filled with you, they gave themselves 100 percent to souls. Many times in my life I have benefited from priests who live only for your flock and you. Bless them, Lord! Today I offer all my works and prayers as support to your priests, pastors, rabbis, and others who serve our heavenly Father.

∼ 76. Moving Into the Light ∼

For once you were darkness, but now you are light in the Lord; walk as children of light (for the fruit of light is found in all that is good and right and true).

EPHESIANS 5:8-9

Contrary to our every merit, we are on the steps of Tabor, by having a firm determination to love and serve his divine goodness well. Therefore, we must have great hope. Let us ascend, my beloved daughter; let us ascend without ever tiring to the heavenly vision of the Savior. Let us, step by step, draw away from earthly affections; let us strip ourselves of the old man and dress ourselves in the new man, aspiring to the happiness that awaits us.

Letters, Vol. 3, 410

I offer my darkness to your purifying light, Lord. Make me a child of light, so that I may do good while I have the time.

∼ 77. Prayer ∼

Pray at all times in the Spirit, with all prayer and supplication. To that end keep alert with all perseverance, making supplication for all the saints.

EPHESIANS 6:18

Prayer is the best weapon we have; it is the key to God's heart. You must speak to Jesus not only with your lips but with your heart; in fact, on certain occasions you should speak to him only with your heart.

Consigli-Esortazioni di Padre Pio da Pietrelcina, 40

Lord, I want to pray, but I get distracted. When I am not thinking of you, Lord, let every beat of my heart be an act of love for you, let my hands sing your praises in their work, however menial, and may every breath I take call to your Spirit.

∽ 78. Let's Laugh ∽

For everything there is a season and a time for every matter under heaven:... a time to weep, and a time to laugh.

ECCLESIASTES 3:1, 4

I laugh at your suffering, as you, many times, laughed at mine.... If you can, laugh at yourself with me, and pray that I too can laugh at myself with you.

Letters, Vol. 3, 118

Yes, Lord, help me not to take myself too seriously but to laugh readily at myself. Even my worst troubles have a ridiculous side.

∽ 79. Doing Good ∽

Do not refuse a kindness to anyone who begs it, if it is in your power to perform it.

PROVERBS 3:27, JB

Let us say to ourselves with the full conviction of telling the truth, "My soul, begin today to do the good works which to this day you have not done." Let us be moved by the presence of God. Let us often say to ourselves, "God sees me, and as he looks at me He also judges me." Let us act in such a way that he sees only good in us.

Letters, Vol. 4, 966

Lord, you want me to follow you by being kind, not just to those who are kind to me but to those who are not. This is tough, Lord! Help me to learn to let incidents of unkindness to me fall into the abyss of your mercy.

∼ 80. The Ocean of Heavenly Goodness ∼

Jesus looked up and said to her, "Woman, where are they? Has no one condemned you?" She said, "No one, Lord." And Jesus said, "Neither do I condemn you; go, and do not sin again."

JOHN 8:10-11

You tell me you went astray ... during the first years.... I don't want to establish what truth there is in this.... I merely insist on telling you, in the Lord, to cast aside this conviction of yours once and for all.... Trust in the Lord, in his forgiveness and protection. Oh yes! You can even rest tranquilly on the bosom of divine mercy, as a tender little child rests in the arms of its mother.

Letters, Vol. 3, 151–52

Divine mercy, may my past, my present, and my future all be lost in this ocean of your goodness. Keeping my eyes on you rather than my sins, may I become more and more like you.

～ 81. Intercessory Prayer ～

Continue steadfastly in prayer, being watchful in it with thanks-giving.

COLOSSIANS 4:2

Oh, how I hope that my poor [prayers] for you will all be granted by the Lord! I know it is only Jesus who probes the depths of your soul; only Jesus has a full knowledge of your desires and needs. Therefore, I constantly present and recommend you to him, and I beg him to satisfy your desires.

Letters, Vol. 3, 371

In the mystery of your providence, you call me to intercede in prayer for certain people. You alone know the depths of their souls and their true needs. Time and again I lift them, Lord, into your transforming light and nourishing, redemptive love. And I cry for them, as for myself, "Heal us, O Lord, and bless us!"

～ 82. Our Blessed Hope: Increasing in Virtue ～

For the grace of God has appeared for the salvation of all men, training us to renounce irreligion and worldly passions, and to live sober, upright, and godly lives in this world, awaiting our blessed hope, the appearing of the glory of our great God and Savior Jesus Christ, who gave himself for us to redeem us from all iniquity and to purify for himself a people of his own who are zealous for good deeds.

TITUS 2:11-14

You who have received many gifts and graces from Jesus, continue to increase always in the life of virtue, and your piety and zeal will recall those who are far from the right path, and thus you will praise the Lord along with our common father, St. Francis, in all the works of the creation, obtaining copious reward on earth and in heaven.

Letters, Vol. 3, 1105

You have blessed me in so many ways, Lord, from the gift of faith to the gift of people I love and am loved by. What can I do in return but love and praise you as much as I can?

Because you deserve so much more love and praise than I can muster, I ask you for more love. St. Maximilian Kolbe said the whole world would be converted when believers' hearts were on fire with love. Set my heart aflame, Lord!

～ 83. Take This Cup Away ～

He said to them, "My soul is very sorrowful, even to death; remain here, and watch." And going a little farther, he fell on the ground and prayed that, if it were possible, the hour might pass from him. And he said, "Abba, Father, all things are possible to thee; remove this cup from me; yet not what I will, but what thou wilt."

MARK 14:34-36

Live totally in God, and for the love He holds for you patiently bear yourself in all your miseries. Remember that in order to be a good servant of God, it is not necessary always to be consoled, always to be in a state of sweetness, always without aversion or repugnance for good. Because if this were true, neither St. Catherine of Siena, St. Teresa, nor

St. Paul would have served the Lord well.

Letters, Vol. 3, 932

Lord, you know the aversion and repugnance I feel toward the event coming up. I have prayed repeatedly that you would take this cup from me. I still have hopes for a last-minute rescue, but I also abandon myself to your loving plan and say, with Jesus, "Not what I will but what you will." I thank you ahead of time, Lord, however this turns out; for I know that wherever you lead me it is always for my good and brings blessings.

∼ 84. Multiplication ∼

They said to him, "We have only five loaves here and two fish." And he said, "Bring them here to me." Then he ordered the crowds to sit down on the grass; and taking the five loaves and the two fish he looked up to heaven, and blessed, and broke and gave the loaves to the disciples, and the disciples gave them to the crowds. And they all ate and were satisfied. And they took up twelve baskets full of the broken pieces left over.

MATTHEW 14:17-20

Once there was nothing but a loaf of bread in the monastery.... Their appetites burned the poor sisters' stomachs. Having triumphed over everything, they still could not always ignore the imperious necessities of life.

Sr. Cecilia, the housekeeper, turned to the holy Abbess [St. Claire] in this emergency, and ... [Claire] ordered the bread to be divided in two; to send half to their brothers [St. Francis and his followers] ... and to keep the rest. This was then to be divided into fifty portions, in accordance with the number of sisters, and each sister was to be given her portion on the table of poverty. But as the devout daughter replied that one of Jesus' miracles would be necessary for such a small amount of bread to be divided into fifty portions, the Mother Superior replied: "My daughter, do what I tell you with certainty."

The obedient daughter hastened to obey, and Mother Claire immediately had recourse to Jesus through prayers and pitiful sighs for her little daughters. Through divine grace, the bread then increased in the hands of she who broke it, and each one received a large portion.

Letters, Vol. 3, 1103–4

Jesus, Padre Pio humbly tells of St. Claire's multiplications when he could have spoken of his own. Studying your saints, I find physicists are right: Matter is energy and with the power of love and prayer can be recombined in new and bigger ways. In giving half the food away when her daughters were so hungry, St. Claire pressed the spring that opens the treasures of heaven.

Help me, Lord, to never be afraid to give lavishly! And help me to always have Claire's confidence that you will provide.

∼ 85. Seeing God ∼

... The angel of the Lord appeared to him [Moses] in a flame of fire out of the midst of a bush;... and lo, the bush was burning, yet it was not consumed. And Moses said, "I will turn aside to see this great sight, why the bush is not burnt." When the Lord saw that he turned aside to see, God called to him out of the bush, "Moses, Moses!" And he said, "Here am I." Then he said, "Do not come near; put off your shoes from your feet, for the place on which you are standing is holy ground." And he said, "I am the God of your father, the God of

Abraham, the God of Isaac, and the God of Jacob." And Moses hid his face, for he was afraid to look at God.

EXODUS 3:2-6

I am convinced that I must speak to you [God] in the midst of thunder and hurricanes, that I should see you in the burning bush amid the fire of tribulations, but to do all this I see that it is necessary to take off one's shoes and give up entirely one's own will and affections.

Letters, Vol. 1, 933

Sometimes, Lord, it seems that I see everyone except you. Transform me, Lord, so that, wherever and at whomever I look—even in the mirror—I shall see only you.

～ 86. Grateful Prayer ～

I give thanks to my God, always making remembrance of thee in my prayers.

PHILEMON 1:4, Challoner-Rheims

May the heavenly Child always be in the midst of your heart; may he sustain it, enlighten it, vivify it, and transform it to eternal charity.... I will continually say this prayer ... for you before Jesus in my prayers, which are certainly poor, but none the less assiduous, as long as I live. Therefore, accept these prayers and good wishes as the most beautiful expressions of the heart of he who loves you with paternal and fraternal tenderness in the most loving heart of our Lord, Jesus Christ. Accept this prayer and good wish of mine as a very small repayment for all you have done for me.

I would like to offer you still more before Jesus, but ... I have nothing more. Never mind! Jesus will reward you for everything and a thousand times.

Letters, Vol. 3, 839–40

How many of your good friends, Lord, have come to my aid, along with others who do not know you but live in your Spirit. I have only my prayers with which to reward them. But you! Lord, you are Master of the Universe. Repay, O Lord, with your great kindness those who have helped your child. Let your blessings pour upon them, pressed down and overflowing. Answer all their prayers, Lord. Give them health of soul and body. And let their days be peaceful, long, and filled with love!

∼ 87. Building the Kingdom ∼

Let each of us please his neighbor for his good, to edify him.

ROMANS 15:2

Fear nothing. Jesus is and will always be totally yours, and nobody will take him from you. Do not allow yourself to be overcome by discouragement if you don't always visibly see your every effort crowned. Jesus sees, rewards, and commands good will and not good success, because the latter does not depend on human efforts and work.

Letters, Vol. 3, 792

Lord, trying to help someone I love today, through my insensitivity I hurt him instead. I have tried to make amends, Lord. Thank you for reminding me through this that even all the goodwill in the world cannot keep me from annoying or even angering others. Help me to be conscious of the fact that my view is not the only view. My perceptions of events and people may be skewed or, even if right, not acceptable to others. Let me follow that saint, Lord, who said, "To help others one must be very, very humble."

~ 88. Searching for God ~

As a doe longs for running streams, so longs my soul for you, my God.
PSALM 42:1, JB

But what is this painful searching for God that occupies your heart incessantly? It is the effect of the love that draws you and the love that impels you.

Letters, Vol. 3, 634

My soul longs for you because you call me through your Spirit, speaking wordlessly in my heart; you call me through the beauty of the natural world; and you call me through my inner demand for love and meaning. Speak, Lord, I am listening!

~ 89. A Way to Look at Suffering, Desolation, and Contradiction ~

For it is better to suffer for doing right, if that should be God's will, than for doing wrong.

1 PETER 3:17

Consider that we are always in the presence of God, to whom we have to give account for our every action, both good and bad.... [Meditating on Jesus' Passion will help] ... when the most sweet Jesus sends you suffering, places you in a state of desolation, or wishes to make you a subject of contradiction.

Letters, Vol. 3, 60–61

Lord, when I study the lives of your saints, I find so many whom you permitted to suffer for doing good and to become signs of contradiction to their societies. How small I see myself with all my conventional desires to "look good," "to fit in," "to not make waves." I wish, Lord, that I were bolder and that I did not hate controversy and disharmony so much! You changed St. Gaspar del Bufalo from a timid man into an apostolic giant. Can't you do something about me?

∼ 90. Belonging to God ∼

With my whole heart I seek thee.

PSALM 119:10

He who belongs only to God seeks nobody but God himself, and given that he is equally great in times of tribulation and prosperity, one lives calmly in the midst of adversity.

He who belongs only to God continually thinks of him in the midst of all the events of this life and always tries to become better in the eyes of God, and finds and admires God in all creatures, exclaiming with St. Augustine: "All creatures, O Lord, tell me to love you."

Letters, Vol. 3, 527

Lord, St. Thérèse of Lisieux said, I only have today—this moment even—to love you. So, as the old prayer says, may every beat of my heart today be an act of love for you.

～ 91. Avoid Haste to Drive Away Faults ～

Set your heart right and be steadfast, and do not be hasty in time of calamity. Cleave to him…. Trust in him, and he will help you…. You who fear the Lord, wait for his mercy, and turn not aside, lest you fall.

SIRACH 2:2-3, 6-7

… Try as best you can, without excessive anxiety, to do what you must and wish to do with perfection. But once it is done, think no more about it, but rather attend only to what you must and want to do or to what you are doing. Walk with simplicity in the ways of the Lord and do not torment your spirit. You must hate your faults, but with a quiet hate, not troublesome and restless. We must be patient with them and gain from them through holy humility. Without that patience … instead of diminishing, your imperfections will increase constantly, as there is nothing that nourishes our defects like restlessness and the haste to drive them away.

Letters, Vol. 3, 582–83

Lord, help me to be patient with my faults and weaknesses and, as Pio says, gain from them through humility, while I await your mercy that can free me when you deem it best.

∼ 92. Freedom to Be Real ∼

Live as free men, yet without using your freedom as a pretext for evil; but live as servants of God.

1 PETER 2:16

Let nature resent suffering because, when there is no sin, there is nothing more natural than this. With divine help, your will, will always be superior to it [your feelings of repugnance and resentment], and divine love will never diminish in your soul if you do not cease to pray.

Letters, Vol. 3, 82

How consoling that Padre Pio understood human nature! He is not seeking to form repressed plaster "saints" who cannot own that they feel resentment in suffering. A feeling, I remind myself, Lord, is never a sin. Sin enters when my feeling of anger or resentment is expressed in a deliberate malicious act. I do not want to sin, Lord, but I want to always have an honest dialogue with you, free to be angry, free to be frightened, free to be the complex mix of feelings that is ME.

∼ 93. Lord, Save Me! ∼

But when the disciples saw him walking on the sea, they were terrified, saying, "It is a ghost!" And they cried out for fear. But immediately he spoke to them, saying, "Take heart, it is I; have no fear." And Peter answered him, "Lord, if it is you, bid me come to you on the water." He said, "Come." So Peter got out of the boat and walked on the water and came to Jesus; but when he saw the wind, he was afraid, and beginning to sink he cried out, "Lord, save me."

*Jesus immediately reached out his hand and caught him, saying to
him, "O man of little faith, why did you doubt?"*

MATTHEW 14:26-31

O daughter of little faith, I also repeat to you with the divine Master,
Why are you afraid? No, do not fear; you are walking on the sea amid
the wind and waves, but be sure that you are with Jesus. What is there
to fear? But if fear takes you by surprise, you too shout loudly: "O
Lord, save me!" He will stretch out his hand to you; and this hand is
precisely that tenuous ray of trust in him which you feel in the depths
of your soul. Squeeze his hand tightly and walk joyfully, at least in the
apex of your soul.

Letters, Vol. 3, 178

*Tonight I am afraid, Lord. Take my childlike hand, and lead me through
this dark hour. Jesus, I trust in you! Help my lack of trust!*

～ 94. Jesus My Hope ～

*Therefore we must pay the closer attention to what we have heard,
lest we drift away from it. For if the message declared by angels was
valid and every transgression or disobedience received a just retribu-
tion, how shall we escape if we neglect such a great salvation? It was
declared at first by the Lord, and it was attested to us by those who
heard him, while God also bore witness by signs and wonders and
various miracles and by gifts of the Holy Spirit distributed according to his own will.*

HEBREWS 2:1-4

Keep Jesus Crucified present to your imagination; in your arms and on your breast, and kissing his side, say a thousand times: "This is my hope, the living source of my happiness; this is the heart of my soul; nothing will ever separate me from his love. I possess him and will not leave him, until he places me in a safe place."

Often say to him: "What can I have on earth, or what can I expect in heaven, if not you, O my Jesus? You are the God of my heart and the inheritance I desire for all eternity."

Letters, Vol. 3, 508

Lord, I see you in the garden in your agony. I am too poor and weak to support you. Like your disciples, I fall asleep rather than let myself truly enter into your sufferings. But I will *to be with you, Lord, and offer you my mite of understanding, love, and appreciation. Accept my will, Lord, and increase my ability to love you, since on my own I can do nothing to stretch my narrow heart beyond its self-centeredness.*

∼ 95. When Heaven Is Silent ∼

Being in an agony he prayed more earnestly; and his sweat became like great drops of blood falling down upon the ground.

LUKE 22:44

Listen, dear daughters, don't waste time. Tell Jesus that it is by now time he came to my aid. I truly cannot bear it any longer. May he grant me what I have been asking of him for some time now, and quickly; otherwise I will inevitably be overwhelmed by the enemies. I am suffering the most atrocious agony. Tear from him, quickly, what I am asking; otherwise it will be too late. I deserve nothing more from divine mercy, I know, but I am waiting for my prayers to be granted through the merits of Jesus and the prayers of good souls. Will I not be heard even for this? If not, I will be lost.... Dear God, I feel I am dying under this heavy weight!

Letters, Vol. 3, 390–91

Dear God, how good to know that even a saint like Padre Pio at times experienced the feeling that he could not take any more suffering. I know he was young at the time he wrote those words to some of his spiritual daughters. I am much older and should be much more accepting of my crosses. But I too am asking you to take away my trouble through the merits of your Son, your saints like Pio, and all those good people who are praying for me. Divine Mercy, I am waiting for your healing touch!

∼ 96. Walk Humbly Without Rancor ∼

Have this mind among yourselves, which you have in Christ Jesus, who, though he was in the form of God, did not count equality with God a thing to be grasped.

PHILIPPIANS 2:5-6

I beg you not to take to heart the incident that took place yesterday. I did what I did not because I took your complaint badly—that is to say, because I held some rancor against whomsoever. May God protect me from that! He is a witness to what I am doing. And my intention was always upright before him. But I withdrew from you and everybody because they are matters that hurt my soul deeply, and I am unable to quell a certain interior sadness, which hurt me precisely in the most delicate and sensitive part, in the center of my heart.

Don't hold anything against me, because I bear nobody any rancor. On the contrary, all are very dear to me, and I love them as I love my own soul.

Letters, Vol. 3, 525

Oh dear Lord, you know I was pretty crisp and full of myself when I got that third telemarketing call in two days from the same company, just as I was pondering those words from Philippians about your emptying yourself. You do have a way of gently pointing out how poorly I follow your example. Sorry! Help me be more charitable to the least of your children, among whom telephone sales folk surely qualify.

∼ 97. Cling to Hope ∼

Why so downcast, my soul, why do you sigh within me? Put your hope in God: I shall praise him yet, my savior, my God.

PSALM 42:5, JB

I cannot go on any longer. My eyes are becoming veiled with tears, and my heart is crushed under this heavy weight.... If you want to give me a word of encouragement, and if Jesus still permits you to have dealings with this person who is dead among the living, I will be grateful to you.

Letters, Vol. 3, 391

Lord, things look pretty black just now. But however unrealistic it seems at this point to hope, I WILL HOPE! Jesus, I trust in you.

Pray for me, Padre Pio, that when cast down I may still reach out, as you did, to God and friends for help and encouragement.

～ 98. Do Good Whenever You Can ～

Do not withhold good from those to whom it is due, when it is in your power to do it. Do not say to your neighbor, "Go, and come again, tomorrow I will give it"—when you have it with you.

PROVERBS 3:27-28

Each one loves according to his own tastes; few, however, live according to their duty and the will of the Lord. From this there arises that tearful state whereby many start out on the path to perfection but few arrive at the summit.

Letters, Vol. 3, 289

Lord, help me not to hold back from loving with all my heart EVERY-ONE you put in my path, those who wish me good and those who wish me ill. Help me also to never fear to give my material goods to others. Surely by now I should know that the more I give, the more you see I receive. I am ashamed that still sometimes I feel hemmed in by caution or by fear masquerading as "prudence." Give me a holy "foolishness" in your regard, that in the way I relate to others I may become a Christian in deed as well as name.

～ 99. Flowers ～

For lo, the winter is past, the rain is over and gone. The flowers appear on the earth, the time of singing has come, and the voice of the turtledove is heard in our land.

SONG OF SONGS 2:11-12

One day a friar whose birthday it was heard a small noise outside the closed door of his cell. Curious, he opened the door and caught Padre Pio, who was shyly leaving the flower he had picked to wish his confrere a happy feast day.

Patricia Treece

(Padre Gerardo of Deliceto's remembrance of Pio's feast day gift can be found in *The Voice of Padre*, Vol. 27, Summer Number, 1997, 5.)

Oh, the flowers, Lord! You place beauty everywhere, from the daffodils of spring to the roses of summer, from chrysanthemums of autumn to the primroses in winter. You did not have to create the world in color; you did not have to give us flowers. Thank you, Lord! Thank you!

~ 100. Living in God's Love ~

Charity never fails.

1 CORINTHIANS 13:8, Challoner-Rheims

May Jesus fill you with his holy love, and may he transform you totally in him!

Letters, Vol. 3, 827

May our most sweet Savior extirpate your heart, as he did with his servant St. Catherine of Siena, in order to grant you his most divine heart, through which you can then live totally of his holy love.

Letters, Vol. 3, 824

Lord, I know that the transformation you offer me and that I long for is all about love. Giving up revenge, giving up even justice sometimes in order to "cover" enemies' misdeeds—such aspects of true forgiveness are the strongest proof of love that is not cheap words but the real thing. How hard it is to love like you, to truly let the rain of one's mercy fall upon the just and the unjust. I cannot do this unless you totally transform me, Lord. Do it soon!

∽ 101. Paying Our Debts in Prayer ∽

I remember you constantly in my prayers.... I long night and day to see you, that I may be filled with joy.

2 TIMOTHY 1:3-4

My dear daughter, write to me always with the confidence of a daughter.... In order that you be directed well, it is not sufficient for me to know only the general state of your soul; I also want to know of new events that take place and also accidentals. If you were more greatly convinced of the holy affection I have for you in the Lord, and knew of the fire with which my soul burns for your sanctification, I would not have thought it necessary to request this of you, to encourage you to do what I say.

How can I repay—I don't say you—but your family, for what you and they have done for me. I do my best to repay this debt in some way with my assiduous prayers before the Lord, and for this reason I offered the Mass I sang last Saturday to the heavenly Father for you and your family.

... How happy I would be if I could personally thank you and your family.

Letters, Vol. 3, 866–67

Oh, the wonder of the communion of saints! As John Donne instinctively saw, "no man is an island." Isolated as we are, all who do not definitively opt out are connected in God's family. And we can enrich and succor each other with prayer, the thread that binds us more closely to another soul than ties of blood. As God's child I rejoice to be in communion with others, even beyond such "boundaries" as life and death, time and space.

Bless, Lord, all my living and dead benefactors. Bless all the living and the dead who need my prayers and support. Bless those for whom I have been a gift in any way. Bless those who dislike me or whom I have hurt. Thank you, Lord, for this glorious family of yours and my little place in it!

⁓ 102. On Pride and Humility ⁓

When pride comes, then comes disgrace; but with the humble is wisdom.

PROVERBS 11:2

On the way they had discussed with one another who was the greatest. And he sat down and called the twelve; and he said to them, "If any one would be first, he must be last of all and servant of all."

MARK 9:34-35

Lovingly humble yourself before God and men, because God speaks to those who are humble. *Hear, O daughter,* he says to the bride in the Sacred Song [of Solomon], *and incline your ear; forget your people and your father's house.* Thus loving sons prostrate themselves when they speak to the heavenly Father and await the reply from his divine oracle.

The Lord will fill your vessel with his balm when he sees it empty of the perfumes of the world; and the more you humble yourself, the more he will exalt you.

Letters, Vol. 3, 866

Lord, you gave Padre Pio such great gifts that you had to blind him to his spiritual state and let him worry all his life if he had been pleasing to you or had used properly what you had given him. No need for that with a small soul like me! I find it easy most of the time to see my good points and gifts. Help me to as readily see my faults and weaknesses. Let me know the truth about myself—good and bad. Above all, let me see your perfection and glory, so that seeing myself in the light of your love, beauty, and wisdom, I may become humble.

∼ 103. God's Healing Power Through His Saints ∼

Jesus said to him, "Rise, take up your pallet, and walk." And at once the man was healed.

JOHN 5:8-9

In 1974 I was the recipient of what my husband and I consider a miracle from Padre Pio. I was told in July 1974 [that] I would be opened up for major cancer. Since I was also a nurse at the hospital, I knew the score. The surgeon told me quite bluntly: "We are opening you up for major cancer, with the expectation of finding it, and praying we don't."

The night before surgery my husband awakened about 2:00 A.M. to the scent of roses (a miracle in itself since he was just out of the hospital from nose surgery and could smell nothing at all). He followed the scent to the living room, where on the mantel was a continuous candle burning in front of a statue of Padre Pio. Suddenly he heard a voice, and it said, "Rudolph, don't worry; they won't find cancer: she'll be all right." My husband was stunned.

The next morning I was in surgery six hours. Then the doctor came into my room smiling and said to me, "Do you know you had a miracle? There isn't a trace of cancer in your body anywhere. A large tumor was removed, and it was benign."

Testimony of Rita M. DeNitti from friary archives quoted in
Patricia Treece, *Apparitions of Modern Saints,* 148–49

Healing is yours, Lord, but you seem to love to deliver it through your saints, just as you once sent out seventy-two disciples to bring blessings in your name. Since nothing is impossible with you, Lord, let me always be both conformed to your will and open to miracles when I am ill.

∼ 104. Safe in Jesus' Arms ∼

The God who made the world and everything in it, being Lord of heaven and earth, does not live in shrines made by man, nor is he served by human hands, as though he needed anything, since he himself gives to all men life and breath and everything.... He is not far from each one of us, for "In him we live and move and have our being."

ACTS 17:24-28

You say you are anxious about the future, but don't you know that the Lord is with you always and that our enemy has no power over one who has resolved to belong entirely to Jesus?... Humble yourself, then, at the delightful thought that you are in the divine arms of Jesus, the best of fathers, like a little infant in its mother's arms, and sleep peacefully with the certainty that you are being guided toward the destination that will be to your greatest advantage.

Letters, Vol. 2, 68–69

Lord, I am anxious about the future. Please help me to feel that I do live, move, and have my being in you. Help me to feel like a loved child in the best of fathers' arms, as Padre Pio counseled. I don't feel it. I want to. Heal my anxiety, Lord.

∼ 105. The Holy Spirit: Bringer of Good to Those Who Seek God ∼

But it is God who establishes us with you in Christ, and has commissioned us; he has put his seal upon us and given us his Spirit in our hearts as a guarantee.

2 CORINTHIANS 1:21-22

Never fall back on yourself alone, but place all your trust in God, and don't be too eager to be set free from your present state. Let the Holy Spirit act within you. Give yourself up to all his transports and have no fear. He is so wise and gentle and discreet that he never brings about anything but good. How good this Holy Spirit, this Comforter, is to all, but how supremely good he is to those who seek him!

Letters, Vol. 2, 70

Come, Holy Spirit, Comforter, Guide. Fill me with your wisdom and your peace. I surrender my life to your loving guidance.

~ 106. Seeking Deliverance ~

Finally, brethren, pray for us, that the word of the Lord may speed on and triumph, as it did among you, and that we may be delivered.

2 THESSALONIANS 3:1-2

I understand that our enemies are strong, very strong, but when one fights along with Jesus, how can one have any doubt about winning the battle? Oh, isn't our God stronger than all the others? Who can hold out against him? Who can oppose his decrees or his will?

Letters, Vol. 2, 435–36

Help me, Lord, when it seems that the forces of darkness are plunging the world into wars, epidemics, acts of terrorism and other disasters, to cling to hope that in the end you will triumph over every evil.

~ 107. Imperfect Love ~

Let all that you do be done in love.

1 CORINTHIANS 16:14

Jesus, you always come into my soul. With what food must I feed you? With love! But my love is false. Jesus, I love you very much. Make up for my love ['s deficiencies].

quoting Pio in *Diary of Padre Agostino da San Marco in Lamis,*
one of Padre Pio's spiritual directors, 36

Lord, I so often tell myself that real love goes beyond words to deeds. But Sts. Paul and Pio remind me that I must go deeper. Even great deeds may be empty if the motive is not right. Purify my heart, Lord, so that my deeds may be rooted and grounded in true charity rather than ego.

~ 108. The Sure Path to Heaven ~

Happy is he who trusts in the Lord.

PROVERBS 16:20

Do your best to conform always and in everything to the will of God in all eventualities, and do not fear. This is the sure path to heaven.

Letters, Vol. 3, 452

With all my heart, Lord, I wish to let go of fear and simply trust you. Yet time and time again I give in to either fear or anxiety. When will you heal these traits, Lord? Soon, please, soon! Jesus, I trust in you to transform me.

~ 109. Reject Sadness, Cultivate Joy ~

A glad heart makes a cheerful countenance, but by sorrow of heart the spirit is broken.

PROVERBS 15:13

When you are overcome by sadness,... then more than ever must you renew your trust in God.... Cast far from you all thought of things that cause you to be sad, refuse to harbor all such thoughts just as you would reject temptations against holy purity. You must not dwell any longer on these tormenting thoughts.

... In addition you must endeavor to occupy your mind with happy things. Try to dwell, for example, on the goodness of the heavenly Father in giving you his Only Begotten Son, on the beauty of our holy faith, on the happiness reserved for us in paradise, on the resurrection and ascension of Jesus, on the glory he enjoys in paradise and which, if we remain faithful to him, he has reserved one day for us also. Try to have other people keep you company, moreover, and avoid topics that tend to make you sad. Let your speech be edifying, and confine yourself to cheerful topics.

Letters, Vol. 2, 402

Give me a glad heart, Jesus, and help me to habitually cultivate happy thoughts instead of anxious ones. May the beauty of your world, the goodness of other people, and the wonders of faith visible in lives like Padre Pio's keep me so amazed and grateful that I have no room in my heart for sadness.

～ 110. The Will ～

And they went to a place which was called Gethsemane; and he said to his disciples, "Sit here, while I pray." And he took with him Peter and James and John, and began to be greatly distressed and troubled. And he said to them, "My soul is very sorrowful, even to death; remain here, and watch." And going a little farther, he fell on the ground and prayed that, if it were possible, the hour might pass from him. And he said, "Abba, Father, all things are possible to thee; remove this cup from me; yet not what I will, but what thou wilt."

MARK 14:32-36

God, who has bestowed so many benefits on us, is satisfied with such a very insignificant gift as that of our will. Let us offer it to him along with the divine Master himself in that most sublime prayer, the *Our Father*.... Don't let us make our offering like those children who, when they have given away something precious as a gift, immediately or very soon regret what they have done and begin to cry and ask to have it back.... The total offering of our will is unfortunately very difficult.

Letters, Vol. 2, 356–57

Jesus, how grateful I am, how consoled, that you, too, felt human repugnance toward your passion and begged God to take it away before you could offer yourself to God's will. For me, it is so difficult to make a total offering of myself in all circumstances. My anxieties, especially, get in the way. Lord, I do commit, with all my will, to your will being done in my life and for all my loved ones. Help me, Lord, to be steadfast in this stance, even when human nature cries out, "Take this cup from me!"

～ 111. God—Rich in Mercy ～

I would have you wise as to what is good and guileless as to what is evil; then the God of peace will soon crush Satan under your feet.

ROMANS 16:19-20

But God, who is rich in mercy, out of the great love with which he loved us, even when we were dead through our trespasses, made us alive together with Christ (by grace you have been saved), and raised us up with him, and made us sit with him in the heavenly places in Christ Jesus, that in the coming ages he might show the immeasurable riches of his grace in kindness toward us in Christ Jesus.

EPHESIANS 2:4-7

Once more, get rid of all those doubts which are clouding the heavens of your soul, such as the idea that you are deaf to the divine call, that you resist his tender invitations, that you yourself are the only obstacle in the way of perfection on the part of your sister, for this does not come from the good spirit but consists in the devil's cunning attempts to turn you aside from your purpose, or at least to make you pause in your [spiritual] progress ... and lose heart.

Letters, Vol. 2, 98

You are the God of mercy to those who seek you, Lord. Concern for my sins or failings, when I am in relationship with you, leads to more gratitude for your mercy, more humble acceptance of myself, more charity, and refusal to judge others. It is the evil one who wishes to make me hate myself, doubt your forgiveness, and fall into despair. Deliver all of us, Lord, from such snares.

～ 112. A Healing Mystery: Relics ～

And wherever he came, in villages, cities, or country, they laid the sick in the market places, and besought him that they might touch even the fringe of his garment; and as many as touched it were made well.

MARK 6:56

During the lifetime of Padre Pio the Lord healed many sick, even terminally ill, people through the prayers or appearances of Padre Pio, sometimes through bilocation. Since his death, many people have been healed through asking his prayer intercession with God while touching something that Pio once wore or used, such as the bandages from his stigmata or a piece of his Franciscan habit. [Such items are called relics.]

A typical testimony: I have a nephew who was born blind. The doctors said he would never see. I asked Fr. Fanning if I might have one of Padre Pio's relics for a short time. He lent it to me, and I applied it to the baby's eyes. In about two weeks we noticed that he was following objects. His parents took him to the eye specialist, who said the child could see, but he had no medical explanation for why.

> Testimony from a letter to the friary quoted in
> *Meet Padre Pio,* 140

Lord, I thank you that you have given and are giving so many miracles of your healing through St. Pio. You have certainly kept your promise that your disciples would do the same works you did on earth.

Padre Pio, pray for all us who need physical healing!

~ 113. "The Abominable Vice": Self-Righteousness ~

The Pharisee stood and prayed thus with himself, "God, I thank thee that I am not like other men, extortioners, unjust, adulterers, or even like this tax collector."

LUKE 18:11

You must be careful and always keep a vigilant watch over yourself, especially as regards the abominable vice of vainglory, which is the woodworm, the consuming moth, of devout souls. You must watch out for this vice, all the more so since it is easier for it to enter the soul and make headway unobserved and hence it is much less easily recognized. We must always be on our guard, and we can never fight too hard against this tireless enemy, who is always there on the doorstep of our every action.

> *Letters,* Vol. 1, 114,
> quoting a letter dated September 5, 1915

Jesus, I beg you to keep me safe from the self-righteousness that is the sin of those who try to be good. I know in the past I have fallen into this "abominable vice." If I do so again, please apply a swift kick in the pants so I can see how ridiculous it would be for an ordinary human sinner like myself to feel superior to anyone!

∼ 114. "Something Mysterious" in Us ∼

For I know that nothing good dwells within me, that is, in my flesh. I can will what is right, but I cannot do it. For I do not do the good I want, but the evil I do not want is what I do.

ROMANS 7:18-19

For all who are led by the Spirit of God are sons of God. For you did not receive the spirit of slavery to fall back into fear, but you have received the spirit of sonship.... We cry, "Abba! Father!"

ROMANS 8:14-15

I see something mysterious in myself: I am constantly sorry for the sins I have committed, I resolve continually never to commit them again, yet I must admit with bitter tears that in spite of all this I am still very imperfect, and it seems to me that I very often offend the Lord. At times I am almost in despair because it seems to me almost impossible that Jesus should forgive so many sins; again, more often than not, it seems impossible that Jesus should let me go astray. Oh, what on earth is all this? Explain it to me a little.

However, all this happens to me without my perceiving it, for I have by no means the will to offend God even to the slightest extent.

Letters, Vol. 1, 51

Heavenly Father, Abba, you know that, like Padre Pio, I do not wish to offend you in anything, but still I often fail through my weakness. I choose to believe that it is impossible that you should let me be separated from you or go too far astray. Lead me, Lord, all the way home to you! And forgive my sins.

∼ 115. Equal to God's Majesty: His Mercy ∼

Those who fear the Lord will prepare their hearts, and will humble themselves before him. Let us fall into the hands of the Lord, but not into the hands of men; for as his majesty is, so also is his mercy.

SIRACH 2:17-18

Take heart, then, my beloved daughter, even when you feel oppressed by the great number and the atrocity of your offences. Then more than ever should you come to the feet of Jesus Christ, who is fighting and enduring agony for us in the Garden. Humble yourself, weep, entreat with him, and like him ask with loud cries for God's mercy—his forgiveness of your faults—for help to walk all the time in his sight. Do this and have no doubt that this merciful and clement God will stretch out a compassionate hand, as he has always done, to lift you up out of your poverty and spiritual desolation.

Letters, Vol. 2, 506

Lord, I thank you that your mercies fall upon us all, the just and the unjust.

～ 116. On Human Weakness ～

For we all make many mistakes.

JAMES 3:2

My only regret is that, involuntarily and unwittingly, I sometimes raise my voice when correcting people. I realize that this is a shameful weakness, but how can I prevent it if it happens without my being aware of it? Although I pray, groan, and complain to Our Lord about it, he has not heard me fully. Moreover, in spite of all watchfulness, I sometimes do what I really detest and want to avoid.

Letters, Vol. 1, 1305

You kept Padre Pio humble, Lord, by refusing to change his human personality with its particular weakness: this tendency to be brusque or "raise his voice," as he put it. That gives me hope that my human weaknesses, which I so often demonstrate in spite of my desire to do better, can be useful at least for humility.

～ 117. The Paradox: Joy and Anguish Can Coexist ～

Count it all joy, my brethren, when you meet various trials.

JAMES 1:2

Infinite praise and thanks to Jesus, King of souls.... Seeing you subjected by Jesus to this fresh trial, the higher part of my soul rejoices with all the children of God, for I see very plainly the fulfillment of God's plan for you and the crown that is being fashioned for you up above in the heavenly homeland.

I do not deny that in the lower part of my soul I feel as if my heart were being torn to pieces to see you plunged in such a very harsh trial.

Letters, Vol. 2, 384

Lord, the great saints can take the longer, the eternal view—even when their humanity cries out to see human suffering, as St. Pio does in this letter to his beloved spiritual daughter. I can't do that today, Lord. Yes, I recognize that my past trials have given me strength and maturity, but today I will settle for less growth and your removing the trouble that is pressing on me. Sorry. I can't "count it all joy" today, Lord, but that joy has to come from you. So send it, or take away the trial. I count on you!

∼ 118. Obliged to Love My Creator ∼

Then said Jesus, "Were not ten cleansed? Where are the nine? Was no one found to return and give praise to God except this foreigner?"

LUKE 17:17-18

Filled with the keenest gratitude, my soul is led to testify to the Lord that he grants me this grace ["a great peace" and a burning desire to please God] without any merit on my part…. By means of this grace he has given me such a clear view that I see myself obliged more than anyone else to love my Creator.

Letters, Vol. 1, 431

Lord, I don't have the heroic virtues of your saints, so help me practice the humble virtues—above all, gratitude. It is impossible to list all the gifts and graces for which I am grateful: the gift of life, the gift of your Church,

the gifts of my loved ones, such health as I have, the gift of nature's beau-
ties, my daily bread, and on and on. Let me each day express gratitude to
you for something.

~ 119. A Trick of Love ~

Upon my bed by night I sought him whom my soul loves; I sought
him, but found him not; I called him, but he gave no answer. "I
will rise now and go about the city, in the streets and in the squares;
I will seek him whom my soul loves." I sought him, but found him
not.... Scarcely had I passed them, when I found him whom my soul
loves. I held him, and would not let him go.

SONG OF SONGS 3:1-2, 4

If Jesus manifests himself, thank him, and if he remains hidden, thank
him just the same: All is a trick of love.

Letters, Vol. 2, 99

Lord, I remember when you seemed so close, and my prayer was easy and
full of joy. Now for a long time my prayer is as dry as the desert, and you
seem to have left me on my own. I remind myself frequently that "all is a
trick of love." If you did not appear to withdraw, I would still be loving
you for the sweetness showered on me; now I have a chance to hope against
hope and to love when it appears love is not returned. Bring me through
this purification, Lord, so that I may again delight in your presence.

~ 120. Intercessory Love ~

For I wrote you out of much affliction and anguish of heart and with many tears, not to cause you pain but to let you know the abundant love that I have for you.

2 CORINTHIANS 2:4

When I know that a person is afflicted in soul or body, what would I not do to have the Lord relieve him of his sufferings! Willingly would I take upon myself all his afflictions in order to see him saved, and I would even hand over to him the benefits of such sufferings if the Lord would allow it. I see quite clearly that this is a most singular favor from God, because in the past, although by divine mercy I never neglected helping those in need, I had little or no pity in a natural way for their suffering.

Letters, Vol. 1, 519

Lord, I thank you for the magnitude of love seen in your saints. St. Paul, St. Pio, and all your saints "love without limits," as Auschwitz martyr St. Maximilian Kolbe put it. Let their example inspire me to ask you to give me more love—love for you and for each person who comes my way.

~ 121. Jesus, Draw Me After You! ~

With my whole heart I cry; answer me, O Lord!... I cry to thee; save me, that I may observe thy testimonies. I rise before dawn and cry for help; I hope in thy words. My eyes are awake before the watches of the night, that I may meditate upon thy promise. Hear my voice in thy steadfast love; O Lord, in thy justice preserve my life.

PSALM 119:145-49

I urge you to pray continually to the heavenly Father that he may always keep you close to his divine heart, that he may make you hear his loving voice more and more clearly and lead you to correspond with increasing gratitude. Ask Jesus with boundless confidence ... to draw you after him ... wherever he goes.

Letters, Vol. 2, 98

Prayer is the oxygen of the soul.

Padre Pio, as recalled by his spiritual son
and fellow Capuchin Fr. Joseph Pius Martin

Lord, I cannot pray for a long time, so help me send little prayers your way all the time. And when my mind and mouth are too weary to pray, let every task of my hands and every beat of my heart be a prayer that draws me after you.

～ 122. Pray for Me ～

I appeal to you, brethren, by our Lord Jesus Christ and by the love of the Spirit, to strive together with me in your prayers to God on my behalf.

ROMANS 15:30

Continue steadfastly in prayer, being watchful in it with thanksgiving; and pray for us also, that God may open to us a door for the word, to declare the mystery of Christ, on account of which I am in prison, that I may make it clear, as I ought to speak.

COLOSSIANS 4:2-4

While thanking you most earnestly for the prayers you offer to the Lord for me, may I ask you to keep me informed, if you don't mind, when you have finished the three novenas to Our Lady of the Rosary of Pompeii and if you have been so good as to offer your Communions to the Lord for my intentions. Forgive me if I am taking too much advantage of your kindness.

Letters, Vol. 2, 123–24

I am encouraged, Lord, that your saints too know they need prayer to accomplish their life's work. It means so much to me when people pray for my health, my work, and all my special needs. Help me to always be eager to pray for others, especially my benefactors.

～ 123. Anxiety: "A Waste of Time" ～

Rejoice in the Lord always; again I will say, Rejoice.... The Lord is at hand. Have no anxiety about anything, but in everything by prayer and supplication with thanksgiving let your requests be made known to God. And the peace of God, which passes all understanding, will keep your hearts and your minds in Christ Jesus.

PHILIPPIANS 4:4-7

I beg you, beloved Father, to calm your anxiety with regard to your spiritual state, for this seems to me to be a real waste of time on our way to eternity. What is worse, due to the great number of these anxieties, which in themselves may be holy, and due to our own weakness and the continual powerful urgings of the devil, all our good actions are invariably soiled, if I may use the expression, by a certain lack of confidence in God's goodness.

Letters, Vol. 1, 455

Dear Lord, I thank you that as I get older my anxieties are so much less. Forgive this weakness, and keep increasing my trust in you.

~ 124. Do Not Fear; Trust More ~

You will have confidence, because there is hope....

JOB 11:18

[Anxiety over one's spiritual state, actually a lack of confidence in God's goodness] ... is a very slender thread, it is true, which keeps the spirit tied down, but it prevents the soul to a great extent from taking flight in the way of perfection and from acting with holy freedom.

Letters, Vol. 1, 455

Dear Lord, increase my confidence in you so that one day I, too, may live in "holy freedom."

~ 125. Trust More and More ~

Cast all your anxieties on him, for he cares about you.

1 PETER 5:7

May the good Jesus always console you ... and give you even more strength to overcome and defeat our common enemy, who is always intent on laying traps for us, in order to make us betray trust. Do not fear him at all; trust more and more in the most sweet Lord, our Jesus Christ, who never leaves you alone.

Letters, Vol. 3, 68

Lord, I bring you my financial worries, my health worries, my safety worries—the whole shebang. Take care of me until you lead me safely home!

~ 126. Blessing Enemies ~

But I say to you that hear, Love your enemies, do good to those who hate you, bless those who curse you, pray for those who abuse you.

LUKE 6:27-28

It makes my heart ache to hear that the conflicts with your brother show no sign of coming to an end. Let us adore in silence God's designs when he allows this situation to continue as a further test of faithfulness on the part of both of you. Pray to the Lord that all may work out for his glory and for the good of souls.

Letters, Vol. 2, 190

Lord, your ways are surely not the way of the world. You tell me that, rather than getting back at or even demanding justice of those who mistreat me, I should do good to them, pray for them, and bless them. I know you are right, Lord. But can I do it? I look to you for the grace.

~ 127. Myself—A Mystery ~

For now we see in a mirror dimly, but then face to face. Now I know in part; then I shall understand fully, even as I have been fully understood.

1 CORINTHIANS 13:12

To put it briefly: My belief is a great effort of my poor will, against all human reasoning on my part. Perhaps it is for this reason that I will never be able to receive any solace.... This, my dear Father [and spiritual director], is not a matter of several times a day but is continual, and if I were to act differently I could not help becoming unfaithful to my God. The night is growing ever darker, and I don't know what the Lord has in store for me.

There are so many things that I would like to tell you, Father, but I am unable to do so. I realize that I am a mystery to myself.

Letters, Vol. 1, 855

Lord, let me remain a mystery to myself so long as you become clearer and clearer in my spiritual vision, to lead me away from sin and ego into the person you want me to be.

∼ 128. Test the Spirits ∼

Beloved, do not believe every spirit, but test the spirits to see whether they are of God; for many false prophets have gone out into the world.

1 JOHN 4:1

The other night the devil appeared to me in the likeness of one of our fathers and gave me a very strict order from Father Provincial not to write to you [my spiritual director] anymore, as it is against poverty and a serious obstacle to perfection.... I wept bitterly, believing this to be a fact. I should never have even faintly suspected this to be one of the ogre's snares if the angel had not revealed the fraud to me.

Letters, Vol. 1, 362

Lord, it is hard for me to grasp the spiritual world in which people like Pio live, a world of visible guardian angels and of devils posing as people or spirits of light. This sort of thing may never happen to me, but let it teach me that, even in the spiritual world, I must tread warily. As your Scripture says, "not all who cry Lord, Lord" have any real part in you. I thank you, Lord, for your Church, where I can get the same guidance that kept saints like Pio from illusion and delusion.

～ 129. On Using Medical Means ～

Honor the physician with the honor due him, according to your need of him, for the Lord created him; for healing comes from the Most High.

SIRACH 38:1-2

Your behavior up to the present with regard to this new illness to which the Lord has been pleased to subject you hurts me more than a little. Do you mean to say you don't know that anyone who refuses human remedies exposes himself to the danger of offending the Lord? And do you not know that God tells us through the Sacred Scriptures to love the physician for love of himself?

I don't intend to rebuke you, but I am certainly displeased with you. Please take note that I want you to have a medical examination without delay. In conscience you have a serious obligation to do this.... Obey me then, and be at peace, for it is only the obedient man who cries victory. Have yourself examined, and let me know what the doctor says about it.

Letters, Vol. 2, 511

Lord, help us submit to medical help when we need it, and help all doctors realize they need you.

~ 130. Encourage! ~

Jesus then said to them, "Truly, truly, I say to you, it was not Moses who gave you the bread from heaven; my Father gives you the true bread from heaven. For the bread of God is that which comes down from heaven, and gives life to the world." They said to him, "Lord, give us this bread always." Jesus said to them, "I am the bread of life; he who comes to me shall not hunger, and he who believes in me shall never thirst."

JOHN 6:32-35

Through your good will and the cooperation of others [in the Third Order of St. Francis], you should, on some free day you have during the month, gather together all your sisters and encourage them, with a little spiritual talk, to be faithful to the propositions made by frequenting the sacraments. You must assure them that, in the most holy sacrament of the Eucharist, in this sacrament of love, we have true life, a blessed life, and true happiness. Because in it we receive not only those graces that perfect us but the very author of these graces.

Letters, Vol. 3, 1101

Lord, I see that the people who most wholeheartedly encourage and give themselves in service to others are often the people who quietly sacrifice sleep and ease to receive you in the Word of your Scriptures and your Eucharist each morning. Give me the health to join them, Lord!

114

∼ 131. Kissing Jesus: Living What We Profess ∼

O that you would kiss me with the kisses of your mouth!
SONG OF SONGS 1:2

I urge you to unite with me and draw near to Jesus with me, to receive his embrace and a kiss that sanctifies and saves us.... The prophet Isaiah said: *For to us a child is born, to us a son is given* (Is 9:6). This child ... is the affectionate brother, the most loving Spouse, of our souls, of whom the sacred spouse of the Song, prefiguring the faithful soul, sought the company and yearned for the divine kisses: *O that you were like a brother to me ... If I met you outside, I would kiss you ... O that you would kiss me with the kisses of your mouth!* (Song 8:1; 1:2).

This son is Jesus, and we can kiss him without betraying him, give him the kiss and the embrace of grace and love he expects from us and which he promises to return. We can do all this, St. Bernard tells us, by serving him with genuine affection, by carrying out in holy works his heavenly doctrine, which we profess by our words.

Let us not cease, then, to kiss this divine Son in this way, for if these are the kisses we give him now, he himself will come to take us in his arms and give us the kiss of peace in the last sacraments at the hour of death. Thus we shall end our life in the holy kiss of the Lord,... which, according to St. Bernard, is not a matter of approaching face-to-face and mouth-to-mouth. Rather does it mean that the Creator draws close to his creature, and man and God are united for all eternity.

Letters, Vol. 2, 506–7

Lover of my soul, when will I love you enough to receive your kiss?

～ 132. Keep Growing ～

Brethren,... one thing I do, forgetting what lies behind and straining forward to what lies ahead, I press on toward the goal for the prize of the upward call of God in Christ Jesus.

PHILIPPIANS 3:13-14

I see that you are far advanced in this love of God, and I merely urge you to grow more and more in it.

Letters, Vol. 2, 304

Lord, today may I grow in love, ending the day more yours and more pleasing to you than I began it.

～ 133. The Great Cloud of Witnesses ～

Therefore, since we are surrounded by so great a cloud of witnesses, let us also lay aside every weight, and sin which clings so closely, and let us run with perseverance the race that is set before us, looking to Jesus the pioneer and perfecter of our faith.

HEBREWS 12:1-2

For ourselves who have been called, through the goodness of the Most High God, to reign with the divine Bridegroom, whose minds are enlightened by God's true light, let us fix our gaze constantly on the splendor of the heavenly Jerusalem.

Let the consideration of all those good things to be possessed in that realm provide us with delightful food for our thoughts. Enchanted by these eternal delights, our minds will then inflame our hearts with love for them. Only then, despite the fact that we are pilgrims in a foreign land, in a valley of tears, surrounded by apparent beauty, by enticements and illusions, only then shall we be able to repeat with full conviction along with the indomitable martyr St. Ignatius: *Oh, how worthless is the earth when I look at heaven!*

Letters, Vol. 2, 203

Lord, how wonderful the love that binds your saints living and dead, that great "cloud of witnesses" of whom Paul speaks! St. Pio turned to the early martyr St. Ignatius of Antioch to advise a woman born almost two thousand years later. Now we turn to the words of Pio to help us follow you. Thank you, Lord, for all your holy people, canonized saints and the saints I meet in my daily path, who uphold me with prayer and encouragement.

∼ 134. A Truth About Temptation ∼

Lead us not into temptation but deliver us from evil.
MATTHEW 6:13, Challoner-Rheims

I understand that temptations seem to stain rather than purify the soul, but this is not really the case. Let us hear what the saints have to say about it. For you it suffices to know what the great St. Francis de Sales says, namely, that temptations are like the soap which when spread on the laundry seems to soil but in reality cleanses it. It is well for you to pray continually to Jesus, however, that he may not allow you to be tempted, and I too, although very feebly, will pray for the same purpose.

Letters, Vol. 2, 76

Lord, I am often tempted to say what is better left unsaid. And how many times I fail! I beg you to give me better control of my tongue.

∼ 135. Love of the Beloved ∼

God is love, and he who abides in love abides in God, and God abides in him.

1 JOHN 4:16

Dear Father, I feel I am drowned in the immense ocean of the love of my Beloved. I am being surfeited continually with it. Yet the bitterness of this love has a sweetness, and its burden is light, but this does not prevent my soul from feeling the immense transport of this love. I have no means to bear its immense weight, so that I feel annihilated and vanquished. My small heart is incapable of containing this immense love. It is true that it is inside and outside me. But, dear God, when you pour yourself into the little vase of my being, I suffer the agony of not being able to contain you. The inner walls of this heart feel as if they were about to burst, and I am surprised this has not happened already.

Letters, Vol. 1, 1249–50

Lord, I feel so deficient in love as a feeling: I neither feel your love nor my own for you or others. All has dried up. Yet I will to love you and everyone without limits. Accept my desire, Lord, and overlook my powerlessness to feel as I would like.

～ 136. Padre Pio's Tact ～

At that time Jesus went through the grainfields on the sabbath; his disciples were hungry, and they began to pluck ears of grain and to eat. But when the Pharisees saw it, they [rebuked Jesus].... He said to them ... "if you had known what this means, 'I desire mercy, and not sacrifice,' you would not have condemned the guiltless."

MATTHEW 12:1-3, 7

His tact knew no limits; at the end of one Lent (1923), the friars were astounded to hear—and on Good Friday!—that he wanted a cup of chocolate and fruit, but he knew that one of those present had been indiscreet and over-zealous in fasting during Holy Week and [he added] "Or rather bring two cups of chocolate ... one also for this brother tertiary." And because the friars scoffed, [thinking Padre Pio would never break his fast on this day of all days], Padre Pio added, "We will eat together."

The Voice of Padre Pio, Vol. 27, Summer Number, 1997, 7

St. Pio, thank you for this moving reminder that true holiness knows when not to follow the rules and regulations of religion that lesser spirits can mistake for the essence of faith—forgetting that is really charity. Help me, dear saint, to aspire to being good and not settle for looking good.

～ 137. Don't Worry ～

And now, little children, abide in him.

1 JOHN 2:28, Douay-Rheims

Pray, hope, and don't worry. Worry is useless. God is merciful and will hear your prayer.

Consigli-Esortazioni di Padre Pio da Pietrelcina, 39

Lord, keep me in your peace, free from anxiety and worry, which accomplish nothing and only sap my strength. I do trust in you, Lord, with all my will. Help me when my feelings, against my will, succumb to anxiety.

∽ 138. Use the Fleeting Moment ∽

Therefore do not be anxious about tomorrow, for tomorrow will be anxious for itself. Let the day's own trouble be sufficient for the day.
MATTHEW 6:34

Make hay while the sun shines. Do not put off till tomorrow what you can do today. It's easy enough to be wise after the event; besides, who can assure us that we will be alive tomorrow? Let us listen to the voice of our conscience, to the voice of the royal prophet: "Today, if you hear the voice of the Lord, do not turn a deaf ear." Let us arise and make use of the fleeting moment, which alone is ours.

Letters, Vol. 4, 965–66

Oh, for the grace to live in the present moment—to use it well and to neither look back in regret nor forward with anxiety. Lord, I beg you, let me seize this day that you have made and given to me.

～ 139. Patiently Waiting on God ～

The eyes of all look to thee, and thou givest them their food in due season. Thou openest thy hand, thou satisfiest the desire of every living thing.
PSALM 145:15-16

By all means desire what you told me, but let this be in a calm manner, and be patient in awaiting the Lord's mercy.

Letters, Vol. 3, 837

How hard it is sometimes, Lord, to await your "due season," your time of mercy. Since I cannot do this of myself, I ask for the grace to always look hopefully to you with the calm and patience St. Pio recommends.

～ 140. Don't Doubt Divine Assistance ～

For I, the Lord your God, hold your right hand; it is I who say to you, "Fear not, I will help you."
ISAIAH 41:13

I repeat, my dear Raffaelina [Cervase, a spiritual child], that you are not to be afraid. The One who has helped you so far will continue his work of salvation. Don't have any doubts about the divine assistance, don't turn in upon yourself because of the many calamities that continually surround you, for everything will turn out for God's glory and the salvation of your soul.

Letters, Vol. 2, 423

Today, Lord, I want to rest upon your heart of mercy, claiming your help in my troubles, your stamina for my work, and your Holy Spirit to guide me.

∼ 141. Food ∼

And day by day, attending the temple together and breaking bread in their homes, they partook of food with glad and generous hearts, praising God and having favor with all the people.

ACTS 2:46-47

Food will not commend us to God. We are no worse off if we do not eat, and no better off if we do. Only take care lest this liberty of yours somehow become a stumbling block to the weak.

1 CORINTHIANS 8:8-9

Let us make an effort to ensure that the supper by which we satisfy the body may be a preparation for the altogether divine supper of the most holy Eucharist. Let all this be done without excessive spiritual fatigue.... Never rise from the table, moreover, without having given due thanks to the Lord. If we act in this way, we need have no fear of the wretched sin of gluttony.

As you eat, take care not to be too difficult to please in the matter of food, bearing in mind that it is very easy to give in to gluttony. Never eat more than you really need, and endeavor to practice moderation all the time. You should be very ready to refuse what you need rather than what is in excess of your needs. However, I don't mean to say that you should rise from table without eating. No, this is not my intention. Let everything be regulated by prudence, which should be the rule in all our actions.

Letters, Vol. 2, 291–92

Lord, I live in a wealthy country, where huge portions and constant availability of food make gluttony socially acceptable. Forgive me for those times I have been a glutton, like on that vacation when I ate a whole cake. Help me to eat for health and to never eat or drink without thanking you. Today I will make an offering to help the hungry.

～ 142. The Mystery of Jesus as Food and Drink ～

"I am the bread of life. Your fathers ate the manna in the wilderness, and they died. This is the bread which comes down from heaven, that a man may eat of it and not die. I am the living bread which came down from heaven; if any one eats of this bread, he will live for ever; and the bread which I shall give for the life of the world is my flesh." The Jews then disputed among themselves, saying, "How can this man give us his flesh to eat?" So Jesus said to them, "Truly, truly, I say to you, unless you eat the flesh of the Son of man and drink his blood, you have no life in you; he who eats my flesh and drinks my blood has eternal life, and I will raise him up at the last day. For my flesh is food indeed, and my blood is drink indeed. He who eats my flesh and drinks my blood abides in me, and I in him."

JOHN 6:48-56

My heart feels drawn by a higher force each morning before I am united with him in the Blessed Sacrament. I have such a hunger and thirst before I receive him that I almost die, and ... I am incapable of not uniting myself with him.... Moreover, instead of being appeased after I have received him sacramentally, this hunger and thirst steadily increase. When I already possess this Supreme Good, then indeed the abundance of sweetness is so great that I very nearly say to Jesus:

"Enough, I can hardly bear any more."

Letters, Vol. 1, 246

Jesus, I bow before the mystery of your love that makes yourself into sweet and wholesome living food, which sustains my being and nurtures my soul toward holiness.

∽ 143. Regretting Betrayals ∽

And immediately the cock crowed a second time. And Peter remembered how Jesus had said to him, "Before the cock crows twice, you will deny me three times." And he broke down and wept.

MARK 14:72

I shed bitter tears as I write this letter. You must know, Father, that during the past few days I have had the effrontery to offend Jesus once more by telling a lie. Dear God! How ashamed I am!... Meanwhile Jesus himself is always with me, and he is not ashamed to stay with me still, for he continues to manifest himself in me with all the splendor of his heart, with the prodigious effusion of his fatherly love.

Letters, Vol. 1, 266–67

Pardon me, Lord, if in my littleness of soul I rejoice that those you love, like St. Peter and St. Pio, are not flawless and yet you loved them anyway! How encouraging!

～ 144. Oh, We Pharisees! ～

And the Lord said to him, "Now you Pharisees cleanse the outside of the cup and of the dish, but inside you are full of extortion and wickedness. You fools! Did not he who made the outside make the inside also? But give for alms those things which are within; and behold, everything is clean for you.

"But woe to you Pharisees! for you tithe mint and rue and every herb, and neglect justice and the love of God; these you ought to have done, without neglecting the others. Woe to you Pharisees! for you love the best seat in the synagogues and salutations in the market places."

LUKE 11:39-43

From this battle [with vainglory, also called self-righteousness] he does not spare good people, especially those who are striving for perfection.... In order to avoid praise by others we prefer secret and hidden fasts to those which are known, we prefer silence to eloquent speaking, we prefer to be despised than to be held in esteem, we prefer contempt to honors. Alas, my God, in this also vainglory wants to poke its nose ... by inducing us to vain complacency.

St. Jerome was quite right when he compared vainglory to one's shadow. In point of fact, our shadow follows us everywhere and even marks our steps.

Letters, Vol. 1, 446–47

Lord, I see my own shadow side, tainting sometimes my seemingly most charitable acts. If I cannot escape traces of egotism in almost everything I do, let me gain greatly in humility as I meditate on my own flawed love and puny mercy compared to your perfect love and boundless mercy.

∽ 145. God's Goodness—Greater Than My Fears ∽

And Peter answered him, "Lord, if it is you, bid me come to you on the water." He said, "Come." So Peter got out of the boat and walked on the water and came to Jesus; but when he saw the wind, he was afraid, and beginning to sink he cried out, "Lord, save me." Jesus immediately reached out his hand and caught him, saying to him, "O man of little faith, why did you doubt?"

MATTHEW 14:28-31

Is it possible that the Lord will allow my downfall? Unhappily this is what I deserve, but can it be that the heavenly Father's goodness will be outdone by my wickedness? This will never, never be.... I feel again the love of my God rising up like a giant in my poor heart, and I still have the confidence and strength to cry aloud with St. Peter: *Lord, save me, I am perishing!* (Mt 8:25).

Letters, Vol. 1, 618

Lord, even in your presence St. Peter became frightened; St. Pio, too, often felt anxiety as to whether he was corresponding properly to the many graces he had received. Yet each turned to you with confidence. Give me that confidence, Lord. So like another saint I love, St. Thérèse of Lisieux, I can always repent and run to you no matter what sin or imperfection I fall into, knowing you will receive me with open arms.

∽ 146. Thirsting for God ∽

On the last day of the feast, the great day, Jesus stood up and proclaimed, "If any one thirst, let him come to me and drink. He who believes in me, as the scripture has said, 'Out of his heart shall flow rivers of living water.'"

JOHN 7:37-38

Tell me, is it possible that Jesus is far away when you are calling and praying and seeking him and, let us even say, when you possess him?... Is it possible ... that God is not present in that soul, when he has committed himself by his infallible word to be with that soul in the time of tribulation? *I will be with him in trouble* (Ps 91:15). How is it possible that the fountain of living water that issues from the divine Heart should be far from a soul that rushes to it like a thirsty hart? It is true that this soul may also fail to believe it because it feels continually consumed by an unquenchable and insatiable thirst. But what of that? Does this, perhaps, go to show that the soul does not possess God? Quite the opposite. This happens because the soul has not yet reached the end of its journey and is not yet totally immersed in the eternal fountain of his divine love, which will happen in the kingdom of glory.

Let us therefore love to quench our thirst at this fountain of living water and go forward all the time along the way of divine love. But let us also be convinced ... that our souls will never be satisfied here below.

Letters, Vol. 2, 541–42

My soul thirsts for you, my Lord and my God.

～ 147. God Faithfully Cares for Me ～

Cast all your anxieties on him, for he cares about you.

1 PETER 5:7

Has the Lord not told us that he is faithful and promised never to allow us to be vanquished? God is faithful.... How could you persuade yourself of anything else, my dear sister? Isn't our good God far above anything we can conceive? Isn't he more interested than we are in our salvation? How many times has he not given us proof of this? How many victories have you not gained over your very powerful enemies and over yourself, through the divine assistance, without which you would inevitably have been crushed? Let us consider Jesus' love for us and his concern for our well-being, and then let us be at peace.

Letters, Vol. 2, 152

Lord, I cannot conceive the heights and depths of your love and mercy. Let me throw myself into your arms, certain you will catch me and carry me where I need to go.

～ 148. The Flame of Divine Love ～

Beloved, let us love one another; for love is of God, and he who loves is born of God and knows God. He who does not love does not know God; for God is love.

1 JOHN 4:7-8

The human spirit without the flame of divine love tends to reach the level of the beast, while, on the other hand, charity, the love of God, raises it up so high that it can reach even to the throne of God. Give thanks without ever growing weary for the liberality of such a good Father, and ask him to increase holy charity more and more in your heart.

Letters, Vol. 2, 77

You are Love, Lord. I want to love as you do. Your mercies fall on the just and the unjust. You came that we might have life and have it to the full, and you will all people to be saved.

How can my narrow heart expand to this kind of love unless you do it, Lord? Jesus, Lord of mercy, I trust in you to fill my heart with your kind of love.

～ 149. Children—Spiritual or Natural—Are Gifts ～

Thou didst form my inward parts, thou didst knit me together in my mother's womb.... Wonderful are thy works!

PSALM 139:13-14

I cried with emotion and consolation, and I raised my hand many times in the silence of the night, in my little cell, blessing and presenting you all [new members of the Third Order—that is, the lay branch—of St. Francis] to Jesus and our common father St. Francis, so that they might consider you their chosen children.

Letters, Vol. 3, 1092

I thank you, Lord, for the gift of children, both those I have borne in the flesh and those of my spirit. Not all of us may be mothers and fathers in a physical way, but all Christians are called to spiritual paternity like Padre Pio's. I am moved, Lord, when I recall his desire not to enter heaven until the last of his spiritual children was safely across the threshold. I thank you, also, Lord, for those who have been spiritual fathers and mothers to me.

∼ 150. Surfeited With Spiritual Joy ∼

I will extol thee, my God and King, and bless thy name for ever and ever. Every day I will bless thee, and praise thy name for ever and ever. Great is the Lord, and greatly to be praised, and his greatness is unsearchable.

PSALM 145:1-3

Dear God! I cannot describe ... all that I felt in my heart on that most happy night. My heart seemed to overflow with a holy love for our God become man.... I was surfeited with spiritual joy.

Letters, Vol. 1, 1095

Lord, may I praise you, who are way beyond my comprehension. And may I one day overflow with love for you, as did Padre Pio.

∼ 151. Reconciliation ∼

So if you are offering your gift at the altar, and there remember that your brother has something against you, leave your gift there before the altar and go; first be reconciled to your brother, and then come and offer your gift.

MATTHEW 5:23-24

I offer warmest thanks to the goodness of the heavenly Father for the reconciliation with your brother and his wife. I ask you now to put aside your pessimistic judgment on this situation. May the Lord continue to use mercy toward you all and grant you the grace of holy perseverance. Get rid of the diabolical thought that you have been the cause of the disagreement that has existed up to the present with your brother. Have we understood one another?

Letters, Vol. 2, 480

Lord, help me always to be open to reconciliation with anyone, no matter the situation.

∼ 152. God's Holy Love ∼

In this is love, not that we loved God but that he loved us.

1 JOHN 4:10

May God be the center of your heart and set it all on fire with his holy love! I never cease to bless the divine mercy for the most holy love he shows toward your soul.

Letters, Vol. 1, 1009

My love for you, Lord, is so paltry next to your love for me. I thank you with all my heart and ask that you set me, too, on fire with your holy love, so I may love others as you love.

∼ 153. Heartfelt Love ∼

Above all hold unfailing your love for one another, since love covers a multitude of sins.

1 PETER 4:8

Good-bye [for] now, my dear Father [Padre Agostino, one of his two spiritual directors], and who knows if I shall be granted the grace to see you again. I won't send you a kiss, because this is too little for all you have done for me, but I send you all that I have in my heart for you, which is an infinite tenderness. I hold you in veneration, Reverend Father. Francesco, my family, the archpriest, and all your friends send you infinite greetings and regards.

Letters, Vol. 1, 289

Lord, it is wonderful to see that, in his total gift of self to you, Padre Pio only loved all the more the people you placed in his life, loved them with a spotlessly pure, ardent, disinterested love that was still as down-to-earth as "sending a kiss." Give me such a pure love for those you place in my life, Lord!

∼ 154. My Defects and Those of Others ∼

Why do you see the speck that is in your brother's eye, but do not notice the log that is in your own eye?

LUKE 6:41

I cannot tolerate criticism and speaking ill of our brothers. It is true, sometimes I enjoy teasing them, but speaking ill of them makes me sick. We have so many defects in ourselves to criticize, why pick on our brothers? And lacking in charity we damage the roots of the tree of life, with the risk of killing it.

Padre Pio visto dall'interno, Giovannida Baggio, Firenze, 1970, 62

Jesus, help me to see my own faults clearly, and help me never to see the faults of others unless I must do so for some positive purpose. In the latter case, help me discern wisely and keep me from gossip, especially that which hides behind the guise of expressing concern for someone. When I open my mouth to slander even evil people, let me see your agonized face on the cross and hear your voice saying of those who pounded nails through your flesh, "Father, forgive them; they do not know what they are doing."

∼ 155. Suffering for Love ∼

O Jerusalem, Jerusalem, killing the prophets and stoning those who are sent to you! How often would I have gathered your children together as a hen gathers her brood under her wings, and you would not!
MATTHEW 23:37

He who begins to love must be willing to suffer.
Consigli-Esortazioni di Padre Pio da Pietrelcina, 25

Lord, how I suffer to see those I love suffer, especially when I know that they will neither take advice from anyone nor turn to you for guidance. Instead they blame you for the trouble they have gotten themselves into. Lord, I beg you to somehow reach them with the good news that you are not the big meanie in the sky but the One who truly loves them.

∼ 156. On Pestering God ∼

And I tell you, Ask and it will be given; seek, and you will find; knock, and it will be opened to you. For every one who asks receives, and he who seeks finds, and to him who knocks it will be opened. What father among you, if his son asks for a fish, will instead of a fish give him a serpent; or if he asks for an egg, will give him a scorpion? If you then, who are evil, know how to give good gifts to your children, how much more will the heavenly Father give the Holy Spirit to those who ask him!

LUKE 11:9-13

Pray more insistently, daughter, to the most compassionate Heart of Jesus, that he may be pleased to put an end to this most harsh trial [that is, Padre Pio's call to leave the cloister and serve in the army of Italy during World War I]. I expect to be treated with this same charity, through the benevolent influence of yourself, of excellent Francesca, of most pious Annita, and of all those others who love Jesus and whose names are written in my heart. Pray, all of you.

Letters, Vol. 2, 552

At last we can sing the *Te Deum.* Our most compassionate Lord has shown me mercy [in having me put on medical leave], and I am deeply convinced that he has been compelled to do all this because you and the others have pestered him too much with your prayers.

Letters, Vol. 2, 557

Lord, may I always pester you for the health and other needs of my loved ones and myself, until you show mercy in one form or another. Help me to see too, Lord, that you do not promise to give what is asked. You promise the Holy Spirit, in whom all problems find a solution, even if not always the solution expected.

∼ 157. Being Good Shepherds ∼

I am the good shepherd; I know my own and my own know me, as the Father knows me and I know the Father; and I lay down my life for the sheep.

JOHN 10:14-15

But do you perhaps think that while aware of your torment I remain indifferent? No, you are very familiar with the brotherly concern I have had for you up to the present, and you know that Divine Providence has entrusted you to my care. I share everything with you, in times of prosperity and times of trial. Hence my heart cannot fail to be stricken with the most acute pain when I see you, so very dear to me, placed in such harsh conditions by a trial willed by God for your sanctification.

Meanwhile I never cease to pray to our merciful God to make haste and bring to a speedy end this period of trial. At the same time I neglect no effort with our most tender Lord to induce him to alleviate now and then your torment in this time of trial. I am praying, or rather I am continually pestering the heart of the divine Master, to allow me to feel, if not all at least a part of your torments, on condition that he lessen and lighten your own sufferings.

Letters, Vol. 2, 325

Jesus, St. Pio, like so many of your saints who are priests or other shepherds of souls, wants to take on the suffering of one of his spiritual children. Help me too, Lord, to move out of egotism into being willing to suffer that your kingdom come for others.

∼ 158. Heaven ∼

Let not your hearts be troubled; believe in God, believe also in me. In my Father's house are many rooms; if it were not so, would I have told you that I go to prepare a place for you? And when I go and prepare a place for you, I will come again and will take you to myself, that where I am you may be also.

JOHN 14:1-3

Let us always keep before our eyes the fact that here on earth we are on a battlefield and that in paradise we shall receive the crown of victory; that this is a testing-ground, and the prize will be awarded up above; that we are now in a land of exile, while our true homeland is heaven, to which we must continually aspire. Let us live, then,... with a lively faith, a firm hope, and an ardent love, with eyes fixed on heaven and the keenest desire, as long as we are travelers, to dwell one day in heaven whenever this is pleasing to God.

Letters, Vol. 2, 470

Yes, Lord, how I look forward to heaven, whenever you are pleased to call me home! To be with you! To be with my loved ones! To all be one in you! How sweet!

∼ 159. The Tempter ∼

And he took him to Jerusalem, and set him on the pinnacle of the temple, and said to him, "If you are the Son of God, throw yourself down from here; for it is written, 'He will give his angels charge of you, to guard you,' and 'On their hands they will bear you up, lest you strike your foot against a stone.'" And Jesus answered him, "It is said, 'You shall not tempt the Lord your God.'" And when the devil had ended every temptation, he departed from him until an opportune time.

LUKE 4:9-13

[Satan] is whispering to me continually, and, what is more painful, he insinuates into my mind extremely disturbing thoughts. But praise be to Jesus! For even in the midst of these gloomy ideas which ought to drive me to despair, I maintain in the depths of my heart a peace such as I have seldom experienced.

Letters, Vol. 1, 326

The ogre won't admit defeat. He has appeared in almost every form [including at times that of one of Pio's spiritual directors]. For the past few days he has paid me visits along with some of his satellites, armed with clubs and iron weapons, and, what is worse, in their own form as devils. I cannot tell you how many times he has thrown me out of bed and dragged me around the room. But never mind! Jesus, our dear Mother, my little angel, St. Joseph, and our father St. Francis are almost always with me.

Letters, Vol. 1, 284–85

Lord, your world is much vaster than the material. Spirits do contend for souls. Give me the grace to recognize evil when I see it, whether it disguises itself as something positive or shows its true face. And give me the grace to say no to the temptations Jesus faced, including the infantile desire to be cared for without any responsibility of my own, to have worldly power, and to live for myself alone.

∼ 160. The Treasurer of the Poor ∼

As for the rich in this world, charge them not to be haughty, nor to set their hopes on uncertain riches but on God who richly furnishes us with everything to enjoy. They are to do good, to be rich in good deeds, liberal and generous, thus laying up for themselves a good foundation for the future, so that they may take hold of the life which is life indeed.

1 TIMOTHY 6:17-19

You pity the wretched state of many unhappy and needy people and have always endeavored ... to help them, to dry their tears and relieve their poverty by all those material means with which the Lord has abundantly provided you and of which he has given you charge as the treasurer of the poor.

Letters, Vol. 2, 233

Lord, living in my country in this present age, I am certainly among the rich of the world. Help me to see my role in my surplus as "the treasurer of the poor," so I may be rich in good works.

∼ 161. We're in a War ∼

Be sober, be watchful. Your adversary the devil prowls around like a roaring lion, seeking some one to devour. Resist him, firm in your faith.

1 PETER 5:8-9

Do you know what the devil has resorted to? He didn't want me to inform you in my last letter about the war he is waging on me. And since, as usual, I did not want to listen to him,... they ... (there were several of them although only one spoke) ... hurled themselves upon me, cursing me and beating me severely.

Letters, Vol. 1, 345–46

Lord, it is so easy to believe that the devil is only a myth. But when I study the lives of even very recent saints, it becomes clear that there are not only good angels but bad ones. Help me to not only acknowledge this but to also simply keep my eyes on you, Lord, certain you will lead me on the right paths and keep me from being harmed by spirits or people who do not wish me well.

～ 162. Attachment to One's Own Opinions ～

I appeal to you, brethren, by the name of our Lord Jesus Christ, that all of you agree and that there be no dissensions among you, but that you be united in the same mind and the same judgment.

1 CORINTHIANS 1:10

Complete my joy by being of the same mind, having the same love, being in full accord and of one mind.

PHILIPPIANS 2:2

I'll be certain of your constant progress in the path of holiness to which God, by his goodness alone, has called you ... [if] you ... take care never to quarrel with anyone, never to contend with anyone whomsoever. If you act otherwise, it means good-bye to peace and charity. To be inordinately attached to your own opinion is invariably a source and beginning of discord. St. Paul exhorts us to be united in the same mind.

Letters, Vol. 2, 234

Lord, keep me from thinking "I know best." Make me humble about what I think I know and willing to listen to others' points of view. Especially, Lord, keep me willing to change my opinions when warranted.

∼ 163. Hanging in There ∼

I thank my God in all my remembrance of you, always in every prayer of mine for you all making my prayer with joy, thankful for your partnership in the gospel from the first day until now. And I am sure that he who began a good work in you will bring it to completion at the day of Jesus Christ.

PHILIPPIANS 1:3-6

I beg you, for heaven's sake, to calm your anxiety and apprehension.... Remain at peace, continue to go forward, and don't let your swift course be stopped when I assure you in our most tender Lord that you are already halfway to the summit of Calvary. It is true that this is the darkest hour of the night for you, but may the thought of a bright dawn and a more brilliant noontime sustain you, cheer you up, and induce you to keep on moving forward. Do not doubt that the One who has sustained you so far will continue with ever greater patience and divine kindness to support you on the remainder of your difficult and trying journey.

Letters, Vol. 2, 479–80

I sometimes fear, Lord, I'll be unequal to what the future might hold. Grant me the grace of perseverance and more trust in you.

∼ 164. Of Suffering and Relief ∼

But rejoice in so far as you share Christ's sufferings, that you may also rejoice and be glad when his glory is revealed.

1 PETER 4:13

I have a great desire to suffer for the love of Jesus. How is it, then, that when I am put to the test, altogether against my will I seek relief? What force and violence must I use toward myself in these trials to reduce nature to silence when it cries out loudly, so to speak, for consolation!

Letters, Vol. 1, 640

Me too, Lord. Like Pio when he was young, in suffering I rush for relief, even if I try to say, "Your will be done."

∼ 165. A Fabulous Inheritance ∼

Blessed be the God and Father of our Lord Jesus Christ! By his great mercy we have been born anew to a living hope through the resurrection of Jesus Christ from the dead, and to an inheritance which is imperishable, undefiled, and unfading, kept in heaven for you, who by God's power are guarded through faith for a salvation ready to be revealed in the last time.

1 PETER 1:3-5

Let us pray that he may enlighten us more and more as to the immensity of the eternal inheritance which has been reserved for us by the goodness of the heavenly Father. May our discernment of this mystery turn our hearts away from earthly goods and make us eager to arrive at our heavenly home.

Letters, Vol. 2, 212

Lord, I want an inheritance that is "imperishable, undefiled, and unfading," in St. Peter's words. You had mercy on this bumbling man who loved you in spite of his weaknesses. Have mercy on me too.

~ 166. Beating Down Envy, Irascibility, and Self-Righteousness ~

[He] saved us and called us with a holy calling, not in virtue of our works but in virtue of his own purpose and the grace which he gave us in Christ Jesus ages ago.

2 TIMOTHY 1:9

Do we want to live a spiritual life, moved and guided by the Spirit of the Lord? Let us take care, then, to mortify our selfish spirit, which puffs us up, makes us impulsive, and leads to aridity of soul. In a word, we must be careful to subdue vainglory [today more commonly called "self-righteousness"], irascibility, and envy, three evil spirits to which most men are slaves. These three ... are extremely opposed to the Spirit of the Lord.

Letters, Vol. 2, 218

You know my weakness, Lord. It is not envy or irascibility but vainglory—that is, feeling "above" people who do not know you. But what an idiot that makes me, for I know you only by your grace, and they do not know you only because of your unsearchable designs. If I were a true follower of yours, rather than feel superior I would weep over them as you wept over Jerusalem. I would give myself for their redemption.

Lord, forgive my self-righteousness. And give all people, here or on the other side, an opportunity to see you as you are. For to know you is certainly to love you!

～ 167. On Suffering ～

And after you have suffered a little while, the God of all grace, who has called you to his eternal glory in Christ, will himself restore, establish, and strengthen you.

1 PETER 5:10

Do not fear adversities, because they place the soul at the foot of the cross, and the cross places it at the gates of heaven, where it will find he who triumphed over death and will introduce it to eternal life.

Have a Good Day, 50
quoting Angela Serritelli, *Notizie su Padre Pio,* 42

Lord, I am so afraid of suffering physical pain. Help me to keep the perspective that pain lasts a short time in light of eternity.

～ 168. Physical and Spiritual Beauty ～

Charm is deceitful, and beauty is vain, but a woman who fears the Lord is to be praised.

PROVERBS 31:30

We give much thought and waste much time and effort in trying to correct our superficial bodily defects, even in arranging our hair so that not even a single hair remains out of place....

We are never done trying to improve our appearance.... God in his infinite wisdom has placed in our hands all the necessary means for the embellishment of our souls, even after we have disfigured them by sin. The soul's cooperation with divine grace is all that is required to enable it to develop, to reach such a degree of splendor and beauty as to attract, not so much the loving and astonished gaze of the angels, but the gaze of God himself, according to the testimony of Holy Scripture: *The king*—that is, God—*will desire your beauty* (Ps 45:11).

Letters, Vol. 2, 241

Lord, give me the soul beauty of a Mother Teresa, whose face reminded me of a smiling prune yet glowed with an attractiveness that won all hearts.

∼ 169. Friendship ∼

David rose from beside the stone heap and fell on his face to the ground, and bowed three times; and they kissed one another, and wept with one another, until David recovered himself. Then Jonathan said to David, "Go in peace, forasmuch as we have sworn both of us in the name of the Lord, saying, 'The Lord shall be between me and you, and between my descendants and your descendants, for ever.'"

1 SAMUEL 20:41-42

[Padre Pio writes to his beloved spiritual director, who has been drafted during World War I:]

For several days now I have been without your news, and I leave you to imagine how this silence is weighing on my poor heart. The assurance of heaven should suffice for me only too well, but what can you expect? You can't give orders to the heart.

Letters, Vol. 1, 927

How beautiful a thing, Lord, is true friendship. For thousands of years Jews and Christians have honored the friends David and Jonathan because of their great love for one another. St. Pio, likewise, loved his friends deeply.

Thank you for my friends, who have done so much for me and who are rooted, everlastingly, in my heart. Make me worthy of my friends, Lord!

～ 170. My Heart—Free and Vast As the Sea ～

I was glad when they said to me, "Let us go to the house of the Lord!"
PSALM 122:1

When I read your words, "It seems to me that the end of your earthly exile is not far off," I felt transformed.... For an instant my unbearable sufferings were lessened. I felt my lungs swell; I breathed a pure and refreshing air that penetrated all the fibers of my body, coursed through my veins, and brought life to every corpuscle and every molecule of my blood. I felt delightfully inebriated, a great peace invaded soul and body, a peace like a clear sky, which made me exclaim from the depths of my soul: "Oh, what a beautiful day is this; oh, what a magnificent prospect, to close the eyes of this body and open those of the spirit before the divine Spouse! How wonderful it feels!"

I felt death to be clean and full of elasticity, my heart free and vast as the sea. Troublesome thoughts, painful treatment, the annoyances of life, the whole bundle of troubles, afflictions, vexations, disappointments, and sorrows that distress my soul seemed to vanish as if by magic, and I no longer even remember them.

Letters, Vol. 1, 796–97

Lord, help me to see death as the wonderful moment of liberation, when my heart will be "free and vast as the sea."

～ 171. Grafted to the Savior ～

I am the true vine, and my Father is the vinedresser.... Abide in me, and I in you. As the branch cannot bear fruit by itself, unless it abides in the vine, neither can you, unless you abide in me. I am the vine, you are the branches. He who abides in me, and I in him, he it is that bears much fruit, for apart from me you can do nothing.

JOHN 15:1, 4-5

Shouldn't we perhaps consider ourselves lucky to be able to graft our branches to those of the divine Savior, which is founded on God? As this Sovereign Being is the root of the tree of which we are the branches, and our good works the fruit. Oh, my dear daughter, courage! Let us not cease to place our hearts in God.

Letters, Vol. 3, 706

Jesus, may your kingdom come! I am a small branch, but if you course through me, I too can bear fruit.

~ 172. Humility, Contrition, and Prayer ~

The fear of the Lord is the beginning of knowledge; fools despise wisdom and instruction.

PROVERBS 1:7

Where the struggle of man with God is concerned, the contrary [to man's struggle with another man] takes place. He who trembles before God; he who is oppressed under the weight of tribulation, weighed down at the sight of the deep wounds his sins have made in him; he who rubs his face in the dust; lowers himself, humbles himself, cries, shouts, sighs, and prays—it is he who wins; it is he who triumphs. ... Humility, contrition, and prayer make this distance between man and God disappear and act in such a way that God descends to man and man ascends to God, so that they end up understanding, loving, and possessing one another.

Letters, Vol. 3, 98

Lord, help me to love you so much that I have true humility and long not to hurt you by sin.

~ 173. The Merciful, Painful Light ~

With thee is the fountain of life; in thy light do we see light.

PSALM 36:9

I assure you in the Lord ... that the knowledge of your interior unworthiness and deformity is a most pure divine light by which your ... ability to

147

commit any sin whatsoever, without the help of grace, is placed before you. This light is a great mercy of God ... because it shelters the soul from all ... vanity and pride and consolidates humility, which is the foundation of virtue and Christian perfection. St. Teresa also had this knowledge, and she says it is so painful and horrible that it would cause death if the Lord did not sustain the heart. The knowledge of potential unworthiness must not be confused with real unworthiness.

Letters, Vol. 3, 183–84

Lord, I know I must say "yes" to you, that you force no one into a relationship. Yet I know also that without the light of your grace I cannot say "yes." It is all a mystery, Lord. I do not understand why you have made me your own, but I beg you to never let me go. And any parts of me not yet under your grace I beg you to conquer.

∼ 174. Seeking Knowledge of God ∼

My son, if you receive my words and treasure up my commandments with you, making your ear attentive to wisdom and inclining your heart to understanding; yes, if you cry out for insight and raise your voice for understanding, if you seek it like silver and search for it as for hidden treasures; then you will understand the fear of the Lord and find the knowledge of God.

PROVERBS 2:1-5

St. Bernard, in the scale of values he established for his cloistered monks, recognizes four degrees or means by which to reach God and perfection—namely, reading and meditation, prayer and contemplation. As proof of what he says, he quotes the Divine Master's own words: *Seek, and you will find; knock, and it will be opened to you* (Mt 7:7). He goes on to apply these words to the four means or degrees of perfection and says that by reading Sacred Scripture and other holy and pious books, we are seeking God. By meditation we find him, by prayer we knock at the door of his heart, and by contemplation [we] enter the theatre of divine delights, which has been opened to our mental gaze by reading, meditation, and prayer.

Letters, Vol. 2, 155

Lord, keep me reading and pondering your Word until it has permeated not only my soul but my very bones. Help me too to find models of how to imitate you by reading the lives of saints.

～ 175. The Highest Form of Apostolate ～

Now you are the body of Christ and individually members of it.... Are all apostles? Are all prophets? Are all teachers? Do all work miracles?
1 CORINTHIANS 12:27, 29

All of us are not called by God to save souls and propagate his glory by the noble apostolate of preaching.... One can promote God's glory and work for the salvation of souls by means of a truly Christian life, by praying without ceasing that "his kingdom come," that his name "be hallowed," that "we may not be led into temptation," and that he "deliver us from evil." This is what you ought to do, offering yourself continually to the Lord for this purpose.

Pray for the wicked, pray for the lukewarm, pray even for fervent souls, but pray especially for the supreme Pontiff, for all the spiritual [and] temporal needs of ... [the] Church.... A special prayer also for all those who are working for the salvation of souls and for God's glory in the missions.... You may be perfectly sure that this is the highest form of apostolate.

Letters, Vol. 2, 77

Lord, thank you for my particular little place in your Church. May my work—whether it is doing laundry, gardening, or writing—help to build your kingdom. I offer it all to you this day. May every work of my hands be an act of love for you, and every beat of my heart a prayer that all may know and love you.

～ 176. When God Seems Absent ～

[He] alone stretched out the heavens, and trampled the waves of the sea;... Lo, he passes by me, and I see him not; he moves on, but I do not perceive him.

JOB 9:8, 11

I am praying continually, but my prayer will never rise up from this lowly world. Dear Father, heaven seems to me to have turned to stone; an iron hand rests on my head and thrusts me further and further away.

Letters, Vol. 1, 144

How dry is my prayer right now. You seem deaf, God. But like Pio, I will keep praying.

～ 177. Speaking Out ～

Yahweh, who has the right to enter your tent, or to live on your holy mountain? The man ... who speaks the truth from his heart, whose tongue is not used for slander.

PSALM 15:1-3, JB

I have always hated duplicity, and now I am accused of having recourse to falsehood to excuse myself, simply because I state the truth—namely, that it is almost impossible for me to write. I had no intention of disobeying you, my dear Father, when I let a long time pass without writing to you. I have been ordered to rest my sight completely.

Letters, Vol. 1, 348

It is good to see, Lord, that your saints do not confuse humility with not speaking up for themselves when it is right to do so. Help me learn when to keep quiet and when to speak up. Above all, let me defend myself when necessary without anger or malice.

～ 178. On Sexual Impurity ～

Finally, be strong in the Lord and in the strength of his might. Put on the whole armor of God, that you may be able to stand against the wiles of the devil. For we are not contending against flesh and blood, but against the principalities, against the powers, against the world rulers of this present darkness, against the spiritual hosts of wickedness in the heavenly places. Therefore take the whole armor of God, that you may be able to withstand in the evil day, and having done all, to stand.

EPHESIANS 6:10-13

Even in these holy days the enemy is making every effort to induce me to consent to his impious designs. In particular this evil spirit tries by all sort of images to introduce into my mind impure thoughts and ideas of despair. He shows me a most dismal picture of my life, especially my life in the world.

To put it briefly, dear Father, I am right in the grip of the devil, who is trying with all his might to snatch me from the hands of Jesus. I am alone in this combat, and my heart is filled with terror. What is to become of me, I do not know. I feel very weak in mind and body, Father, but I abandon myself in God's hands.

Letters, Vol. 1, 248–49

Even your saints are tempted, Lord. St. Pio, like St. Francis before him, suffered sexual temptation. Help me, Lord, to live chastely in a licentious era. Give me the strength to graciously avoid books, films, and situations that lead to sexual temptations, even when I seem a fuddy-duddy to those who do not know you.

～ 179. The Suffering of Saints—and of Everyone ～

Five times I have received at the hands of the Jews the forty lashes less one. Three times I have been beaten with rods; once I was stoned. Three times I have been shipwrecked; a night and a day I have been adrift at sea; on frequent journeys, in danger from rivers, danger from robbers, danger from my own people, danger from Gentiles, danger in the city, danger in the wilderness, danger at sea, danger from false brethren; in toil and hardship, through many a sleepless night, in hunger and thirst, often without food, in cold and exposure.

2 CORINTHIANS 11:24-27

You want to know the condition of my health [in 1910 when Pio has been forced by atrocious health to return to his family home, unable to live in the friary, a state which lasted seven years], so here I come to satisfy you. Thanks be to God, I have hardly vomited at all since Christmas, whereas previously I could retain nothing but water. I feel a good deal stronger, so that I can walk a little without much difficulty. But what refuses to leave me is the fever, which pays me a visit almost every day toward evening and is followed by abundant sweating. My cough and the pains in my chest and back are what cause me continual suffering more than anything else.

Letters, Vol. 1, 204

Lord, as St. Teresa of Avila said, "the way you treat your friends, it's no wonder you have so few." Loving you does not keep the saints from illness or harm's way at all. But wait, Lord, non-saints suffer too, and some become bitter and angry, while your saints, even when suffering, have hope in you to sustain them. If life brings suffering to all, then I guess I'd rather be a saint, Lord.

～ 180. One Heart From Two ～

Rejoice always, pray constantly, give thanks in all circumstances; for this is the will of God in Christ Jesus for you.

1 THESSALONIANS 5:16-18

When Mass was over, I remained with Jesus in thanksgiving. Oh, how sweet was the colloquy with paradise.... It was such that, although I want to tell you [my spiritual director] all about it, I cannot. There were things that cannot be translated into human language without losing their deep and heavenly meaning. The heart of Jesus and my own ... were fused. No longer were two hearts beating but only one. My own heart had disappeared, as a drop of water is lost in the ocean. Jesus was its paradise, its king. My joy was so intense and deep that I could bear no more, and tears of happiness poured down my cheeks.

Letters, Vol. 1, 308

Dear Lord, no ecstasies for me, but I too aspire to having my heart lost in yours. Come, Lord Jesus!

～ 181. Doing One's Best in Prayer ～

Continue steadfastly in prayer, being watchful in it with thanksgiving.

COLOSSIANS 4:2

It is true that, given our condition, it is not within our power to keep our thoughts always fixed on God, but let us do our best to keep ourselves, as far as possible, in his presence. This we can and must do, calling to mind every now and then the great truth that God sees us.

Letters, Vol. 3, 257

Lord, I hate to say it, but I know there will be many times today when I forget you. Let me offer the day right now to you, that your will may be done and your kingdom come. And do not forget me, Lord!

~ 182. When God Is Silent: Trust Him Anyway ~

Blessed be the Lord, my rock,... and my fortress, my stronghold and my deliverer, my shield and he in whom I take refuge.

PSALM 144:1-2

I recommended the matter of those two people to Jesus, but he thought fit not to give me an answer.... But although I don't expect an answer, I [am] ... recommending the matter to the Lord, so that everything may be done for the greater glory of God and for the good of the two people concerned....

Letters, Vol. 1, 486

Lord, when praying, even your saints must often simply leave matters in your hands with trust. Today whenever I find myself worrying about my loved one, I will make an act of trust in you and banish such thoughts from my mind by counting ten blessings.

~ 183. On Saints Seeking Suffering ~

Now I rejoice in my sufferings for your sake, and in my flesh I complete what is lacking in Christ's afflictions for the sake of his body, that is, the church.

COLOSSIANS 1:24

If I were to listen merely to the promptings of my heart, I would ask Jesus to give me all the sorrows of men. But I do not do so because I am afraid of being too selfish by desiring the better part, which is

155

suffering. When we suffer, Jesus is closer to us. He looks on, and it is he who comes to beg us for pain and tears, of which he is in need for souls.

Letters, Vol. 1, 305

Lord, I hate suffering, but I see, in the lives of saints like Paul and Pio, that it has a mysterious dimension that enriches them and can, freely offered, help bring about your kingdom and the salvation of souls. In my own life I see how close my sufferings came to making me a bitter, angry person; only by your grace have I found growth in love, in compassion, and in understanding true riches through my trials. I thank you, Lord, for all those graces, and I ask your forgiveness that, in spite of its benefits, I cannot seek to suffer. If it comes, however, I offer it to you.

~ 184. Good Comes From ALL for God's Friends ~

We know that in everything God works for good with those who love him.

ROMANS 8:28

You would like me to be close to you always during this [trial],... and I don't know what I wouldn't do to keep you here at my side. But if you cannot do so, believe that I am always close to you in spirit. And as I am far away from you in the body, the only advice I can give you is to ... simply let the Holy Spirit accomplish what he wants in you. Abandon yourself to his transports, and do not fear. He is so discreet, wise, and sweet that he cannot but do good.

Letters, Vol. 3, 1032

Come, Holy Spirit, and guide me. Rule over my soul, which I freely surrender to your love.

~ 185. Invitation to the Full Life ~

I came that they might have life, and have it abundantly.

JOHN 10:10

Jesus calls the poor and simple shepherds by means of angels to manifest himself to them. He calls the learned men by means of their science. And all of them, moved interiorly by grace, hasten to adore him. He calls all of us with divine inspirations, and he communicates himself to us with his grace.

How many times has he not lovingly invited us also? And with what promptitude have we replied? My God, I blush and am filled with confusion at having to reply to such a question.

Letters, Vol. 4, 977–78

Lord, you called me. I come, sometimes haltingly, often stumbling, but still longing to belong totally to you.

~ 186. Fear Not! ~

Say to those who are of a fearful heart, "Be strong, fear not! Behold, your God will come.... He will come and save you."

ISAIAH 35:4

Don't be bewildered if the night becomes deeper and darker for you. Don't be frightened.... Believe always.... Isn't it God who arranges everything for our greater good? Take heart, therefore;... wait a while and the good Lord will grant our prayers.

Letters, Vol. 3, 404–5

Bless me, Lord. I trust in you.

∼ 187. The Journey ∼

When they had heard the king they went their way; and lo, the star which they had seen in the East went before them, till it came to rest over the place where the child was.

MATTHEW 2:9

Faith also guides us, and we follow securely in its light the way which leads to God, his homeland, just as the holy Magi, guided by the star, symbol of faith, reached the desired place.

Letters, Vol. 4, 980

Lord, how many people, sermons, and books have been the Star in my life, leading me deeper into faith, closer to you. Thank you, Lord. Keep leading me until the happy day when you and I are one.

∼ 188. The Lord, My Shepherd ∼

He will feed his flock like a shepherd, he will gather the lambs in his arms, he will carry them in his bosom, and gently lead those that are with young.

ISAIAH 40:11

They should leave all concern to the most sweet Spouse of souls; let them lay their heads on the breast of this most tender Spouse as beloved disciples and not fear,... for the heavenly Master will not allow a hair of their heads to be touched, just as he did not allow his disciples to be harmed in the Garden of Gethsemane. Then, in the midst of the insolent crowd, they will ascend unobserved with their King.

Letters, Vol. 3, 26

Lord, you are my shepherd. I am your beloved, not from any worthiness of my own but from your merciful, all-encompassing love, which falls like rain on the just and the unjust. Thank you, Lord, for creating me and loving me. I am weary today, so please carry me against your heart.

∼ 189. Help My Unbelief ∼

[The father of the possessed boy said,] "If you can do anything, have pity on us and help us." And Jesus said to him, "If you can! All things are possible to him who believes." Immediately the father of the child cried out and said, "I believe; help my unbelief!"

MARK 9:22-24

There are times ... when I am assailed by violent temptations against faith. I am certain that my will does not yield, but my imagination is so inflamed and presents the temptation in such bright colors that sin seems not merely something indifferent but even delightful. This gives rise to all those dejected thoughts, to diffidence and thoughts of despair, and—please don't be horrified, Father—even to blasphemous thoughts. I am terrified in the face of such a combat, I tremble and do violence to myself, and I am certain that by God's grace I don't fall.

Letters, Vol. 1, 159

Jesus, you know I believe in you. Do not take the immense grace of faith away from me. And in those moments when I doubt you, heaven, everything, do not abandon me but help my unbelief.

～ 190. The Holy Spirit ～

The wind blows where it wills, and you hear the sound of it, but you do not know whence it comes or whither it goes; so it is with every one who is born of the Spirit.

JOHN 3:8

May the grace of the divine Spirit be more and more superabundant in your heart.

Letters, Vol. 1, 730

Come, Holy Spirit, rule over my soul. You're the Life, and you're the Way; yes, you're still the Truth today. Sweet Spirit, rule over my soul.

～ 191. Praying in the Spirit ～

Pray at all times in the Spirit, with all prayer and supplication. To that end keep alert with all perseverance, making supplication for all the saints.

EPHESIANS 6:18

How is it, Father, that when I am with Jesus I do not remember everything I had firmly resolved to ask him? Yet I feel sincerely sorry for this absentmindedness. How is this to be explained?

Letters, Vol. 1, 638

The Lord only allows me to recall those persons and things he wants me to remember. In point of fact, on several occasions our merciful Lord has suggested to me people whom I have never known or even heard of, for the sole purpose of having me present them to him and intercede for them, and in this case he never fails to answer my poor feeble prayers. On the other hand, when Jesus doesn't want to answer me, he makes me actually forget to pray for those persons for whom I had firmly decided and intended to pray.

Letters, Vol. 2, 102

Lord, like Pio, how your Holy Spirit works in my prayer I do not always understand: Some I would like to pray for just fade from my thoughts; others I had no thought of clamor for my attention in prayer. Help me to pray with confidence that you are leading me, Holy Spirit. Make me willing to obey impulses received in prayer to call or write someone, and save me also from the burden of long "must remember" lists. Yes, Holy Spirit, I trust in you.

～ 192. On the Angels ～

Because you have made the Lord your refuge, the Most High your habitation, no evil shall befall you, no scourge come near your tent. For he will give his angels charge of you to guard you in all your ways.

PSALM 91:9-11

I cannot tell you the way these scoundrels [devils] beat me. Sometimes I feel I am about to die. On Saturday it seemed to me that they intended to put an end to me.... I turned to my angel, and after he had kept me waiting a while, there he was hovering close to me, singing hymns to the Divine Majesty....

I rebuked him bitterly for having kept me waiting so long when I had not failed to call him to my assistance. To punish him, I did not want to look him in the face.... But he, poor creature, caught up with me almost in tears and held me until I raised my eyes to his face and found him all upset.

Then, "I am always close to you, my beloved young man," he said. "I am always hovering around you with the affection aroused by your gratitude to the Beloved of your heart. This affection of mine will never end, not even when you die. I know that your generous heart beats all the time for the One we both love; you would cross every mountain and every desert in search of him, to see him again, to embrace him again in these extreme moments, and to ask him to break at once this chain that unites you to the body.... For the present [he cannot give you your desire], but do not cease to ask him insistently for this, because his supreme delight is to have you with him...."

Poor little angel! He is too good.

Letters, Vol. 1, 351–52

Lord, I was not reared to believe in guardian angels, and to this day, while my mind assents, my belief is weak. That you have assigned one of these spirits of light to look after me seems too good to be true. But I want to believe this, Lord. Help my unbelief!

～ 193. Singing the Eternal Song of Praise ～

In the days of the trumpet call to be sounded by the seventh angel, the mystery of God, as he announced to his servants the prophets, should be fulfilled.

REVELATION 10:7

Courage, Father! This day will not be long coming, contrary to all our human forecasts. This beautiful day is already on its way, and happy are those who will be able to shout with joy: *This is the work of the Lord* (Ps 118). All of us will join with them to sing the eternal song of praise to God, for this day will appear wonderful to our eyes: *a marvel in our eyes,* for the triumph of divine justice over iniquity. This beautiful day that is coming cannot be the work of anyone but God, and God will make it be for the resurrection of many and the triumph of his glory. Thanks be to God!

Letters, Vol. 1, 889–90

Lord, you gifted St. Pio with the charism of prophecy. He knew when wars would break out and end, when kings would die, and who would be elected pope. I, on the other hand, have no idea what lies ahead for me, for my loved ones, for the world. But I do know that you, the good God, must triumph in the end. For that I praise you, Lord, and my heart fills with joy.

∼ 194. Yes, Lord ∼

His mother said to the servants, "Do whatever he tells you."

JOHN 2:5

My son, you do not know the effects of obedience. Well, for a yes, for a single yes, *be it done unto me according to Your word,* to do God's will, Mary became the mother of the Most High, professing herself to be his handmaid and keeping her virginity, which was so dear to God and herself. Thanks to this "yes" pronounced by Mary Most Holy, the world obtained salvation, and humanity was redeemed. Let us always do God's will and always say yes to the Lord.

Have a Good Day, 77–78

Tomorrow, Lord, I may be my obstinate wanting-my-own-way self again. But today, Lord, by your grace, I come to do your will.

∼ 195. Let's Thwart Satan—by Forgiving ∼

Any one whom you forgive, I also forgive. What I have forgiven, if I have forgiven anything, has been for your sake in the presence of Christ, to keep Satan from gaining the advantage over us; for we are not ignorant of his designs.

2 CORINTHIANS 2:10-11

You will never complain about offences, no matter where they come from, remembering that Jesus was saturated with ignominy from the malice of men he himself aided. You will excuse everyone with Christian charity, keeping before your eyes the example of the divine Master, who excused even his crucifiers before the Father.

Archives, Our Lady of Grace Friary, San Giovanni Rotondo, quoted in *Have a Good Day,* 135

I am overcome, Lord, thinking of your forgiving those who drove nails into your hands and feet. I want to be like you, Jesus, and I thank you that the older I get the easier it is to forgive. St. Paul says forgiving helps our spiritual children as well as ourselves. That makes sense to me, Lord, and I pray that you will forgive me for the times I held on to injuries and thereby set a bad example to my loved ones. From this moment, Lord, help me to always cast all injuries immediately and irrevocably into the abyss of your mercy.

~ 196. Life: A Brief Pilgrimage ~

But we would not have you ignorant, brethren, concerning those who are asleep, that you may not grieve as others do who have no hope. For since we believe that Jesus died and rose again, even so, through Jesus, God will bring with him those who have fallen asleep.

1 THESSALONIANS 4:13-14

Jesus wants her all for himself. Let her stir up her faith, then, and throw herself with sublime abandonment into the arms of God, and God will carry out the plans he has for her.... This is the path by which Jesus leads strong souls. Here she will gain a better knowledge of our true homeland and will come to see the present life as a brief pilgrimage.

Letters, Vol. 2, 564–65

Lord, help me to have the larger vision of the saints, which sees heaven as well as earth, to hope I will see those I love again, and to abandon myself to you, my guide on this pilgrimage to the Homeland.

~ 197. The Praise of Glory ~

Blessed be the God and Father of our Lord Jesus Christ, who has blessed us in Christ with every spiritual blessing in the heavenly places, even as he chose us in him before the foundation of the world, that we should be holy and blameless before him. He destined us in love to be his sons through Jesus Christ, according to the purpose of his will, to the praise of his glorious grace which he freely bestowed on us in the Beloved.

EPHESIANS 1:3-6

Considering myself unworthy of the divine gaze, on the one hand, and seeing the divine benevolence toward me, my heart cannot contain itself and cannot remain unmoved. May he accept the homage of my gratitude. May he be blessed and honored and glorified a thousand times, praised in heaven and on earth as he deserves.

Letters, Vol. 1, 691

Lord, your goodness exceeds all my just desserts. I thank you for loving me and for the innumerable graces you have poured out on me during my lifetime. May every beat of my heart, Lord, be an act of love and gratitude to you, until I sing your praises in paradise.

∼ 198. True Love: Obeying the Commandments ∼

Every one who believes that Jesus is the Christ is a child of God, and every one who loves the parent loves the child. By this we know that we love the children of God, when we love God and obey his commandments. For this is the love of God, that we keep his commandments. And his commandments are not burdensome.

1 JOHN 5:1-3

How fine a thing it is ... to be able to live according to what the Lord disposes! I feel that this gives me continually new strength to face the severity of the winter. I feel my whole being invaded by a superhuman calm, although I remain in ignorance of everything, despite the fact that my inward gaze is always fixed upon the beloved object in the midst of the fog.

Letters, Vol. 1, 977

Lord, help me to always keep all of your commandments, the difficult ones as well as the easy. And if I am not living as you desire in any way, please make that very clear to me.

∼ 199. The Purifying Light ∼

Again Jesus spoke to them, saying, "I am the light of the world; he who follows me will not walk in darkness, but will have the light of life."

JOHN 8:12

I forewarn you that aridity and privation of the reflected light are not sufficient for spiritual purification. Another painful interior process is also required, which penetrates into the most secret recesses of the soul, pierces it to the depths, and renews it completely. This is nothing but a very bright light, which gives the soul a clearer view of its faults than we can possibly conceive and consequently plunges it into an abyss of darkness and most painful anxiety. In a word, this very bright light penetrates and envelops the soul so thoroughly as to cause it extreme torment and interior agony. And if that person does not die, it is because the Lord keeps him alive by a continued miracle.

Letters, Vol. 2, 315

Jesus, you are the Light of the World. When I see myself in you, I see more clearly my faults and imperfections. But these do not bother me unduly, because my eyes are fixed on you, your glory, your perfection, and your power, which I trust will, bit by bit, refashion me into your image.

∽ 200. The Terrors of God ∽

For the arrows of the Almighty are in me; my spirit drinks their poison; the terrors of God are arrayed against me.

JOB 6:4

The spiritual combats, instead of dying down, are pressing on me relentlessly. Darkness is followed by darkness, and spiritual blindness has become pitch darkness for me.... I haven't the strength to speak to you this time about my spiritual state. My present state of soul is such that I couldn't conceive a more deplorable one, and what is worse, I have lost all hope of seeing the sun rise again before I enter into eternal rest. The feeling is very strong within me that I must arrive at the *Consummatum est.* This feeling pervades my whole being, and if I suffer on this account it is solely due to the fear that I will not be able to bear up under this most harsh trial until the end. Do not tell me that the Lord will help me, because I have only myself to blame and am fully aware of the enormity of my wickedness in the Lord's sight.

Letters, Vol. 1, 861–62

Lord, my "trial," as St. Pio would put it, went on so long that I too lost hope it would ever end. Like Pio, I feared I would not be able to persevere to the end. Yet Pio was very young when he thought all was over and he had lost your favor. He lived almost another sixty years, and he did persevere. Now my trial too is abating.

I ask your intercession, Padre Pio, to help me persevere to life's end, whatever life brings.

~ 201. In Praise of Our Good God ~

O Lord, thou art my God; I will exalt thee, I will praise thy name; for thou hast done wonderful things, plans formed of old, faithful and sure.

ISAIAH 25:1

What will we give to the Lord in return for what he gives us?.... May Jesus be thanked, loved, and blessed by heaven and earth. And may this most sweet God of ours always smile on your heart, my excellent daughter; may he always sustain your spirit, fill you with all his charisms, and lastly, reward you with eternal possession of him.

Letters, Vol. 3, 251–52

Today let me praise you, Lord, for the blessings of your beautiful world, the blessings of human love, the blessings of being a member of your Church, the blessings of being able to live in a free country, and all the special blessings your love gives me.

~ 202. Humble Yourself to Be Enriched ~

Do you know what I have done to you? You call me Teacher and Lord; and you are right, for so I am. If I then, your Lord and Teacher, have washed your feet, you also ought to wash one another's feet. For I have given you an example, that you also should do as I have done to you.

JOHN 13:12-15

Always be lovingly humble before God and man, because God speaks to those whose hearts are truly humble and enriches them with his gifts.

Padre Pio da Pietrelcina: Testimonianze, 54,
quoted in *Have a Good Day*, 125

Lord, you call me to serve others. Lately many help me and I can do nothing for them due to illness. Let my service then be gratitude and prayer for my benefactors.

∼ 203. The Fire of Love ∼

With my whole heart I cry; answer me, O Lord! I will keep thy statutes. I cry to thee; save me, that I may observe thy testimonies. I rise before dawn and cry for help; I hope in thy words. My eyes are awake before the watches of the night, that I may meditate upon thy promise. Hear my voice in thy steadfast love, O Lord.

PSALM 119:145-49

In the last few days more than in the past I have felt within me an indescribable uneasiness. The loving anxiety with which my soul rushes toward God has been deeper and more intense for some days now and produces deep down in me an unspeakable ardor. Moreover, since this fire sometimes leaps up to an enormous height in my soul, I yearn so intensely for God, it seems as if all my bones were dried up by this longing.

Letters, Vol. 1, 983

Lord, hear my poor prayers, that I may love you more and be more and more filled with your Holy Spirit.

～ 204. Real Holiness ～

"I will be a father to you, and you shall be my sons and daughters, says the Lord Almighty...." Since we have these promises, beloved, let us cleanse ourselves from every defilement of body and spirit, and make holiness perfect in the fear of God.

2 CORINTHIANS 6:18; 7:1

Let us keep before our minds what goes to make up real holiness. Holiness means getting above ourselves; it means perfect mastery of all our passions. It means having real and continual contempt for ourselves and for the things of the world, to the point of preferring poverty rather than wealth, humiliation rather than glory, suffering rather than pleasure. Holiness means loving our neighbor as ourselves for love of God. In this connection holiness means loving those who curse us, who hate and persecute us, and even doing good to them. Holiness means living humbly, being disinterested, prudent, just, patient, kind, chaste, meek, and diligent, carrying out one's duties for no other reason than that of pleasing God and receiving from him alone the reward we deserve.

Letters, Vol. 2, 562

Lord, with my own strength I can never achieve holiness. But I recall your words to the mystic Josefa Menendez: "Love will purify you, will consume your defects, and the very strength of that pure and ardent love will lead you to sanctity.... I will do it all" (The Way of Divine Love, *321*).

So come, Lord Jesus, and fill me with the cleansing, sanctifying fire of your love.

～ 205. He Is With Me ～

I have passed out of mind like one who is dead; I have become like a broken vessel ... terror on every side!... But I trust in thee, O Lord.
PSALM 31:12-14

Cast aside worries, dismiss sinister judgments. God is in you and with you. What then do you fear? The anguished fear of having lost him is a sure and evident sign that he dwells within you. Your soul seeks and doesn't find so it suffers, flounders becomes ... exhausted, without ever calming itself down in its despondency. But if for one single minute, it could observe the satisfaction with which he observes your dissatisfied love, what joy!

Letters, Vol. 3, 119

Lord, today my heart is sad. Help me to believe you are with me whatever my feelings.

～ 206. Keep Running ～

For I am already on the point of being sacrificed; the time of my departure has come. I have fought the good fight, I have finished the race, I have kept the faith.

2 TIMOTHY 4:6-7

On the other hand, this knowledge [of God's loving plans for you] must serve as an incentive to lay aside all fear and not come to a halt halfway on your journey, because of the sufferings and trials that must be endured if you are to reach the end of this extremely long road.... Run, then, without growing weary, and may the Lord direct and guide your steps so that you may not fall. Make haste, I tell you, for the road is long and time is very short.

Letters, Vol. 2, 316–17

Lord, even for those who live a long time, life is short. And our day of departure can come anytime. Help me to endure and keep the faith until the end, whenever it comes. Jesus, I place my life in your hands!

~ 207. Let Your Sun Shine on the Good and the Bad ~

Be sons of your Father who is in heaven; for he makes his sun rise on the evil and on the good, and sends rain on the just and on the unjust.

MATTHEW 5:45

Be careful, above all, of charity toward God, your neighbor, and yourself. Refrain from judging anyone whomsoever, except when it is your duty to do so. In this way you will hold everyone in esteem, and you will also show yourself to be a worthy son of the heavenly Father, who makes his sun shine on the evil and on the good.

Letters, Vol. 1, 1263

Dear Lord, you know I want to be like you, good to those who are good to me and good to those who are not. But if it isn't so hard to do good deeds to those I don't like or who don't treat me well, I certainly find it hard not to judge them. And I invite others, at times, to share my judgment. Root these nasty traits out of my heart, Lord, so I may truly become your child.

~ 208. Prescription: Boundless Confidence in God's Mercy ~

But we have this treasure in earthen vessels, to show that the transcendent power belongs to God and not to us. We are afflicted in every way, but not crushed; perplexed, but not driven to despair; persecuted, but not forsaken; struck down, but not destroyed; always carrying in the body the death of Jesus, so that the life of Jesus may also be manifested in our bodies.

2 CORINTHIANS 4:7-10

At times the spirit is willing and the flesh weak, but God wants the spirit more than anything else. Cling closer and closer to him, then, with your will, with the highest point of your soul. Let nature feel [the suffering], and be roused to demand its rights, for nothing is more natural. If nature is also subjected to suffering at present, this is not due to itself, for nature too was made for happiness. These sufferings are due to it because of sin. What criminal is there who, when subjected to what he recognizes as deserved,... does not feel the pain and demand to be freed from it?

Always bear in mind as a safe general rule that while God tries us by his crosses and sufferings, he always leaves us a glimmer of light by which we continue to have great trust in him and to recognize his immense goodness. I urge you, therefore, not to be entirely disheartened in the face of the cross ... heaven bestows on you, but to continue to have boundless confidence in the divine mercy.

Letters, Vol. 1, 461

It heartens me, Lord, that even a great warrior saint like Padre Pio recognizes as simply natural for our human nature—an earthen vessel—to fight against suffering, even if the highest point of the soul is willing to do whatever you will. Help me, in my particular trials and crosses, to always trust in your divine mercy and your tender love for me.

～ 209. Fear of Being a Burden ～

I robbed other churches by accepting support from them in order to serve you. And when I was with you and was in want, I did not burden any one.

2 CORINTHIANS 11:8-9

To the former trials of which you are already aware, there has been added ... the fear of being a burden and a trouble to everyone, especially to my brethren. There is hardly any foundation for this fear, yet it distresses and torments me and prevents me from enjoying spiritual peace even for an instant.... At the height of my torment the following words escaped me: "If I am a burden to you and my work does not please you, then tell me so quite clearly, for pity's sake, and I'll go elsewhere to ask for hospitality."

Letters, Vol. 1, 40

Even your saints, Lord, have to fight self-pity and the related fear of being a burden to those one loves. It is humbling to me, Lord, when the daughter I once diapered has to pass me a bed pan because I cannot get up, or the son I drove to Scouts must drive me to the doctor. Lord, give me and everyone in this situation the humility of quiet acceptance. Help us express love and gratitude, not bitterness or anger. Above all,

keep us cheerful to be around and centered on you and others, not our-
selves.

∼ 210. On Repentance ∼

In that day [when Jerusalem was invaded] the Lord God of hosts
called to weeping and mourning, to baldness and girding with sack-
cloth; and behold, joy and gladness, slaying oxen and killing sheep,
eating flesh and drinking wine. "Let us eat and drink, for tomorrow
we die." The Lord of hosts has revealed himself in my ears: "Surely
this iniquity will not be forgiven you till you die," says the Lord God
of hosts.

ISAIAH 22:12-14

Let us be docile in face of these events [of World War I], which are
apparently harsh but are a sign of true mercy. Let us continue to trust,
for the God who humiliates us and makes us suffer at present is the
God who is still speaking to us, and the God who still speaks to us,...
even if he thunders so unpleasantly and severely, is still the God who
loves us. He is waiting for the voice of our repentance to silence his
thundering. He is waiting for our tears to extinguish his lightning.

Well then, let our tears of true contrition never fail us. Let us lift up
our hands to heaven and implore tears of this kind for all our fellow
travelers.

Letters, Vol. 2, 459

Lord, help me to remember that whether it is war, flood, fires, invasion, or
any evil, it is to you and you alone I must look for deliverance and help.
My country is in deep trouble, Lord, morally, spiritually, and politically.

Help us to repent and change so we may call upon you and be saved from the troubles our sins have brought upon us and upon the world. I do repent, Lord, for all the ways in which I have followed the world and the flesh instead of following only you.

～ 211. On Being Children of God ～

As indeed he says in Hosea, "Those who were not my people I will call 'my people,' and her who was not beloved I will call 'my beloved.'"

ROMANS 9:25

Infinite praise and thanks to Jesus, King of souls, for treating you as a chosen daughter of his own. I cannot fail to be deeply moved and filled with indescribable joy at the sight of all these most singular gestures of love with which Jesus favors your soul.... Rejoice, then, along with me at this outstanding benevolence of our good God. Oh,... how delightful and consoling it is to know that without any merit of our own, this most tender Father has raised us to such high dignity.

Letters, Vol. 2, 384–85

Lord, how can I thank you for calling me "beloved" and "daughter"? You have brought me into your flock through a mystery of grace, for I am surely no better than many who must go through life without knowing you. I offer my prayer, Lord, that all may come to know you and your tender love, perhaps even in those moments between this life and the next.

∼ 212. Temptation: On the Brink of the Precipice ∼

For I delight in the law of God, in my inmost self, but I see in my members another law at war with the law of my mind and making me captive to the law of sin which dwells in my members. Wretched man that I am! Who will deliver me from this body of death? Thanks be to God through Jesus Christ our Lord! So then, I of myself serve the law of God with my mind, but with my flesh I serve the law of sin.

ROMANS 7:22-25

Who will set me free from the miseries in which I am placed? The temptations, especially, pursue me more relentlessly than ever. They are a source of great suffering, not because of the continual violence I must do myself but because they are so repellent and persistently hostile and in view of my great fear of offending God from one moment to the next. For there are moments at which I am right on the brink of the precipice and about to fall.

Letters, Vol. 1, 230–31

Lord, I feel rattled today by temptations to angry acts, to slander, to lust, to jealousy, to sloth. I feel my emotions whirling this way and that. Help the compass of my will in all this turbulence to remain firmly fixed on you, and deliver me from all evils, particularly the one of not recognizing my own potential for evil.

～ 213. The Way to Holiness ～

Let all bitterness and wrath and anger and clamor and slander be put away from you, with all malice, and be kind to one another, tenderhearted, forgiving one another, as God in Christ forgave you.
EPHESIANS 4:31-32

Be watchful, I tell you, and never place too much trust in yourself or count excessively on your own strength. Try to advance more and more on the way to perfection and practice charity more and more, for charity is the bond of Christian perfection.

Letters, Vol. 2, 274

Do not worry, however, for the good we endeavor to do to others will also result in the sanctification of our own souls.

Letters, Vol. 2, 400

St. Paul tells us what we must renounce, Lord. But it is impossible to simply say, "I will not feel angry," or, "I will not feel bitterness." Such things must be gifts of grace. So, Lord, I tell you, I will to not be angry, and I refuse to act out of anger. I renounce malice utterly, and I am practicing compassion, forgiveness, and kindness to everyone in all circumstances as best I can. As to my feelings of fury, those I must accept until your grace heals me, as it healed me long ago of bitterness when I cried out to you.

～ 214. Turn to the Light ～

Once you were darkness, but now you are light in the Lord; walk as children of light (for the fruit of light is found in all that is good and right and true).
EPHESIANS 5:8-9

We are not all called to the same state [of life] and the Holy Spirit doesn't work in all souls in the same way. He "blows as he wills and where he wills" [Jn 3:8]. Live completely at peace because there will be light.

Letters, Vol. 3, 108

Lord, help me to live in your light. And when it appears there is only darkness, let me trust, as Pio says, "There will be light" eventually.

～ 215. O Foolish Pride! ～

For by grace you have been saved through faith; and this is not your own doing, it is the gift of God—not because of works, lest any man should boast. For we are his workmanship, created in Christ Jesus for good works, which God prepared beforehand, that we should walk in them.

EPHESIANS 2:8-10

What have you that you did not receive? If then you received it, why do you boast as if it were not a gift?

1 CORINTHIANS 4:7

When assailed by pride, say to yourself: What good is there in myself that I have not received? And if I have received everything, why should I praise myself? Oh! I would be foolish to praise myself for what is not mine. Do this and have no fear in this regard.

Letters, Vol. 3, 60

Lord, today I found myself feeling quite proud of some work I have done. What an idiot I am! I was only using talent you gave me. Forgive me, please, for not turning to you and thanking you for my gift, Lord. I beg you to help me keep firmly in mind that all I am and have comes from you.

~ 216. A Cure for Impatience ~

And those who passed by derided him, wagging their heads, and saying, "Aha! You who would destroy the temple and build it in three days, save yourself, and come down from the cross!" So also the chief priests mocked him to one another with the scribes, saying, "He saved others; he cannot save himself. Let the Christ, the King of Israel, come down now from the cross, that we may see and believe." Those who were crucified with him also reviled him.

And when the sixth hour had come, there was darkness over the whole land until the ninth hour. And at the ninth hour Jesus cried with a loud voice, "Elo-i, Elo-i, lama sabach-thani?" which means, "My God, my God, why hast thou forsaken me?"

MARK 15:29-34

Let your entire life be spent in resignation [that is, acceptance of God's will], prayer, work, humility, and rendering thanks to the good God. If you happen to notice a feeling of impatience arising, immediately have recourse to prayer.... Above all, turn your thoughts to the annihilation that the Son of God suffered for love of us. I want the thought of the suffering and humiliation of Jesus to be the usual subject of your meditation. If you practice this, as I am sure you will, in a short time you will experience its salutary fruits. Such meditation will act as a shield to defend you from impatience.

Letters, Vol. 3, 60

Lord, may meditating on your sufferings voluntarily taken up for me, sufferings totally undeserved, give me patience in all my troubles and annoyances. I love and adore you, my Lord and my God.

~ 217. God Inspires Bountiful Sowing ~

The point is this: he who sows sparingly will also reap sparingly, and he who sows bountifully will also reap bountifully.

2 CORINTHIANS 9:6

For one who is inflamed with divine love, helping the neighbor in his needs is a fever that consumes him by degrees. He would give his life a thousand times if he could induce a soul to offer one more act of praise to the Lord. I too feel that this fever is eating me up.

Letters, Vol. 1, 464

Lord, inflame me with your love, so that I may always turn to my neighbor with compassion. As I wish to receive compassion, mercy, and love, let me sow them bountifully here through deeds, alms, and prayer. Give me the grace, Lord, to give even when it hurts, as when someone has harmed me, and give me the grace to give alms to your works for the needy when I "cannot afford to," knowing that a claim on your own generosity never goes unpaid.

~ 218. Put Your Spouse First ~

Be subject to one another out of reverence for Christ.

EPHESIANS 5:21

May the Holy Family never withdraw its loving gaze from you and your family. Model yourselves on it, and you will have peace and spiritual and temporal well-being.

Letters, Vol. 4, 1000

Lord, when I think in terms of power and control, I do not want to be subordinate to anybody! But when I think in terms of your love, which calls us to our highest and our best, I feel differently. As Paul says, each of a couple must put the other's welfare first and must do so in light of being both Christ's disciples and God's precious children. Only then can marriage follow your design.

Fill your world, Lord, with holy marriages! And give your grace to all those who are struggling to create them.

~ 219. On Evil's Fruitless Works of Darkness ~

Take no part in the unfruitful works of darkness, but instead expose them.

EPHESIANS 5:11

When the soul grieves and is afraid of offending God, it does not offend him and is very far from committing sin. Divine grace is with you continually, and you are very dear to the Lord. Shadows and fears and convictions to the contrary are diabolical stratagems, which you should despise in the name of Jesus. Do not listen to these temptations. The spirit of evil is busily engaged in trying to make you believe that your past life has been strewn with sins.

Listen, rather, to me when I tell you, just as we are told by the Spouse of our souls, that your present state is an effect of your love for

God and a proof of his incomparable love for you. Cast away those fears, and dispel those shadows which the devil is increasing in your soul in order to torment you.

Letters, Vol. 2, 67

Lord, help me to see "the works of darkness" in myself, particularly those St. Pio speaks of—the shadows, fears, and convictions that you do not love me. I look to your divine mercy, Lord, to help me renounce every type of evil and to expose it fearlessly when necessary for the greater good.

~ 220. Secret Infidelities ~

Your wickedness will chasten you, and your apostasy will reprove you. Know and see that it is evil and bitter for you to forsake the Lord your God; the fear of me is not in you, says the Lord God of hosts.

JEREMIAH 2:19

At the present moment ... my soul is greatly oppressed, and it seems to me that my life is coming to an end. My heart is rent by the most severe pain, which invades my whole person. The thickest darkness is gathering on the horizon of my soul. And only the mercy of the One who causes it can and must dissolve it. Meanwhile my soul will waste away under the weight of its infidelities to the Author of life.

I know that no one is pure in the Lord's sight, but there is no limit to my uncleanness before him. In my present state, when the merciful Lord in his infinite wisdom and justice is condescending to raise the veil and reveal all the malice and ugliness of my secret infidelities, I see myself so disfigured that even my clothing seems to abhor my filthiness. This happens because the dark picture I describe is not shown to me by men, in which case the soul could easily defend itself, but by God.

Letters, Vol. 1, 533

Lord, if a saint like Padre Pio could barely stand to see his "secret infidelities," what hope is there for me? Certainly I would be a liar if I did not acknowledge that, in spite of my desire to never offend you, I often lack the strength to follow you all the way.

Yet I will hope, Lord, for I trust in your mercy more than I trust in myself. Your mercy is surely stronger than my betrayals and weakness. Show me my sins, Lord, and give me true repentance for what I am and have done. Then strengthen me to sin no more!

∼ 221. Out Fear, in Real Love ∼

So we know and believe the love God has for us. God is love, and he who abides in love abides in God, and God abides in him. In this is love perfected with us, that we may have confidence for the day of judgment, because as he is so are we in this world. There is no fear in love, but perfect love casts out fear. For fear has to do with punishment, and he who fears is not perfected in love.

1 JOHN 4:16-18

If we earnestly endeavor to love Jesus, this alone will drive all fear from our hearts, and the soul will find that instead of walking in the Lord's paths, it is flying. The soul in this state is induced to exclaim with the royal prophet: *I will run in the way of thy commandments when thou enlargest my understanding!* (Ps 119:32).

Letters, Vol. 1, 456

Love, Lord, is a word bandied left and right, used to sell cosmetics and send young men to die for country. The more I ponder what love is—the heights and depths, the boundlessness of real love—the more I see its glory and its cost. That glory is you, Lord, who are Love. Real love, the kind you lived and still model both in yourself and your saints like Pio, is the pearl of great price that can only be had by selling everything.

Yet how I cling to my "valuables." I fear to give them up and have—dare I say it?—only you. Wrest them from my grasping hands, Lord, so that I may have you alone and, in having you, receive at your hands everything of real value.

∼ 222. O the Blessed Angels! ∼

Then Jesus said to him, "Put your sword back into its place; for all who take the sword will perish by the sword. Do you think that I cannot appeal to my Father, and he will at once send me more than twelve legions of angels?"

MATTHEW 26:52-53

How consoling it is to know [that] one is always under the protection of a heavenly spirit who never abandons us, not even (what an admirable thing!) when we are actually offending God! How delightful is this great truth to the one who believes! Who is to be feared, then, by the devout soul who is trying to love Jesus, when accompanied by such an illustrious warrior? Was he not, perhaps, one of the multitude who joined with St. Michael ... to defend God's honor against Satan and all the other rebellious angels?... Well, then, let me tell you that he is still powerful against Satan and his satellites. His love has not lessened, and he can never fail to defend us.

Make a habit of thinking of him.... When it seems to you that you are alone and abandoned, don't complain that you are without a friend to whom you can open your heart and confide your woes. For goodness' sake, don't forget this invisible companion who is always there to listen to you, always ready to console you.

Letters, Vol. 2, 420–21

Lord, I know people who have been given the grace to see their guardian angels and the guardian angels of others. Padre Pio saw angels from childhood. Help me to take in this beautiful reality. I thank you for this further proof of your love for me and all humanity.

～ 223. God's Light ～

This is the message we have heard from him and proclaim to you, that God is light and in him is no darkness at all.

1 JOHN 1:5

The finest grace that can be asked by and on behalf of those who aspire to the spiritual life [is] ... an increase of heavenly light. This is a light that cannot be acquired either by prolonged study or through human teaching, but which is directly infused by God. When the righteous soul obtains this light, it comes to know and love its God and eternal things in its meditations with extreme clarity and relish. Although it is nothing but a light of faith, it is still sufficient to produce such spiritual consolation that the earth, in the first place, disappears from view, while all that this world can offer is seen to be worthless.

Letters, Vol. 2, 211

Dear Lord, grant me this light so I may love you, as Pio says, "with extreme clarity and relish."

∼ 224. Imitating Our Saints ∼

Precious in the sight of the Lord is the death of his saints.

PSALM 116:15

I heard of our very dear Francesca's departure for the heavenly home-land before you told me about it. I shed a lot of tears at the loss of such a precious, not to say rare, existence. These tears were and are being shed solely because of the not inconsiderable loss the Church militant [that is, the Christians still on earth] has suffered by her death. An immense sense of veneration surges over me at the thought of this departed one, and almost without my being aware of it, I feel induced to kneel down as if before a sacred image. Holiness shone forth from her and made her the most perfect and most lovable image of God.

You whose enviable lot it was to draw near to this truly holy soul will agree with what I have said about her. How many times when you were close to her, when you heard her speak and considered the way she acted and all that she was, have you not forgotten all about your-self, felt small and wretched, and experienced a strange sense of admi-ration, veneration, and joy that cannot be put into words? How often, I say, when you were beside her, have you not felt closer to God and an indefinable need to become better?

She has now disappeared from our bodily sight, but let us make her live on within us by imitating her in the practice of virtue and holiness.

Letters, Vol. 3, 146-47

Lord, I thank you with all my heart for the now dead holy friends and relatives you have given me over my lifetime. They demonstrated the virtues by the way they lived and made me want to conquer my failings and become a better person. May they bask now in the glory of your presence. And may you make me holy, too, Lord—however impossible that seems at times—so that I may come where they are and be reunited with them in you.

∼ 225. Ask to Be Holy ∼

Blessed be the God and Father of our Lord Jesus Christ, who has blessed us in Christ with every spiritual blessing in the heavenly places, even as he chose us in him before the foundation of the world, that we should be holy and blameless before him.

EPHESIANS 1:3-4

As regards your ... behavior in church, do not fear. The most useful, fruitful, and also the most acceptable way to the Lord is precisely that: To ask Jesus to make us holy is neither presumption nor audacity, because it is the same as desiring to love him greatly. The fears that arise, as to whether you spent your time in the presence of God well or otherwise, are without foundation. And dwelling on this is a true waste of time that could be used for holier and more fruitful matters.

Letters, Vol. 3, 253

Lord, I feel a certain embarrassment when I ask you to make me holy, because I know how far from that state I am. I also feel a slight fear as to what it might cost in pain and suffering. But my own anxiety makes me smile, for I know from experience that life is not stingy with suffering and pain of varied kinds, whether one becomes holy or not. And my study of

189

the saints convinces me that, suffering or not, it is the saints who get the most out of life in terms of joy and peace.

So let this chicken-hearted follower of yours ask, "Please make me a saint, so I may love and serve you in this life and enjoy your company forever in the next."

∼ 226. Keeping Turned Toward God ∼

My eyes are toward thee, O Lord God.

PSALM 141:8

If you want to become perfect, always keep present in your mind what God said to Abraham: "Walk before me, and be blameless" (Gn 17:1).

Let us refer all our actions to him; let us raise our souls to him more often. Let us carry out Christian actions more often along with short prayers.

In short, let us refer everything to God, and let us act and live in him.

Letters, Vol. 3, 257–58

Lord, the other day my friend sent me a card that reads, "If it matters to you, it matters to him." That is how I want to live my life, referring all things to you for your guidance and trusting always in your fatherly care. I trust in your mercy for the graces to live a truly Christian life.

∼ 227. Help for the Troubled Heart ∼

Let not your hearts be troubled; believe in God, believe also in me.

JOHN 14:1

Live calmly, and do not worry excessively, because in order to work more freely in us, the Holy Spirit needs tranquility and calm. And for you, every anxious thought is a mistake, as you have no reason to fear. It is the Lord who works within you, and you must do nothing except leave the door of your heart wide open so that he might work as he pleases.

Letters, Vol. 3, 258

Lord, help me to feel to the bottom of my being that "every anxious thought is a mistake," as St. Pio counseled one of his spiritual children. I cannot always control my feelings, Lord, but I tell you with my will that I love you, trust you, and surrender all that I am and have to you.

∼ 228. Waiting for the Precious Fruit ∼

Be patient, therefore, brethren, until the coming of the Lord. Behold, the farmer waits for the precious fruit of the earth, being patient over it until it receives the early and the late rain. You also be patient.

JAMES 5:7-8

The desire to be in eternal peace is good and holy, but you must moderate this with complete resignation to divine will. It is better to do [the] divine will on earth than to enjoy paradise. To suffer and not to die was St. Teresa [of Avila]'s motto. Purgatory is sweet when one suffers for love of God.

The trials to which the Lord is subjecting you at present and those to which he will subject you in the future are all countersigns of divine love and jewels for the soul. The winter will pass, my dears, and the never-ending spring will come, all the richer in beauty as the storms were strong.

Letters, Vol. 3, 553–54

Lord, help me not to get caught up in the anxieties of the day but to keep my eyes on the prize, the life of joy that will never end. Come, Lord Jesus!

～ 229. Wonderful Dark Light ～

But you are a chosen race, a royal priesthood, a holy nation, God's own people, that you may declare the wonderful deeds of him who called you out of darkness into his marvelous light.

1 PETER 2:9

The darkness you are experiencing is an indication of the closeness of God to your souls. Moses, that great leader of the people of God, found the Lord in the darkness of Sinai. The Jewish people saw him in the form of a cloud, and he appeared in the temple as a cloud also. Jesus Christ, in the Transfiguration on Tabor, was first visible, and then he rendered himself invisible to his apostles, because he was covered by a shining cloud. God's hiding himself in the darkness means his making himself more clear to your gaze, and that from his being visible and intelligible he becomes transfigured into the purely divine....

Speaking of the darkness, I have already replied also, as regards the shadows that seem to thicken within you. They are not shadows, my beloved daughters, but light, and such a strong light that it astonishes the soul, which is accustomed to thinking of God in the usual, almost human manner. Thank the Lord for having allowed you to foretaste, from this life, that vision in which when nothing is seen everything is seen.

Letters, Vol. 3, 554

Lord, help me to learn to pray and to live in you and for you, so that one day I too may see the "no thing" in which is "everything." Come, Holy Spirit, with your graces!

~ 230. When Shuddering With Fear ~

Attend to me, and answer me; I am overcome by my trouble. I am distraught.

PSALM 55:2

[World War I is raging, and Pio is about to be called for military service.] What can I tell you about myself? I feel an emptiness in my heart which makes me constantly suffer agonies. Amid the affectionate care of my family, I see that this state is becoming more frightening. Dear God! The thought of the future makes my blood freeze in my veins!

I rely greatly on your prayers for the happy outcome of this trial, not to mention those of the many other souls who are dear to Jesus. Pray and pray more insistently always. Jesus is good and cannot but hear so many prayers said with complete trust in him.

Letters, Vol. 3, 557

I am always heartened, Lord, to see that even your saints can be frightened or anxious over what the future holds. Of course, Pio worried about being cast into an environment that is potentially harmful to spiritual life. He did not worry about material things, not even that he might be injured or killed. Lord, if I must be anxious, let my anxieties be less about pain and suffering for my body and more about situations that can harm my soul and impede my spiritual destiny.

~ 231. To Love God, Our True Good ~

And above all these [virtues] put on love, which binds everything together in perfect harmony.

COLOSSIANS 3:14

The first virtue required by the person who is striving for perfection is charity. In all natural things the first movement, the first inclination or impulse, is to tend toward the center, in obedience to a physical law. The same thing happens in the supernatural sphere; the first movement of our hearts is a movement toward God, which is nothing more than loving our own true good. With good reason Sacred Scripture speaks of charity as the bond of perfect harmony.

Charity has as its close relatives joy and peace. Joy is born of happiness at possessing what we love. Now, from the moment at which the soul knows God, it is naturally led to love him. If the soul follows this natural impulse, which is caused by the Holy Spirit, it is already loving the Supreme Good. This fortunate soul ... possesses the beautiful virtue of love. By loving God the soul is certain of possessing him. When a person loves money, honors, and good health, unfortunately he does not always possess what he loves, whereas he who loves God possesses him at once.

Letters, Vol. 2, 213–14

Lord, you know that I love you; help me to love you more. And help me to live that love by loving everyone else. To do that, give me the grace to become a me full of you.

~ 232. The Wonder of the Grace in Which We Stand ~

Since we are justified by faith, we have peace with God through our Lord Jesus Christ. Through him we have obtained access to this grace in which we stand, and we rejoice in our hope of sharing the glory of God.

ROMANS 5:1-2

Let us pray to the Father of all light to enable us to penetrate more and more deeply into the mystery of our justification, how wretched sinners like ourselves have been led to salvation. Our justification is such an enormous miracle that Sacred Scripture compares it to the resurrection of our divine Master.

Yes,... our conversion from ungodliness is such that it can well be said that God revealed his power more fully in our justification than in drawing heaven and earth from nothing, since there is a greater contrast between the sinner and grace than there is between nonexistence and being. Nonexistence is less far from God than is the sinner. In point of fact, since nonexistence is the lack of being, it has no power to resist God's will, while the sinner, as a being and a free being, is capable of resisting all God's wishes....

Oh! If all men could only understand the extreme wretchedness and dishonor from which God's omnipotent hand has rescued us. Oh! If we could only perceive for a single instant that which still amazes the heavenly spirits..., namely the state to which God's grace has raised us, to be nothing less than his own children, destined to reign with his Son for all eternity!

Letters, Vol. 2, 212–13

Lord, I thank you for the unspeakable gift of being your child. How many graces you have poured out on me, though I am full of weakness, ego, and have sinned. Make me more worthy of my parentage, Lord!

∼ 233. Submitting to the Good God ∼

Righteous art thou, O Lord; all thy deeds and all thy ways are mercy and truth, and thou dost render true and righteous judgment for ever. [So] ... now deal with me according to thy pleasure.

TOBIT 3:2, 6

If our staying firmly on our feet depended on us, undoubtedly we would fall into the hands of the enemy of our salvation at the slightest breeze. Let us confide always in divine mercy, and thus we will experience more and more, how good the Lord is.

Letters, Vol. 4, 237

Lord, let me echo that righteous man Tobit. I praise your goodness and mercy and surrender myself to you. Do with me as you please.

∼ 234. To Remain in Christ ∼

Who shall separate us from the love of Christ? Shall tribulation, or distress, or persecution, or famine, or nakedness, or peril, or sword?

ROMANS 8:35

Last night I spent the entire night with Jesus in his passion. I ... suffered a great deal ... [but] this was a suffering which did me absolutely no harm. My trust in God increased more and more and I felt increasingly attracted towards Jesus.... Although there were no bonds, I felt myself tightly bound to Jesus. I burned with a thousand flames which made me live and die at the same time. Hence, I suffered, lived and died continually.... I would like to shout, to cry out to everyone at the top of my voice: love Jesus....

Letters, Vol. 1, 330

Yes, Lord, I desire to never be separated from you and to love you. But often I have left you, lured by things of this world. I have placed other relationships ahead of you while proclaiming myself your child. Forgive me, Lord, and heal me of my weaknesses so I may truly love you for yourself, not just the treasures of heaven.

～ 235. To Be Human—What a Drag! ～

Wretched man that I am! Who will deliver me from this body of death?

ROMANS 7:24

I exhort you to live tranquilly as regards your spirit. I clearly see the multiple inclinations that self-love nurtures and plants in your heart, my dearest daughter. And I know well that the condition of your sensitive, delicate, and kind soul greatly contributes to this. But there is nothing to worry a great deal about, because, in the final analysis, they are nothing but inclinations which, given the fact that you feel the disturbance, and that the heart suffers as a result, there is neither a danger nor the appearance of your consenting to them.

No, my good daughter, the fact that you conceived the ardent desire—which God himself instilled in your heart—to be totally his,

makes it not so easy to believe that your will consents to such a war....
Your will is molested, agitated by its own affections and passions, but
you ... don't consent to them, except very rarely, and even then you are
not aware of it.

Letters, Vol. 3, 696–98

Lord, in my many weaknesses and self-love, it is to you that I look for vic-
tory over the world, the flesh, and the devil. I trust in you to be the elevator,
Lord Jesus, that as St. Thérèse put it, lifts me to sanctity and to heaven.

∼ 236. Self-Deception ∼

The way of a fool is right in his own eyes.

PROVERBS 12:15

I cannot hide from you ... my great bewilderment at your complaints
that I have been very different in my attitude toward you for some
time past, that you have found me severe, almost rough, and sometimes quite harsh. On the other hand, I admire and appreciate your
frankness, but for the sake of truth I cannot refrain from raising my
voice to inform you that you are mistaken this time as always. What
you attribute to the light is merely due to your own eyes. Unfortunately,
by this time I ought to have made you begin to feel what you attribute
to me, but this is not necessary for the moment.

We'll meet in Foggia and settle our accounts there. Meanwhile, be
at peace, for with the divine assistance all will work out for your own
good, for God's glory, the salvation of souls, and Lucifer's confusion.

Letters, Vol. 2, 518–19

Lord, when I was very ill, I was sure that I treated everyone taking care of me with saintly patience, kindliness, and good cheer. Now my daughter tells me that when the nurses did not respond to my call bell right away, I would harangue her to go find them and make sure they took care of my need, pronto! How blessed I am to have a daughter who shatters my foolish illusions. Help me, Lord, to become the kind of person I sometimes erroneously think I am! Bless all those who put up with me when I am cantankerous or impatient, especially my daughter.

～ 237. Love Is From God ～

Those who love him will keep his ways.

SIRACH 2:15

You become sad at the little love you feel for God. It seems to you that it is little more than nothing.... But ... don't you yourself feel this love in your soul? What is that doubt, or rather, what is that ardent desire that you yourself express to me?

Well, you should know ... that *in divino* that desire to love is love. Who placed this yearning to love the Lord in your heart? Don't holy desires come from above? Are we perhaps capable of arousing in ourselves one single desire of that kind without the grace of God, which sweetly works within us? If there is nothing but the desire to love God in a soul, everything is present already; God himself is there, because God is not, nor can he be, anywhere except where there is a desire for his love....

And if this desire of yours is not satisfied, if it seems to you that you always desire without possessing perfect love, all this signifies that you must never say "enough!" It means that we cannot and must not stop on the path of divine love.

Letters, Vol. 3, 669–70

Lord, you know that I want to love you more. Send forth your spirit, Lord, to lead, push, and pull me along the way of divine love.

～ 238. True and False Humility ～

A man's pride will bring him low, but he who is lowly in spirit will obtain honor.

PROVERBS 29:23

All that you feel within you at the sight of so many holy people around you, all of them devoted to loving and serving the Lord, is a sign that your soul is itself ardently seeking its Creator. The fact that you feel ashamed of yourself on seeing so many souls who love God is a good sign. I exhort you to humble yourself before the Lord at the sight but to be on your guard against the false humility that brings discouragement with it, for this leads infallibly to despair.

What you must do is to thank the Lord and be very glad that in the midst of an unholy nation, generous souls are not lacking, all intent on loving Jesus. You must make an effort to be more and more careful in observance of the divine precepts and of the duties belonging to your own state.

Letters, Vol. 2, 139

Lord, I thank you for all the saintly people I know. I am saddened that I do not serve and love you as well as so many of them do. But I trust you to bring even slothful, worldly me into your kingdom, because in spite of my failings, this is the place I want to go, to live forever with you who are Love, Truth, and Beauty.

～ 239. Imaginary Christian Perfection ～

And the Lord said: "... This people draw near with their mouth and honor me with their lips, while their hearts are far from me, and their fear of me is a commandment of men learned by rote."

ISAIAH 29:13

Not every one who says to me, "Lord, Lord," shall enter the kingdom of heaven, but he who does the will of my Father who is in heaven.

MATTHEW 7:21

I see, in the Lord, that you have almost completely abandoned this dangerous behavior you had in the past [i.e. desiring quickly to arrive at a total perfection that could only be feigned]....With that imaginary perfection in sight always, you multiplied useless desires which, similar to the drone hornet and the bumblebee, devour the honey in the beehive so that those true and good desires remain devoid of any sort of consolation.... Be suspicious of all those desires that ... cannot be attained. And to be more precise, these are all those desires for some Christian perfection that can be imagined and admired but not practiced, and about which many speak without putting it into practice.

Letters, Vol. 3, 683–84

Lord, how easy it is to be deluded in my spiritual life. Forgive me for the times that I think too well of myself. And forgive me when, like the Pharisee, I look down on someone else. Help me to laugh at my own pretensions and refuse to judge the foibles of others.

～ 240. Trusting Surrender ～

We have hope in God.

2 MACCABEES 2:18

As regards the spiritual afflictions and battles, I can assure you that they keep pace with my bodily sufferings. When the latter are multiplied, the former also increase. I do not know where I shall end up if things go on like this. I thank the Lord, though, that despite the fact that particularly in certain contacts with others I suffer moments of real anguish I am invariably cheerful though I must do great violence to myself, and it seems to me that fresh courage is gently invading my heart. Meanwhile I cast myself trustfully into the arms of Jesus. Then let whatever he has decreed take place and he must certainly come to my aid.

Letters, Vol. 1, 243

Lord, grant to me and all those I pray for that trust in you which, as Padre Pio testified, can exist even when we are also experiencing many sufferings, even anguish.

～ 241. Be Patient With Yourself ～

And we desire each one of you to show the same earnestness in realizing the full assurance of hope until the end, so that you may not be sluggish, but imitators of those who through faith and patience inherit the promises.

HEBREWS 6:11-12

Be fully convinced, my dear, that what ... greatly assures our perfection is the virtue of patience. And if it is necessary to practice this virtue with others, it is useful to firstly practice it on ourselves. Those who aspire to pure love of God have no need to be patient with others to the degree we should be with ourselves. We must resign ourselves, my dear daughter, to bearing our imperfections in order to arrive at perfection.

I say to bear our imperfections with patience, and not at all to love and caress them, because humility is nourished in this suffering.

Letters, Vol. 3, 684–85

Lord, I thank you for Padre Pio's counsel to be patient with myself. When I see myself trying to wring my desires from you instead of sweetly surrendering to your will, I could despair that my ego will ever submit fully to grace. Even the good I do seems tainted by traces of ego. Do I ever act out of complete purity of intention and love for you, my God? It seems not. Help me to bear my imperfection, Lord, by fixing my attention ever more upon you and ever less upon myself, while still trying to improve.

∼ 242. The Word of the Lord ∼

You have been born anew, not of perishable seed but of imperishable, through the living and abiding word of God; for "All flesh is like grass and all its glory like the flower of grass. The grass withers, and the flower falls, but the word of the Lord abides for ever."

1 PETER 1:23-25

As regards your reading, there is very little to be admired and hardly anything by which to be edified. It is absolutely necessary for you to add to such reading that of the holy books [Scripture and the lives or writings of saints] so highly recommended by all the holy Fathers of the Church. I cannot dispense you from such spiritual reading, for I have your perfection too much at heart.... It will be well to rid yourself of the prejudice you have with regard to the style and form in which these holy books are set forth. Get to work, then, make an effort in this respect, and don't neglect to ask the divine assistance with all humility.

Letters, Vol. 2, 153–54

Lord, like Padre Pio's spiritual daughter, I sometimes feel a repugnance toward delving into your Scriptures; yet when I do I find they are always fountains of living water for my soul.

Do not let the dark angels keep me from reading your Word daily, Lord, by suggesting I don't have time or that Scripture is dry and uninteresting. I know these are both lies. Deliver me from all that could separate me from your life-giving words.

∽ 243. Reading the Scriptures ∽

Blessed are those who ... seek him with their whole heart.

PSALM 119:2

... [St. Bernard] ... tells us that reading is, as it were, spiritual food applied to the palate of the soul; meditation chews it by its reasoning, while prayer savors it. Contemplation is then the very sweetness of this spiritual food, which restores the soul entirely and comforts it. Reading stops at the bark or outer covering of what is read; meditation penetrates into its core; prayer goes in search of it by its questions; while contemplation enjoys it as something already possessed.

Letters, Vol. 2, 155

Lord, teach me to pray, to meditate, and to contemplate your goodness, truth, and beauty until I see you face-to-face.

～ 244. Nourish the Soul With God's Word ～

But Jesus answered them, "You are wrong, because you know neither the scriptures nor the power of God."

MATTHEW 22:29

The esteem which St. Jerome had for the reading of holy books is incredible. He exhorts Salvina to have holy books always at hand, for these are a strong shield to ward off all the evil thoughts which attack people.... He teaches the same thing to St. Paulinus: "Always keep the holy book in your hands," he tells him, "that it may nourish your soul by devout reading." To the widow Furia he suggests frequent reading of Sacred Scripture and the writing of those Doctors whose doctrine is holy and wholesome, in order to avoid the fatigue involved in searching for the gold of holy and healthful teachings in the quagmire of false documents.

Letters, Vol. 2, 155–56

Lord, I am amazed at the wisdom of St. Jerome, quoted by Padre Pio. How true it is that indiscriminate reading has at times introduced the confusion of false values into my life, so that distinguishing the "true gold" of truth from insidious errors becomes difficult. How much easier my spiritual life would be if I had never read anything but Scripture, the writings that bear the Church's seal of approval, and the right biographies of the saints. But that is impossible in our society, where even grammar school texts contain ideas that lead people astray. Since I live in the world and relate to people with every type of belief system, including hedonists and materialists, help me, Lord, to fortify my soul by the right kind of reading. And give me the strength to put down books that prove an occasion of sin.

~ 245. The Benefits of Spiritual Reading ~

Adorn the doctrine of God our Savior.

TITUS 2:10

St. Gregory expressed himself in the same way [St. Jerome did], using the allegory of the mirror: "Spiritual books are like a mirror which God places before us in order that we may see ourselves in them and hence correct our faults and adorn ourselves with every virtue. Just as vain women look at themselves frequently in the mirror and there remove every blemish from their face, adjust their hair, and adorn themselves in a thousand ways in order to appear charming in the eye of others, so too the Christian must frequently place the holy books before his eyes in order to perceive the faults he must correct and the virtues by which he must adorn himself so as to be pleasing in the sight of God."

Letters, Vol. 2, 156

Lord, Padre Pio found in Scripture and the writings of the saints the impetus to correct faults and strive for more virtues. May your Word prove fruitful in me too, Lord.

~ 246. Freed From Sexual Bondage ~

Let us then cast off the works of darkness and put on the armor of light; let us conduct ourselves becomingly as in the day, not in reveling and drunkenness, not in debauchery and licentiousness, not in quarreling and jealousy. But put on the Lord Jesus Christ, and make no provision for the flesh, to gratify its desires.

ROMANS 13:12-14

I point out to you the power of holy reading to lead even worldly persons to change their course and enter on the path of perfection.... Consider the conversion of St. Augustine.... His ultimate conqueror was neither his mother by her tears nor the great St. Ambrose by his divine eloquence, but ... reading....

What a desperate battle, what violent conflicts he endured in his poor heart because of his enormous reluctance to give up his lewd sensual pleasures. He says of himself that he was compelled to utter groans and laments while his will was bound as if by a strong chain and that the infernal enemy confined his will in the fetters of a cruel necessity. He goes on to say that he experienced mortal agony in abandoning his loose morals and adds that when his mind was almost made up, his former follies and pleasures pulled him back....

But while the saint battled with such tumultuous feelings, he heard a voice which said to him: Take up and read. He at once obeyed,... and as he read a chapter of St. Paul, the thick darkness in his mind was dispelled, all the hardness vanished from his heart, and he became perfectly calm and serene. From that moment he made a clean break with the world, the devil, and the flesh ... and became the great saint who is honored today.

Letters, Vol. 2, 156–57

Lord, in this lewd society of ours, help me to live a chaste and pure life in my thoughts and deeds despite the many temptations to do otherwise. Especially, Lord, let me be vigilant in what I read and what I see on big or small screens.

～ 247. From Above: Every Perfect Gift ～

Do not be deceived, my beloved brethren. Every good endowment and every perfect gift is from above, coming down from the Father of lights with whom there is no variation or shadow due to change.

JAMES 1:16-17

You need to be a little more docile. You are still a rather capricious daughter and somewhat unmanageable, but will it be possible to make you an entirely faithful servant? Jesus desires this, and with his grace all will be achieved. You are still very much afraid of life, and this is what you must set right. Do you know what means to use? Perfect abandonment of your whole self to the divine goodness. Ask Jesus with holy insistence for this grace, for every perfect gift is from above. I promise you that I will do the same in my own poor feeble prayers.

Letters, Vol. 2, 177

I abandon myself, Lord, to your goodness.

～ 248. Away With Discouragement ～

Then David said to Solomon his son, "Be strong and of good courage, and do it. Fear not, be not dismayed; for the Lord God, even my God, is with you. He will not fail you or forsake you."

1 CHRONICLES 28:20

I beseech you wholeheartedly not to waste time in thinking about the past. If it was used well, let us give glory to God; if badly, let us detest it and confide it to the goodness of the heavenly Father. In fact, I exhort you to tranquilize your heart with the consoling thought that [the] part of your life not well spent has already been forgiven by our most sweet God.

Flee with all your strength the perturbations and anxieties of the heart, otherwise all your efforts will bear little or no fruit at all. We may be sure that if our spirit is agitated, the devil's assaults will be more frequent and direct, because ... he plays on our natural weaknesses. We must be careful on this important point. As soon as we are aware of becoming discouraged, we must revive our faith and abandon ourselves in the arms of the divine Father, who is always ready to receive us—always, that is, if we go to him sincerely.

Letter to a fellow priest called to serve in World War I,
February 9, 1916

Lord, I thrust all my past mistakes and sins into the abyss of your mercy; I commit my future into your hands. For today, I trust in your help to do something worthwhile in your sight.

～ 249. The Frivolous, Inconstant Heart ～

Man that is born of a woman is of few days, and full of trouble.
Job 14:1

"Wretched man that I am!" exclaimed the chosen vessel, the apostle of the people [Paul]. It cannot be doubted that this apostle is one of the greatest saints.... How he was persecuted!... How much agony he suffered for Jesus Christ! What charity he had; what a flame of love, what ardent zeal!... How many revelations, visions, ecstasies. He was taken away even to the third heaven!

209

But even so, this holy apostle, rich [in] such great virtue and such excellent gifts, complains.... He felt within himself an army made up of his humors, aversions, habits, and natural inclinations, which conspired for his ruin, for his spiritual death.... [But he knows] ... that the grace of God, through Jesus Christ, will preserve him, not from fear,... not from battles,... but rather from defeat....

It is impossible for us to be in this mortal body and not to feel its weight, with the movement of our passions.... The Holy Spirit said through the mouth of Job, speaking of our pilgrim condition, that one is never in the same condition....

You tell me about the frivolity and inconstancy of your heart,... agitated by the winds of the passions and consequently ... always vacillating. But I also [see] ... in your heart ... [that] the standard of the cross is always hoisted.

Letters, Vol. 3, 697–99

Lord, the frivolity and inconstancy of my heart could depress me, so thank you for the reminder that this is the human condition. And I look to your mercy and love for victory over my sins and weaknesses.

∽ 250. Purifying Trials ∽

Blessed is the man who endures trial, for when he has stood the test he will receive the crown of life which God has promised to those who love him.

JAMES 1:12

You ask me to pray to the Lord that he may deign in his infinite goodness to manifest what he desires from you. Well, then, Jesus wants to toss and shake you, to thresh you like wheat in order that your spirit may be cleansed and purified as he wishes. Could grain be stored in the barn if it were not free from all husk or chaff? Could linen be stored in the owner's cupboard if it had not first been made quite spotless? So, too, must it be with the chosen soul.

Meanwhile you must by no means fear that the Lord will leave you at Satan's mercy.... He gives our enemy just as much power to torment you as serves his own fatherly plan for [your]... sanctification.... Hence ... be strong and cheerful in spirit, for the Lord is in the depths of your heart: He will fight along with you and for you.

Letters, Vol. 2, 75–76

Lord, I am tempted today by impure thoughts. I keep turning away from them, but again and again they rear their ugly head. Mary, you to whom the angel said, "Blessed are you among women," pray for me now.

~ 251. The Mercy of God ~

Everyone who calls upon the name of the Lord will be saved.

ROMANS 10:13

I remind you of balance, patience, and sweetness. Quell your excessively vivacious and ardent actions from the outset. I don't know why you are so apprehensive at the trials your soul is sustaining. The soul that fears offending God and has the sincere desire not to do so, but to love him, does not offend him in fact, but loves him. And as this desire is always constant, your every fear is useless and ... imaginary.

My daughter, live tranquilly in the presence of God, who has loved you for a long time now, granting you his holy fear and the desire for his love. And if you have not corresponded well up to now, there is a remedy: Do better in [the] future. Your miseries and weaknesses should not frighten you, because he has seen more serious ones within you and did not reject you for this, due to his mercy. So even less ... can he reject you now that you work untiringly for your perfection. God does not reject sinners but rather grants them his grace, erecting the throne of his glory on their abjection and vileness.

Letters, Vol. 3, 756–57

How great you are, Lord. How incredible your mercy and grace. I thank you that you did not say whoever is without sin or whoever is perfect will be saved, but simply whoever calls on you. You alone are the holy one, Lord. I thank you today for your mercy to all your human family, whether we have been baptized by water or only by our desire for God. I offer this day, Lord, for all missionaries struggling to bring your kingdom to fruition.

~ 252. God Is With Me ~

It is the Lord who goes before you; he will be with you, he will not fail you or forsake you; do not fear or be dismayed.

DEUTERONOMY 31:8

My dear sister, calm the tormenting anxieties of your heart, and banish from your imagination all those distressing thoughts and sentiments which are all suggested by Satan in order to make you act badly. Jesus is always with you, even when you don't feel his presence. He is never so close to you as he is during your spiritual battles. He is always there, close to you, encouraging you to fight your battle courageously. He is there to ward off the enemy's blows so that you may not be hurt.

For pity's sake, I beseech you by all that you hold sacred not to wrong him by entertaining the slightest suspicion that he has abandoned you even for a single moment. This is really one of the most diabolical temptations which you must drive far from you as soon as you are aware of it.

Letters, Vol. 2, 168

Lord, help me to take these words of Padre Pio to heart. Today help me to be so filled with your Holy Spirit that there is no room for anything but trust.

∼ 253. Jesus and We Sinners ∼

And when Jesus heard it, he said to them, "Those who are well have no need of a physician, but those who are sick; I came not to call the righteous, but sinners."

MARK 2:17

Always remember the reason why the Son of God came to earth, that it was in order to save men. Jesus says that he came into the world not to save the just but rather sinners; not to cure the healthy but to heal the ill. Having stated this, I now come to reply to your question—that is, whether those who have had the misfortune to sin can be accepted into the Third Order of St. Francis.*

I say, yes, as long as they have truly repented and have given proof of this repentance. May God be pleased to see that these poor creatures truly repent and return to him! One must truly be a mother toward all

---

* People who do not wish to become nuns, priests, or brothers but wish to live for Jesus with the particular spiritual approach of St. Francis of Assisi.

those people, and for this reason, have great care for them, because Jesus tells us that there is more festivity in heaven for the sinner who repents than for the perseverance of ninety-nine just people. These words of the Redeemer are truly comforting to many souls who unfortunately sin and who then want to repent and return to Jesus.

Letters, Vol. 3, 1094–95

Thank you, Lord, that you have come to us sinners.

~ 254. Cling to Jesus ~

But even if you do suffer for righteousness' sake, you will be blessed. Have no fear of them, nor be troubled, but in your hearts reverence Christ as Lord.

1 PETER 3:14-15

I know of your sufferings, and what would I not do to relieve you a little. But what I am unable to do, Jesus will do. Always be calm ... and do not fear. Jesus is and always will be totally yours. Be strong and overcome everything with your constancy. My spirit assists you always and follows you everywhere, and I always think of you before Jesus. The little angel gave me your message. I thank you with all my heart.

Letters, Vol. 3, 1074

Lord, take away my troubles if you will. If I must suffer, give me your grace and peace, so I may not lose but gain eternally from what you permit to happen to me.

～ 255. On Seeking Relief From One's Cross ～

And he called to him the multitude with his disciples, and said to them, "If any man would come after me, let him deny himself and take up his cross and follow me."

MARK 8:34

I blush at this point. I know quite well that the cross is a token of love, an earnest of forgiveness, and that love which is not fed and nourished by the cross is not true love but merely a flash in the pan. Yet in spite of this knowledge, this false disciple of the Nazarene feels the cross weighing enormously on his heart, and very often (don't be scandalized or horrified, Father, by what I am about to say) he goes in search of the compassionate Cyrenean who relieves and comforts him.

What value can this love of mine have with God? I am very much afraid on this account that my love of God is not true love.

Letters, Vol. 1, 639–40

Lord, the young Padre Pio found that his spirit was willing to take up his cross but his weak humanity cried out against suffering. Later he accepted this as human and counseled others just to cling to God's will "at the apex of your soul."

I am much older than he was then, and I still cry out for relief in pain or trouble. Condescend, Lord, to accept me in my weakness. If I cannot be the hero of the faith Padre Pio became, let me be the least of your servants.

~ 256. Sin: Awareness Needed ~

We know that any one born of God does not sin, but He who was born of God keeps him, and the evil one does not touch him.

1 JOHN 5:18

You ask me if in this business of your brother, which torments you so grievously, it is possible that you yourself are the cause of such painful consequences. I don't see any fault of yours in this. What do you say yourself? Are you aware before God of your guilt in this respect? It's about time for you to calm yourself and put an end to these fantastic doubts. My dear, we don't commit a sin without first being aware of it.

Undoubtedly, even after all these assurances you still have doubts, and thus you begin all over again. There is need for a little more docility in your attitude. For the second time I tell you, and very much to the point, that you are still a rather capricious daughter and somewhat unmanageable. I hope you now thoroughly understand this expression of mine. If not, don't hesitate to let me know.

Letters, Vol. 2, 190

Lord, St. John says that if we say we are without sin, we deceive ourselves; yet here John says that those living in you do not sin. Enlighten me, Lord. I have no desire to sin, so I hope I don't. But if I have sinned or am sinning in my life, show me my misdeeds. So fill me with your Holy Spirit that there will be no room in me for sin.

∼ 257. Love One Another ∼

If we love one another, God abides in us and his love is perfected in us.

1 JOHN 4:12

Deep down in my soul, it seems to me, God has poured out many graces of compassion for the sufferings of others, especially with regard to the poor and needy. The immense pity I experience at the sight of a poor man gives rise deep down in my soul to a most vehement desire to help him, and if I were to follow the dictates of my will, I should be driven to strip myself even of my clothing to cover him.

Letters, Vol. 1, 519

Dear Lord, you poured out your graces of compassion and charity on Padre Pio, who sought to love and serve you. Help me to grow in love day by day—for you and for fellow members of your human family.

∼ 258. Ecstasy ∼

I know a man in Christ who fourteen years ago was caught up to the third heaven—whether in the body or out of the body I do not know, God knows. And I know that this man was caught up into Paradise—whether in the body or out of the body I do not know, God knows—and he heard things that cannot be told, which man may not utter.

2 CORINTHIANS 12:2-4

The occasions on which I can use my intellect in discursive prayer and avail of the activity of my senses are becoming increasingly rare.... The soul placed in this state by the Lord and enriched with much heavenly knowledge ought to be more eloquent, but it isn't; it has become almost speechless. I don't know if this is something which happens to me alone. In very general terms and more often than not in words which are empty of meaning, my soul succeeds in expressing some small part of what the Spouse of souls is accomplishing within it.... All this is no slight torment for my soul.

It is like what might happen to a poor little shepherd boy who found himself brought into a royal chamber where there was an infinite number of precious objects such as he had never seen before. On coming out,... the little shepherd would undoubtedly have in mind all those beautiful and valuable objects but would certainly be unable to say how many there were or to name them correctly one by one. He would like to tell others about all he had seen; he would muster all his intellectual and cognitive powers to do so, but finding all efforts useless to make himself understood, he would prefer to keep silence. This is what usually happens to my soul, which by divine goodness alone has been raised to this degree of prayer.

Letters, Vol. 1, 518

Lord, how wonderful that saints of my time have known the same prayer delights as your apostle Paul. This increases my faith in the reality of the spiritual life. I do not ask, Lord, that you give me an ecstasy. But I do ask that you give me the purity of life that marked Paul and Pio.

∼ 259. When Love of God Seems to Grow Cold ∼

He who says "I know him" but disobeys his commandments is a liar,
and the truth is not in him; but whoever keeps his word, in him truly
love for God is perfected. By this we may be sure that we are in him.

1 JOHN 2:4-5

You are trying to measure, understand, feel, and touch this love which you have for God, but, my dear sister, you must accept as certain that the more a soul loves God the less it feels this love. The thing seems too strange and impossible in the case of transient love for creatures in this poor world, but when it is a case of love for the Spouse of the soul, things are very different. I am not able to explain this truth very clearly, but you can take it as certain that the matter is as I have said. God is incomprehensible and inaccessible; hence the more a soul penetrates into the love of this Supreme Good, the more the sentiment of love toward him, which is beyond the soul's knowledge, seems to diminish, until the poor soul considers that it no longer loves him at all....

But ... events prove the very opposite. That continual fear of losing one's God, that holy circumspection which makes one look carefully where to place one's feet so as not to stumble, that courage in facing the assaults of the enemy, that resignation to God's will in all life's adversities, that ardent desire to see God's kingdom established in one's own heart and in the hearts of others, are the clearest proof of the soul's love for the Supreme Good.

Letters, Vol. 2, 99–100

I thank you, Lord, for these words of Padre Pio. They comfort me, since I
have a great desire to keep your commandments; yet my love for you seems
to have grown so flat, dry, and cold, lacking all its former consoling sweet-
ness, that it seems I no longer love you at all.

∼ 260. Faith in the Lord ∼

And one of the crowd answered him, "Teacher, I brought my son to you, for he has a dumb spirit; and wherever it seizes him, it dashes him down; and he foams and grinds his teeth and becomes rigid; and I asked your disciples to cast it out, and they were not able." And he answered them, "O faithless generation, how long am I to be with you? How long am I to bear with you? Bring him to me." And they brought the boy to him; and when the spirit saw him, immediately it convulsed the boy, and he fell on the ground and rolled about, foaming at the mouth. And Jesus asked his father, "How long has he had this?" And he said, "From childhood. And it has often cast him into the fire and into the water, to destroy him; but if you can do anything, have pity on us and help us." And Jesus said to him, "If you can! All things are possible to him who believes." Immediately the father of the child cried out and said, "I believe; help my unbelief!"

MARK 9:17-24

Thanks to the favors with which God fills me incessantly, I have greatly improved as regards my trust in him. In the past it sometimes seemed to me that I needed the help of others, but this is no longer the case. I know from my own experience that the best way to avoid falling is to lean on the cross of Jesus, with confidence in him alone, who for our salvation desired to be nailed to it.

Letters, Vol. 1, 519

Lord, even your great friends, saints like Padre Pio, must grow in trust and faith. How encouraging! Lord, help me to trust you more and more, until my trust in you equals that of your saints.

∼ 261. Mercy Amid Misery ∼

Give thanks to the Lord, for he is good, for his mercy endures forever.
DANIEL 3:67

What am I to say about my own wretched soul? Alas, it has been too unfaithful to its Beloved. Praise be to God, however, who never withdraws his mercy from me.

There are certain moments at which dense clouds appear in the heavens of my soul, so thick and dark that they do not allow me to perceive even a feeble ray of light. It is deep night for my soul. All hell is turned loose upon it with cavernous roars, with all the evil of its past life, and what is most terrifying is that my own fantasy and imagination seem determined to conspire against my soul. The beautiful days spent in the shadow of the Lord vanish completely from my mind. The spiritual torment I endure is such that I should be unable to distinguish it from the atrocious pains of ... hell. This torment does not last long, nor could it, for if my soul lives through it, this is only by a remarkable favor from God.... In the midst of such confusion the apex of my soul is by no means disturbed but remains extremely tranquil, a fact of which the lower part is only faintly aware.

Letters, Vol. 1, 523–24

Lord, it is a mystery to me that someone who suffered as much as Padre Pio physically, emotionally, and spiritually was able to remain steadfast in his belief in your mercy and love, while we others often blame you for every hardship. Make me more like Padre Pio, Lord. In troubles or pains, let me believe in your mercy and love.

~ 262. True Love Is Not About Consolations ~

And Mary said, "Behold, I am the handmaid of the Lord; let it be to me according to your word." And the angel departed from her.
LUKE 1:38

Take heart and be sure that God is pleased with you, and that he finds *his peaceful dwelling place* within you. Do not wait for Tabor in order to see God. You are already contemplating him on Sinai without realizing it. I don't think the interior stomach is troubled and indisposed to tasting good. It can desire nothing greater than the Supreme Good in itself, and not his gifts.

Spiritual distractions, involuntary distractions, temptations, etc. are the merchandise offered by the enemy, but you reject them and therefore they do you no harm. When the enemy makes a noise, it is an excellent sign: It is a sign that he wants your will and therefore is still outside it. What must terrify you, my beloved daughter and sister, is his peace and concordance with a human soul.

During the period of spiritual aridity, be humble, patient, and resigned to divine will, and do not give up anything you used to do in times of spiritual joy. Because true love does not consist in receiving many consolations at the service of God, but rather in always having a ready will to do all that God is pleased to order for our spiritual advantage and his glory.

Letters, Vol. 3, 665

Lord, your incarnation took place when Mary, a lowly creature like me, freely put herself at God's service. Mary acted out of love and never looked back, no matter the cost. When a sword pierced her heart as she stood at the foot of the cross, she remained steadfast.

I am so unlike her when my children suffer, Lord. But I do wish to offer

THROUGH THE YEAR WITH PADRE PIO

them to you as Mary offered Jesus. Help me, Lord, to make no idol of even those I love most. Let me love you in deed, not words, by always accepting your will for me and my loved ones.

∼ 263. Let Zeal Be Free of Defects ∼

By your patience you will win your souls.
                                    LUKE 21:19, Challoner-Rheims

[I] praise and bless the Lord more and more for the steadfastness he gave your soul in courageously bearing all those trials, to which the heavenly Father's goodness subjected you. I exhort you, then, my good daughter, to do, on your part, whatever you possibly can, to carry out your plan which truly is God's will.... Let your zeal for such a work be devoid of any defect. Let it not be bitter, fussy, aggravating, or uneasy, but let it be sweet, benevolent, gracious, pacific, and uplifting.

Oh, my dear daughter, who does not see the dear little Babe of Bethlehem, whose zeal for souls is incomparable? He came to die in order to save, but nevertheless his zeal is so humble, sweet, and lovable. Therefore, when you have placed everything in the hands of your bishop, you must then do nothing but wait patiently, avoiding any little worry or uneasiness which impedes the effects of patience.... Patience is most perfect when it is less mixed up with anxiety and worry. I hope that God will free you from these two inconveniences.

Letters, Vol. 3, 835–36

What insight your saint has, Lord, to see that good works can so easily be occasions for doers to become irritable and anxious about their projects. I am certainly guilty, Lord, as you well know, of giving in at times to anxiety over a project. Lord, thank you for letting me do this book for those who wish more of Padre Pio's counsel. I give it to you, Lord. May it be done if and when you will.

～ 264. Free to Be Holy ～

Jesus said to the ruler of the synagogue, "Do not fear, only believe."
MARK 5:36

In this [lack of confidence in God's goodness] the soul greatly offends our heavenly Spouse, and ... our most sweet Lord deprives us of many graces, simply because the door of our heart is not thrown open with holy trust.

Letters, Vol. 1, 455

Lord, may I have greater and greater confidence in your goodness, until I become a huge rock that nothing can move.

～ 265. Loving God ～

How blessed are those who love you! They will rejoice in your peace.
TOBIT 13:14

May you be consoled, dear Father, by the sweet thought of your love for Jesus and of being loved by him much more in return. Let us ask him for the grace to love him and to see him loved more and more. Let us ask him this with the spouse of the holy Canticles: *O that you would kiss me with the kisses of your mouth! For your love is better than wine* (Song 1:2).

How often do we priests especially receive from Jesus this kiss of peace in the most holy Sacrament! Yes, let us ardently desire this kiss of the divine mouth, and still more let us show our gratitude for it. What more precious gift can we wretched mortals desire from God?

Letters, Vol. 1, 455–56

Lord Jesus, love me so much that in return I am swept away by love for you. Then do with me as you will.

～ 266. So Many Reasons to Be Humble ～

Have this mind among yourselves, which you have in Christ Jesus, who, though he was in the form of God, did not count equality with God a thing to be grasped, but emptied himself, taking the form of a servant, being born in the likeness of men. And being found in human form he humbled himself and became obedient unto death, even death on a cross. Therefore God has highly exalted him and bestowed on him the name which is above every name, that at the name of Jesus every knee should bow, in heaven and on earth and under the earth, and every tongue confess that Jesus Christ is Lord, to the glory of God the Father.

PHILIPPIANS 2:5-11

I want you to meditate every day on the humiliations of the Son of God and the glory to which they led. Let us consider how the divine Word abased himself. As St. Paul says, *Though he was in the form of God, for in him the whole fullness of deity dwells bodily,* he did not disdain to lower himself to our level in order to raise us up to fullness of life in God. Of his own free will ... [he hid] his divine nature beneath the veil of human flesh. In this way, says St. Paul, the Word of God humbled himself to the point of emptying himself, as it were ... *taking the form of a servant.*... He was pleased to ... take on the likeness of man in everything, even exposing himself to hunger, thirst, and weariness and, to use the very words of the apostle of the nations, *in every respect tempted as we are, yet without sinning.*

The climax of his humiliation ... is found in his passion and death, where he submitted his human will to the will of his Father, endured great torments, and suffered the most infamous death.... *He humbled himself,* says St. Paul, *and became obedient unto death, even death on a cross.*... He was not induced to obey by any fear of punishment. Neither did he obey for the sake of reward, as he himself was God and equal in all things to the Father.

Letters, Vol. 2, 236–37

Lord, when I ponder your humility and your obedience at such a great cost, my heart fails me, for I see my nothingness, the paucity of my love, the feebleness of my adherence to you, the cowardice of my spirit. Lord, have mercy on me, remembering that you have purchased me at a great price. You have made a bad bargain, Lord; but be like the mother who loves best her most helpless child. Hold me close, and save me by filling me with your Spirit.

～ 267. The Vast Spiritual World ～

Jesus saw Nathanael coming to him, and said of him, "Behold, an Israelite indeed, in whom is no guile!" Nathanael said to him, "How do you know me?" Jesus answered him, "Before Philip called you, when you were under the fig tree, I saw you."

JOHN 1:47-48

No thanks are due to me for the visit which the Lord allowed me to pay you in spirit, so let your thanks and praise be directed to God alone. You ask me to tell you the day and the hour of this visit. I am very reluctant to reveal this to you, but as I don't want to distress you, I'll stifle the repugnance I feel. If I am not mistaken, a visit of this kind took place on 4 October [1914], the feast of our Seraphic Father, St. Francis, and in the early hours of the following day.

I cannot tell you any more about that visit. I can only tell you that it was quite a long one. I beseech you not to say a word about it to a living soul on this earth. In fact, I don't deny that I should very much like you to burn this letter as well as mine of the tenth. What do you say to that? Will my desire be satisfied? However, do as you please in this, for I wouldn't wish to trouble you in the slightest way. Whatever you decide to do in this matter, will you please be so good as to let me know.

Letters, Vol. 2, 221

Heavenly Father, nothing is impossible with you. Jesus could see afar, and his saint Padre Pio, "always tied to the thread of God's will," as he put it, was many times permitted by you to see at a distance. At other times he could actually be somewhere else to carry out errands of your mercy, whether healing or the guidance of souls. I thank you for the special gifts you give your saints, Lord. They increase my belief in the vast spiritual universe, which is so much greater than my limited senses and intellect can take in.

∼ 268. Joy to All of Good Will ∼

And there were shepherds ... living in the fields and keeping watch over their flock by night. And behold, an angel of the Lord stood by them and the glory of the Lord shone about them, and they feared exceedingly. And the angel said to them, "Do not be afraid, for behold, I bring you good news of great joy which shall be to all the people...." And suddenly there was with the angel a multitude of the heavenly host praising God and saying, "Glory to God in the highest and peace on earth among men of good will."

Luke 2:8-14, Challoner-Rheims

Live joyfully and courageously, at least in the upper part of the soul, amid the trials in which the Lord places you. Live joyfully and courageously, I repeat, because the angel who foretells the birth of our little Savior and Lord ... sings, announcing that he brings tidings of joy, peace, and happiness to men of good will. So ... there is nobody who does not know that in order to receive this Child, it is sufficient to be of good will.... He came to bless good will, which little by little he will render fruitful and effective, as long as we allow ourselves to be governed by it. And I hope that we ... will do so.

Letters, Vol. 3, 470

Lord, cleanse my soul, so that in it may be nothing but good will to all people, good and bad, kind and unkind, appealing and repulsive. In short, Lord, make me like you.

∼ 269. Tried Like Gold ∼

Having been disciplined a little, they will receive great good, because God tested them and found them worthy of himself; like gold in the furnace he tried them.

Wisdom 3:5-6

The light increases and soon it is midday, when the soul is dilated in the sun. But when the sun goes down and darkness follows, one no longer remembers the light, and the Lord withdraws even the memory of the consolation enjoyed, so that the shadows may be complete. Calm yourself, and be quite certain that these shadows are not a punishment proportioned to your wickedness. You are not wicked, nor are you blinded by your own malice. You are merely one of the chosen ones who are tried like gold in the furnace.

Letters, Vol. 3, 720

Lord, help me to always believe that whatever I suffer is only from your desire that I grow, learn, and become the utmost I can be spiritually.

~ 270. A Paradox of Love ~

Come, let us take our fill of love till morning; let us delight ourselves with love.

PROVERBS 7:18

For love is strong as death.... Its flashes are flashes of fire, a most vehement flame.

SONG OF SONGS 8:6

I tremble.... I find it almost impossible to explain the action of the Beloved. In the immensity of his strength, Infinite Love has at last overcome my hardheartedness, leaving me weak and powerless. He keeps pouring himself completely into the small vase of this creature, and I suffer an unspeakable martyrdom because of my inability to bear the weight of this immense love. How can I carry the Infinite in this little heart of mine? How can I continue to confine him to the narrow cell of my soul? My soul is melting with pain and love, with bitterness and sweetness simultaneously. How can I endure such immense suffering inflicted by the Most High? Because of the exultation of possessing him in me, I cannot refrain from saying with the most holy Virgin: *My spirit rejoices in God my Savior.* Possessing him within me, I am impelled to say with the spouse of the Sacred Song: *I found him whom my soul loves; I held him and would not let him go.*

But then when I see myself unable to sustain the weight of this Infinite Love, and when I confine him to the smallness of my being, I am filled with terror in case I must leave him because of my incapacity to sustain him in the narrow space of my heart. This thought ... is not ... unfounded (I consider my strength is very limited, incapable, and powerless to constrict this divine Lover). It tortures me and afflicts me to such an extent that my heart seems about to burst out of my chest.

Letters, Vol. 1, 1238–39

In Padre Pio, Lord, I see the paradox that your love is both the greatest delight and a torture in this life due to human smallness next to your immensity. I look forward to heaven, Lord, where we will be free of the constrictions of the heart and enjoy your love in all its heights and depths.

~ 271. Our Food: The Flesh and Blood of Jesus ~

Jesus said to them, "Truly, truly, I say to you, unless you eat the flesh of the Son of man and drink his blood, you have no life in you; he who eats my flesh and drinks my blood has eternal life, and I will raise him up at the last day. For my flesh is food indeed, and my blood is drink indeed. He who eats my flesh and drinks my blood abides in me, and I in him."

JOHN 6:53-56

You are distressed that your illness obliges you to fast from the most holy Eucharist. This I understand, and I do not blame you for it. It is well to be resigned and not to cease imploring Jesus to come to visit you spiritually. When sacramental Communion becomes impossible, spiritual Communion makes up for it to some extent.

I don't hide from you the fact that you are quite wrong to believe that your Communions are neither good nor acceptable to the Lord and that as a punishment for this he deprives you of the Eucharistic food on many mornings. Am I to praise you for this? By no means, and I am sorry that in this matter, rather than accept my assertions and assurances, you readily listen to the devil's promptings, for it is really the devil who suggests this to you.... Since he cannot deter you from receiving Communion, he would like to deprive your soul of the serenity and childlike trust required in those who approach the most holy Sacrament to receive Jesus' embrace.

Letters, Vol. 2, 221–22

Dear Lord, I know there are people whom you feed solely by your Word. But how I thank you that you also offer me your body and blood in the Eucharist. When I receive you in Communion, I become a minnow in the quiet sea of your being, as a friend wrote, even as you live in both my soul and every sinew of my physical being. How great this mystery of love! How unspeakable your ways! How my heart sings with gratitude!

～ 272. Praying That the Kingdom Come ～

And he said to them, "When you pray, say: Father, hallowed be thy name. Thy kingdom come."

LUKE 11:2

I give heartfelt thanks to the heavenly Father, through our Lord, Jesus

Christ, for the constantly new graces with which he continues to enrich your soul. Oh, may he always be blessed by all his creatures.... May God's reign come soon; may this most holy Father sanctify his Church; may he abundantly shower his mercy on those souls who have not known him up to now.

May he destroy the reign of Satan and reveal, to the confusion of this infernal beast, all his evil snares; may he reveal, to all slaves of this awful wretch, what a liar he is. May this most tender Father enlighten the intelligence and touch the hearts of all men, so that the fervent may not become cooler or slow down in the ways of salvation, that the lukewarm may become more fervent, and those who have moved far from him may return. May he also ... confuse all the wise of this world, so that they do not wage war and inhibit the propagation of his reign.

Finally, may this most holy Father banish from the Church all the dissension that exists and impede the birth of more so that there will be only one sheepfold and only one Shepherd. May he multiply a hundredfold the number of chosen souls, send us many saints and learned ministers, and sanctify those we already possess. May he, through them, make fervor return to all Christian souls. May the number of Catholic missionaries increase as we once again have reason to complain to the divine Master: "The harvest is plentiful, but the laborers are few...." Don't ever forget to pray for these needs.

Letters, Vol. 3, 63–64

Lord, Padre Pio's prayers of intercession for the world, the Church, and individuals went up before you night and day. Make me also, Lord, a person of prayer. And may your kingdom come!

~ 273. The Infant Jesus: God's Tender Mercy ~

Through the tender mercy of our God,... the day shall dawn upon us from on high to give light to those who sit in darkness and in the shadow of death, to guide our feet into the way of peace.

LUKE 1:78-79

O most divine Spirit, give feeling to my heart to adore and love; give light to my intellect to contemplate the sublimity of the great mystery of charity of a God made child; give fire to my will so that I can use it to warm the One who is shivering for me on the straw. My Mother Mary, take me with you to the grotto of Bethlehem, and make me contemplate the greatness and sublimity of what is about to take place in the silence of this greatest and most beautiful night which the world has ever seen.

Letters, Vol. 4, quoted in *The Voice of Padre Pio*, 9

Lord, help me to grasp something of the mystery of divine love, which humbly lowers divinity into a vulnerable infant so every infant may have a chance to become like you. Lord, I pray for all the world's children. Give them mothers and fathers who will help them know your unconditional love.

~ 274. Keep Your Eyes on the Lord ~

To thee I lift up my eyes, O thou who art enthroned in the heavens! Behold, as the eyes of servants look to the hand of their master, as the eyes of a maid to the hand of her mistress, so our eyes look to the Lord our God, till he have mercy upon us.

PSALM 123:1-2

We need do no more than we are doing at present; that is, to love divine Providence and abandon ourselves in his arms and heart.

Letters, Vol. 3, 425

Lord, just for today let the eyes of my heart never stray from your face.

~ 275. To Keep the Heart Uncontaminated ~

Lose your silver for the sake of a brother or a friend, and do not let it rust under a stone and be lost. Lay up your treasure according to the commandments of the Most High, and it will profit you more than gold. Store up almsgiving in your treasury, and it will rescue you from all affliction.

SIRACH 29:10-12

Let us keep our gaze fixed on the heavenly home reserved for us; let us constantly contemplate it and aim at it with the greatest care. Let us withdraw our gaze, moreover, from those good things that are visible to our eyes, by which I mean worldly goods, the sight of which fascinates and distracts the soul and contaminates the heart. Worldly goods prevent us from keeping our eyes fixed on our heavenly home.

Let us listen to what the Lord tells us on this subject by the mouth of his holy apostle Paul: *We look not to the things that are seen but to the things that are unseen.* It is quite right that we should contemplate heavenly things while attaching no importance to those of this world, since the former are eternal while the latter are merely transient.

What should we say if we were to behold a poor peasant almost stupefied as he continued to gaze at a swiftly flowing river? Perhaps we should just begin to laugh at him and with good reason. Is it not folly to fix our gaze on something that is rapidly passing? This, then, is the state of a person who fixes his eyes on visible things. For what are these things in reality? Are they perhaps different from a swiftly flowing river, on whose waters we have no sooner laid eyes than they disappear from our sight, never to be seen again?

Letters, Vol. 2, 202–3

Lord, all you have made is good and beautiful. Yet the very beauty of life and nature can absorb me so that I forget spiritual beauties. As I am a being of flesh, it is hard not to fix on the things of this world for satisfaction. It is hard not to find security in material things, such as bank accounts and property.

Yet you call us, while praising the wonders you have given us in this life, to fix our gaze on that which is eternal and to count money given to good works as the real money "set aside for a rainy day." Draw me up, Lord, to where your saints live.

∼ 276. Consolation in Violent Temptation ∼

But this people has a stubborn and rebellious heart; they have turned aside and gone away.

JEREMIAH 5:23

The Christian sanctified by baptism is not exempt from the rebellion of the senses and passions; hence the impelling need to mortify our passions as long as we live. The holy apostle [Paul] himself suffered considerable interior distress from the rebellion of his senses and passions, which led him to utter the following complaint: *I of myself serve the law of God with my mind, but with my flesh I serve the law of sin*

(Rom 7:25), (that is, the law of concupiscence). It is as though he intended to say: "I am mentally subject to God's law, but my flesh is subject to the law of sin."

This is to be said for the spiritual consolation of many unfortunate people who experience the sharp conflict within themselves to which a hot temper or lustful desires give rise. They do not want to feel or to harbor those impulses, that ill feeling toward others, those vivid pictures presented by their imagination, those sensual promptings. Poor things! Quite involuntarily these feelings surge up.... Some ... think they are offending God when they feel this violent interior inclination to evil. Take heart, you chosen souls, for in this there is no sin.... Even when carnal impulses are violently felt, there can be no sin when the will does not consent to them.

Letters, Vol. 2, 243–44

Lord, sometimes I recall my child who, at five, asked me, "But why can't God just make us be good?" With my small soul, I cringe at the great and glorious destiny to which you have called humanity, giving us the freedom to choose you or reject you. But why, Lord, do you leave even us who choose you so inclined to do what, with our will, we do not want to do? I do not understand your ways, Lord. But I will struggle to die to my passions and do your will.

∼ 277. Call to God in Trouble ∼

To thee, O Lord, do I lift up my soul. For thou, O Lord, art good and forgiving, abounding in steadfast love to all who call on thee. Give ear, O Lord, to my prayer; hearken to my cry of supplication.

PSALM 86:4-6

War has been declared upon you,... and you need to be watchful at every moment, to put up a strong defense, with the eye of faith always fixed on the God of hosts, who is fighting along with you and for you. You must have boundless faith in the divine goodness, for the victory is absolutely certain.

How could you think otherwise? Isn't our God more concerned about our salvation than we are ourselves? Isn't he stronger than hell itself? Who can ever resist and overcome the King of the heavens? What are the world, the devil, the flesh, and all our enemies before the Lord?

Letters, Vol. 2, 87

Jesus, today I place everything that could worry me or cause anxiety in your hands. Jesus, Father, Spirit, I trust in your kindness.

~ 278. Grace Will Suffice ~

God is faithful, and he will not let you be tempted beyond your strength, but with the temptation will also provide the way of escape, that you may be able to endure it.

1 CORINTHIANS 10:13

Even St. Paul was restless and besought the Lord to free him from the trial of the flesh; he too was very much afraid that he would yield, but did he not receive the assurance that grace would always be sufficient for him? Our enemy, who plots against us, wants to persuade you that the very opposite is the case, but despise him in the name of Jesus and laugh heartily at him. This is the best way to make him beat a retreat.... When anyone takes up a weapon and faces him, he becomes a coward.

You may fear, if you like, but it must be that holy fear—I mean to say the fear that is never separated from love. When fear and love are united, they help each other, like sisters, to remain on their feet and to walk securely in the Lord's paths. Love makes us hasten with rapid strides, while fear ... makes us watch prudently where we place our feet and guides us so that we may never stumble on the road leading to heaven.

Letters, Vol. 2, 85

Lord, I fear to hurt your feelings because I love you. Help me not to disappoint you today.

～ 279. Put Your Trust in God ～

Trust in the Lord for ever, for the Lord God is an everlasting rock.
ISAIAH 26:4

Meanwhile do not lose faith in God's providence. Put your trust in God, abandon yourself to him, and let him take care of you both, then rest assured that you will not be confounded.

I understand and am deeply aware that the trial is hard and the battle fierce. But I also understand that the fruit you will gather in due course is very abundant. The crown that is being woven for you up above is far greater than can be humanly conceived. You will perhaps laugh at me for saying such things, which you will consider quite mistaken, but I know quite well what I am saying. Judge me as you think fit, but what I want from you is that as the trial increases, your abandonment and trust in God may also increase. Immerse yourself ever more deeply in humility and in blessing the Lord, who in his goodness deigns to visit you in this way so as to prepare you to share in building up the heavenly Sion!

Letters, Vol. 2, 410

Lord, I will trust you in this frightening thing I face. Help my lack of trust, Lord! When I grab the burden back, remind me to lay it again on your altar and say, "My Jesus, who loves me, I trust you will take this burden from me and give me back a blessing."

～ 280. Hope in God ～

Happy [those] whose help is the God of Jacob, whose hope is in the Lord [their] God, who made heaven and earth, the sea, and all that is in them; who keeps faith for ever; who executes justice for the oppressed; who gives food to the hungry. The Lord sets the prisoners free; the Lord opens the eyes of the blind. The Lord lifts up those who are bowed down;... The Lord watches over the sojourners, he upholds the widow and the fatherless;... The Lord will reign for ever.

PSALM 146:5-10

I ... exhort you again to be trustful. A soul who trusts in her Lord and places all her hope in him has nothing to fear. The enemy of our salvation is always around us to snatch from our hearts the anchor that is to lead us to salvation, by which I mean trust in God our Father. Let us keep a very firm hold on this anchor and not relinquish it for a single moment. Otherwise all would be lost. Repeat continually, and more especially in the darkest hours, those most beautiful words of Job: *Even if you are to slay me, O Lord, I will still hope in you.* Always be on your guard and don't become puffed up, considering yourself to be good in any way or above others. Don't imagine that you are better than them or at least as good, but consider all to be better than yourself. The enemy ... overcomes the presumptuous and not the humble of heart.

Letters, Vol. 2, 410–11

Lord, I call upon you for help today. Guide me to the person who can help me, and keep me away from those who will cause me trouble. May your Holy Spirit, through me, be a blessing to all I have contact with this day.

∼ 281. Eyes on the Lord! ∼

My eyes are ever toward the Lord, for he will pluck my feet out of the net.

PSALM 25:15

You wrote that you were bewildered, frightened, and discouraged because you do not correspond adequately to the great graces that Jesus is bestowing on you. Pay attention and be very watchful on this point. Your sentiment, in itself, is holy from a certain point of view, but you know very well that the devil invariably tries to turn things upside down. I want you to refrain from dwelling on this matter, because the discouragement you feel when you deplore your failure to correspond with grace comes from the enemy. Even if he doesn't want to make you turn back, he wants at least to bring you to a standstill....

What I want you to do is to keep your soul at rest, as far as possible, in contemplation of the infinite treasures of the heavenly Spouse, which he is pouring with a lavish hand into your soul. Rejoice in his riches, and stimulate within you the desire to possess them.... Imitate in this the brides of this poor world, who admire and take pleasure in ... the fine gifts and qualities of their husbands, without bothering in the least whether or in what manner they correspond to their husbands' demonstrations of affection. If ... you follow this suggestion of mine, your soul will derive great profit from it.

Letters, Vol. 2, 130–31

Today, Lord, I will try to think much on you, your love, your mercy, your loveableness, and your kindness. I will try not to think about myself at all.

～ 282. God Alone ～

Preserve me, O God, for in thee I take refuge. I say to the Lord, "Thou art my Lord; I have no good apart from thee...." The Lord is my chosen portion and my cup.

PSALM 16:1-2, 5

Don't be discouraged if you experience spiritual dryness. This does not mean that the Lord has abandoned you.... All that is happening in your soul is due to the exquisiteness of Jesus' love for you. He wants you entirely for himself, he wants you to place all your trust and all your affection in him alone, and it is precisely for this reason that he sends you this spiritual aridity, to unite you more closely to him, to rid you of certain little attachments which do not appear as such to us and which, in many cases, we do not even recognize or detect.

Letters, Vol. 2, 141

Lord, you know my unholy attachments better than I do. Heal me. Wash me, Lord, and I shall be whiter than snow. To you alone I look for deliverance from all false gods and attachments. May I love others only in you, so I will love them without egotistic concerns and without making idols of them.

~ 283. Serve and Love God Even in Spiritual Bleakness ~

And I will ... refine them as one refines silver, and test them as gold is tested.

ZECHARIAH 13:9

[Sometimes] ... it really seems to us that all is ended and that the Lord has left us for good because he is tired of bearing with us. Instead, things are quite different. The Lord is never so pleased with us as he is at such times as this. He is always there, close to us, or rather within us, invisibly encouraging us to endure the combat. Don't worry, then, because the Lord will fight for you and will never withdraw from you.

What you must do when Jesus, in his goodness, puts your faithfulness to the test is to show at all times great promptitude in the observance of your duties, without neglecting any of the practices which you perform in times of consolation and [spiritual] prosperity, without paying any attention to your lack of all pleasurable feelings, since such feelings are merely accidental and can often be quite dangerous in the end. True and substantial devotion consists in serving God without experiencing any sensible consolation. This means serving and loving God for his own sake.

Letters, Vol. 2, 141

Jesus, I know that when you test me through the spiritual dryness that goes on and on, it is so I can grow to be more like you, who served your Father both when you experienced the ecstasy of Transfiguration and when you cried out from the cross, "My God, my God, why have you abandoned me?" Lord, you know everything. You know that I love you as much as I can. If you want me to love you more, give me more love.

~ 284. Producing Good Fruits ~

Truly, truly, I say unto you, unless a grain of wheat falls into the earth and dies, it remains alone; but if it dies, it bears much fruit.

JOHN 12:24

Oh,... how lovable is the eternity of heaven, and how miserable are the moments of earth! Continually aspire to the former, and despise comfort and the moments of this mortality. Do not be apprehensive over past errors, nor by fears for future difficulties in the life of the cross, because we must be hidden with a crucified God. Beware of saying, How can I forget the world and everything that belongs to it while I still live in the world? Because our heavenly Father knows you are in need of this oblivion, and he will grant it to you, as long as you abandon yourself with confidence in his arms.

I know well ... that you have extremely good natural inclinations. Therefore, take care to employ them well in the service of him who gave them to you. Plant here the plant of eternal delight, which God will grant you if you are willing to receive it, with a perfect denial of yourself.

Oh ... let us rest our hearts in God alone, and no longer take them away from here. He is our peace, our consolation, and our glory. And let us make every effort to unite ourselves more rightly to this most sweet Savior, so that we can produce good fruits for eternal life.

Letters, Vol. 3, 705–6

Lord, help me to die to all those things that could prevent my bearing good spiritual fruit.

∼ 285. The Necessity of Prayer and the Eucharist ∼

I, O Lord, cry to thee; in the morning my prayer comes before thee.

PSALM 88:13

I am absolutely unable to consider in an indulgent manner your neglecting Holy Communion, not to mention holy meditation. Remember ... that the only way to gain your health [of soul] is through prayer; you cannot win the battle without prayer. So the choice is up to you.

Letters, Vol. 3, 418

Lord, I thank you that I was able to receive Communion today. Keep me always close to you through Jesus' Body and prayer.

∼ 286. Reading God's Word ∼

Thy word is a lamp to my feet and a light to my path.... O Lord,... teach me thy ordinances.

PSALM 119:105, 108

Help yourself mainly during this period [of spiritual dryness] by reading holy books. I earnestly desire to see you reading such books at all times, for this reading provides excellent food for the soul and conduces to great progress along the path of perfection, by no means inferior to what we obtain through prayer and holy meditation. In prayer and meditation it is we ourselves who speak to the Lord, while in holy reading [the Scriptures or holy fathers of the Church] it is God who speaks to us. Try to treasure these holy readings as much as you can, and you will very soon be aware of a spiritual renewal within you. Before beginning to read,... raise your mind to the Lord and implore him to guide your mind himself, to speak to your heart and move your will.

But this is not sufficient. It is also advisable before you start to read, and from time to time in the course of your reading, to declare before the Lord that you are not reading for the purpose of study or to satisfy your curiosity but solely to give him pleasure and enjoyment.

Letters, Vol. 2, 141–42

Help me, Father, to love the Word of God, your Son, and Your Holy Word, the Scriptures. Open my ears, Father, to hear your Word; then strengthen my heart and will to keep it.

～ 287. The Finest Grace ～

All things were made through him, and without him was not anything made that was made. In him was life, and the life was the light of men.

JOHN 1:3-4

Unworthy as I am, although I pray continually for your growth in the spiritual life, I promise you that on your feast day I will send up my feeble pleas to God's throne with greater confidence and filial abandonment, imploring him and doing gentle violence to his divine heart so that he may grant me the grace of increasing heavenly wisdom in your soul, so that you may have a clearer knowledge of the divine mysteries and of God's immensity. Yes, ask for this grace yourself, and ask the heavenly Father to grant it also to me. Do this through the intercession of the saint whose name you bear and through your good guardian angel as well.

Let the consideration of all those good things to be possessed in that realm provide us with delightful food for our thoughts. Enchanted by these eternal delights our minds [will be able] to distinguish what is valuable from what is worthless. As for ourselves ... whose minds are enlightened by God's true light, let us fix our gaze constantly on the splendor of the heavenly Jerusalem.

Letters, Vol. 2, 211, 203

Lord, may your light shine upon me and all those I love and pray for, that we may know you better and so love you more. Come, kingdom of God, kingdom of light and glory!

∼ 288. Be Careful! ∼

I write this to you about those who would deceive you.
1 JOHN 2:26

Your desire to see me in order to tell me many things, all of which concern Jesus, is a holy one. Do not be afraid that in this you are going against God's will. I warn you, however, not to abandon yourself excessively to this desire to see me even miraculously, for this could be dangerous for you. When such a desire stirs in your soul, drive it away at once.

In this way you will close the door to any deception by that wretch. The devil, as you know, is a great artificer of evil, in which he has been engaged only too long. When he sees how keenly you desire it, he could deceive you by some diabolical illusion or apparition disguised as an angel of light. Who would believe it? This unhappy apostate even knows how to disguise himself as a Capuchin and to act the part quite well. I beg you to believe one who has undergone an experience of this nature.

Letters, Vol. 2, 150–51

Lord, you permitted Padre Pio to appear as your messenger through bilocations and other phenomena. But he also knew from experience that anything extraordinary must be examined with great caution. I think of the various cults and sects that purport to have the "real truth" about you because their founder had a vision. I thank you, Lord, that I am not a visionary, and I ask you to bless, guide, and protect those who are.

∼ 289. God Is God ∼

[God] ... does great things beyond understanding, and marvelous things without number.... Behold, he snatches away; who can hinder him? Who will say to him, "What doest thou?" ... He is not a man, as I am, that I might answer him.

JOB 9:10, 12, 32

[About two months after his stigmatization Padre Pio laments to his spiritual director, Fr. Benedetto]:

Ah, my dear Father, for the love of heaven, don't leave at its own mercy a life that is petering out in the thickest darkness of night, deprived of every least glimmer of light! I feel I am about to die of the torment I experience in the deepest recesses of my soul. Alas, what a sharp thorn there is in the depths of my soul, which makes me suffer agonies of love day and night! What acute pain I suffer in hands and feet and heart! These are pains that keep me in a continual state of infirmity, which although delightful, is nonetheless painful and poignant.

In the midst of such torment, which is lovable and painful at the same time, two conflicting feelings are present: one which would like to cast off the pain and the other which desires it. The mere thought of having to live for any length of time without this acute yet delightful torment terrifies me, appalls me, and causes me to suffer agonies. In the midst of this torment I find the strength to utter a painful *fiat* ["thy will be done"].

Letters, Vol. 1, 1227–28

Lord, Padre Pio could not explain the mystery of his stigmatization, which left him in both great pain and delight. He had to simply live it. I do not understand many things in my life either. Help me, as you did Pio, to surrender to your will but never pretend to feel happy about it when my feelings are ambivalent.

～ 290. Cling to the Lord ～

Thy name, O Lord, endures for ever, thy renown, O Lord, throughout all ages. For the Lord will vindicate his people, and have compassion on his servants.

PSALM 135:13-14

I bless and pray to the Lord at every moment ... on your behalf. I give thanks to him incessantly for the many gifts and favors granted to yourself and your sister. May the Father of orphans be blessed forever for having in his infinite goodness brought poor Giovina back to life....

She has been snatched from the jaws of death....

I am revealing this to you, not because I want to cause you unnecessary fear and terror, but to arouse in you a sense of liveliest gratitude toward the giver of all good things and exhort you to confide more and more and abandon yourself to Divine Providence. Oh, how good our God is, my dear. He has been pleased to spare you such a great misfortune. Once again, then, I urge you to have ever greater confidence in God, for it is written that those who trust in him will never be forsaken.

Don't turn in on yourself, as so often happens, unfortunately. In the midst of the trials which may afflict you, just place all your confidence in our Supreme Good, in the knowledge that he takes more care of us than a mother takes of her child.

Letters, Vol. 2, 259–60

Lord, another new day, another chance to trust you with all my cares and trials. Father, Son, and Spirit, I trust in you.

∼ 291. In a Time of Loss ∼

Thy dead shall live, their bodies shall rise.... Come, let us go up to the mountain of the Lord ... that he may teach us his ways.

ISAIAH 26:19; 2:3

A word of comfort for your extremely great suffering on the departure of your father. May Jesus be pleased to instill a little comfort in your hearts through these poor words of mine. But ... shouldn't we adore in all circumstances the Supreme Providence of the heavenly Father, whose advice is holy, good, and lovable? He was pleased to recall from this miserable exile your excellent and very dear father, in order to unite him to himself. Let us confess, my good daughters and sisters, that God is good and that his mercy is eternal. His every will is just, and his decrees are full of lofty mysteries; his pleasure is always holy, and his plans, lovable.

I confess ... that I fully understand what the departure of your dear father means. He was a model and example of Christian virtue in our times, when the tendency is to desert the ways of the Lord. This is the confession of my weakness, after having done the will of God. But nevertheless, this resentment was truly vivid, but also perfectly tranquil, because I said along with the prophet David: "I remain silent, O Lord, and don't open my mouth because it is you who have done this" (Ps 39:9)....

But you would like to know how things went for your dear father before Jesus. What doubt can there be on the eternal kiss that this most sweet Jesus accorded him? Wasn't he a fervent Christian, a practicing Catholic, a model father? Come on.... Away with doubts and fears, which are the fruits of your imaginations, because they have no reason to exist. The virtues that adorned the soul of your dear departed one were too obvious.

Letters, Vol. 3, 483–84

What a test of faith, Lord, is the death of a loved one. If I really believe in you and in eternal happiness with you, I must rejoice for the one I have lost. Yet what a void for myself! As to the judgment, I will think only on your mercy, which my dear one so consistently lavished on those who did her great injuries. May her merits and prayers help me to persevere!

～ 292. Leave All to God's Mercy ～

You who fear the Lord, wait for his mercy; and turn not aside, lest you fall. You who fear the Lord, trust in him, and your reward will not fail; you who fear the Lord, hope for good things, for everlasting joy and mercy.

SIRACH 2:7-9

You must turn to God when you are assaulted by the enemy; you must hope in him and expect everything that is good from him. Don't voluntarily dwell on what the enemy presents to you. Remember that he who flees wins, and at the first sign of aversion for those people, you must stop thinking of it and turn to God. Bend your knee before him, and with the greatest humility say this short prayer: "Have mercy on me a poor weakling." Then get up and with holy indifference go on about your business.

Letters, Vol. 3, 418

Lord, thank you for reminding me that when I feel resentment, hostility, or anger—any kind of aversion to anyone—over some injustice to myself or others, I need to not dwell on it. If there is something I can do to make things right, give me the grace to do it with whatever firmness is necessary but without sin. If there is nothing I can do, give me the grace to thrust the problem into the abyss of your divine mercy, knowing one day all will be made right in you.

~ 293. Gaining Ground ~

What does it profit, my brethren, if a man says he has faith but has not works? Can his faith save him? If a brother or sister is ill-clad and in lack of daily food, and one of you says to them, "Go in peace, be warmed and filled," without giving them the things needed for the body, what does it profit? So faith by itself, if it has no works, is dead.

JAMES 2:14-17

Yes, let us do good. Now is the time for sowing, and if we want to reap an abundant harvest, it is not so necessary to sow a lot of seed as to scatter it in good ground. We have already sown a lot of seed, but it counts for very little if we want to be gladdened at harvest time. Let us sow now and continue to sow, my dear, and let nothing grieve us on this account. Let us make sure that this seed falls in good soil, and when the heat arrives to burst it open and bring forth a plant, we must still be on the watch and take good care that the weeds do not smother the young plants.

Letters, Vol. 2, 274–75

Dear Lord, help me to live my faith in deeds, not just pious words. Let my love bear fruit in good works that help the needy brothers and sisters of your human family. Especially, Lord, give me the gift of kindness.

~ 294. Love Above All ~

[Peter said] "I had scarcely begun to speak when the Holy Spirit came down on them in the same way as it came on us at the begin-

ning and I remembered that the Lord had said, 'John baptised with water, but you will be baptised with the Holy Spirit'. I realised then that God was giving them the identical thing he gave to us when we believed in the Lord Jesus Christ."

ACTS 11:15-17, JB

Be watchful, I tell you, and never place too much trust in yourself or count excessively on your own strength. Try to advance more and more on the way to perfection and practice charity more and more, for charity is the bond of Christian perfection. Throw yourself confidently into the arms of the heavenly Father with childlike trust, and open wide your heart to the charism of the Holy Spirit, who is only waiting for a sign from you in order to enrich you.

Letters, Vol. 2, 274

Come, Holy Spirit, Come!

～ 295. Death, Where Is Thy Sting? ～

When the perishable puts on the imperishable, and the mortal puts on immortality, then shall come to pass the saying that is written: "Death is swallowed up in victory." "O death, where is thy victory? O death, where is thy sting?"

1 CORINTHIANS 15:54-55

I have been here in Trinity Hospital [in Naples] for the past three days [during World War I], sent here for treatment by the captain doctor of my platoon. My illness has reached its utmost limits, so they finally decided to send me here. My dear Father, is this the beginning of the end for me? Am I to be set free? Let us hope so and wish for every blessing from the divine heart and from the maternal goodness of [Mary,] the one who can obtain all things at the throne of the Most High.

Letters, Vol. 1, 1060–61

Lord, how wonderful the thought that death is freedom. Help me to see my own death with the same joy Padre Pio evidenced.

～ 296. Keep Praying ～

And will not God vindicate his elect, who cry to him day and night? Will he delay long over them?

LUKE 18:7

My dear Father, I am making a nuisance of myself with the Lord for all, especially for you! When will I see my prayers adequately answered? When will that most happy moment arrive in which we can sing together a hymn of thanksgiving? If the mere thought of this most happy day takes me out of myself, what will happen when this day is a reality, an accomplished fact? Ah, Father, take heart, because this day is drawing near, and we are coming to the end of these stormy times.

Letters, Vol. 1, 1141

Lord, reading Pio's words and remembering a holy Protestant who prayed thirty years for another individual's conversion, I thank you for encouraging me not to give up my prayers even when the answer seems a long time coming. So today I ask again, Lord, for two people in particular to stop smoking and so preserve their health.

∼ 297. On Nincompoops ∼

Weep for the fool, for he lacks intelligence.

SIRACH 22:11

A man from Brindisi named Alberto Del Sordo, a Latin teacher at that time, had written to Padre Pio when his mother was very sick and received a postcard reply that Padre Pio would pray for her. From this Alberto somehow understood that his mother would not be healed. She was not and died. Sometime later Del Sordo made a trip to Padre Pio's friary. Encountering Pio, he says he tested the saint's charisms by asking, "How is my mother?"

He writes: "Padre Pio fixed me with those eyes of his that penetrated one's very soul and answered me: 'Your mother is about to go to her reward in Paradise [from Purgatory], which you, my nincompoop, will not, if you don't mend your ways.'"

The quote from Del Sordo is found in
The Voice of Padre Pio, Vol. 28, No. 4, 1998, 12

Dear Padre Pio, pray for me and all us nincompoops, that we may mend our ways and merrily meet you in heaven.

∼ 298. The Saints Intercede for Us ∼

Simon, Simon, behold, Satan demanded to have you, that he might sift you like wheat, but I have prayed for you that your faith may not fail; and when you have turned again, strengthen your brethren.

LUKE 22:31-32

I have prayed to the good Jesus that he might manifest to me the storm that is raging in your soul at the present time! This most tender Jesus of ours has made me understand that he would never show me your present afflictions, because only with difficulty would I be able to go on living if they were revealed to me.... But I cannot hide from you the fact that I feel all your sufferings as if they were my own and am induced as if by a blind instinct to entreat the divine mercy [for you]....

But even while I ceaselessly pray in this manner, I see with very great spiritual joy this behavior of the Lord toward you. May it be of salutary consolation to you, my dear Father, to know that all will work out to the glory of his divine Majesty.... Courage, then, and go forward. By this trial Jesus intends to cleanse your soul a little, so be grateful to him for it. However, I have infinite trust in the heavenly Father that before this letter reaches its destination the combat you are enduring will be at least partially subdued and easier for you to bear, because our most sweet Jesus, in response to my voluntary offering, has given me a share in it.

Letters, Vol. 1, 543–44

How sweet it is to know, heavenly Father, that Jesus, my friends, and my loved ones are tirelessly interceding for me with you. How sweet that you have from the beginning, when Peter's command in your name healed the sick, permitted your saints to also intercede for us as carriers of your graces. Padre Pio and St. Peter, pray that I may be healed and may become holy.

～ 299. Hoping Against Hope ～

He trusted in the Lord the God of Israel; so that there was none like him among all the kings of Judah after him, nor among those who were before him.

2 KINGS 18:5

[Padre Agostino ordered Padre Pio to keep a diary so he could give him better spiritual guidance. Padre Pio was able to obey for less than a month due to trouble with his eyes and weakness. Following is his entry from July 12, 1929:]

After fifteen days of painful suffering, this morning after holy Mass, during my thanksgiving, for a brief instant I heard Jesus within me saying, "Be calm, do not be agitated: I am with you." What effect these brief words produced, said with such gentleness, so penetratingly and authoritatively I am unable to express. I only know that I felt my life come back, which had been crushed by the long martyrdom suffered over the last fifteen days. [During that time] everything seemed to me devastated, everything in me pulverized, everything made me nauseous, everything irritated me, and everything in me was in rebellion, except my concupiscence. I felt an extreme compassion for souls, so that every least suffering was for me a martyrdom. I wanted to help them, but I felt myself in the most absolute powerlessness. And all this caused me mortal pains.

I turned to Jesus, but who answered me? No one, absolutely no one. In the depth of my soul I felt an echo that seemed to say to me: You are damned for ever; think of destroying yourself for always from this hell, from which you will never again be free. Curse everything, because everything is and always will be against you.

My God! Even though I saw you as a judge, I also looked at you with extreme trust, even though I felt I could hope in no mercy. And while I looked on God in this way, the occurrence of this morning took place. Deo Gratias.

Oh, the beauty, Lord, of the heroic trust of your saints, who cry out to you with Job, "Though you slay me, yet will I trust you." Lord, I am ashamed of my puny trust. Increase it, please.

∽ 300. Oh, the Wonderful Works of God! ∽

You are the light of the world. A city set on a hill cannot be hid. Nor do men light a lamp and put it under a bushel, but on a stand, and it gives light to all in the house. Let your light so shine before men, that they may see your good works and give glory to your Father who is in heaven.

MATTHEW 5:14-16

As I have told you on a previous occasion, while *it is good to guard the secret of a king* (the King of heaven), it is also good, according to the words of Sacred Scripture, *gloriously to reveal the works of God* (Tb 12:7). May it please heaven, my good daughter, that these souls who announce the wondrous works of the Lord may be multiplied like the sands on the seashore and the atoms which make up all heavenly and earthly bodies!

Do you perhaps think that these generous souls, inflamed with divine love, have not achieved much good by recounting the marvelous works which the Lord has done in themselves? If this is what you think, you are greatly mistaken. Very many tepid souls have become fervent, very many fervent souls have become even more fervent, and very many sinful ones have repented when they heard these souls in love with heaven telling of the marvelous things done within them by the Lord. Do not cease, therefore, you too, to proclaim in a loud voice that what is going on within you is entirely the Lord's work.

Letters, Vol. 2, 530

Lord, let whatever good I may do glorify your name. And give me your Holy Spirit so that I may be able to do good.

～ 301. Privation Fosters Appreciation ～

*And as they were eating, he took bread, and blessed, and broke it,
and gave it to them, and said, "Take; this is my body."*

MARK 14:22

You are tormented by the fact that you are unable to leave the house because of your delicate health and are therefore deprived of the immaculate Flesh of the divine Lamb. Moreover, you believe, or rather the enemy tries to make you believe, that this is a punishment from God. No, no, don't listen to him.

I tell you in all sincerity that this is a particular predilection of the heavenly Father toward you. He wants to make you similar to his beloved Son, who fasted from earthly food in the desert for forty days. By depriving you of this beneficial food, he wants to inspire you more and more with great reverence toward his Son in this sacrament, to enkindle within you an ever greater love for the sacred table, for it is at the moment of privation, when God himself brings this about, that the soul has a deeper appreciation of the greatness of this gift.

Letters, Vol. 2, 86

Lord, deepen my appreciation for the heavenly food that is your own body and blood. Forgive me the many times I have received you into my heart and almost immediately drifted away in my thoughts, instead of resting my head on your heart and communing with you. If that is the avoidance of fear sometimes, Lord, give me the perfect love that casts out all fear; if it is sloth, heal me.

∼ 302. Faith and Hope—Arms for the Struggle ∼

Because he himself has suffered and been tempted, he is able to help [others].

HEBREWS 2:18

I know that you are suffering more spiritually than physically, that the latter is a reflection of the former.... Out of holy love I am pleased that your spirit is on Calvary, nailed to the cross of Jesus amid the darkness and sufferings. But do not fear. After having been nailed to the cross with Jesus and after having descended to the sepulchre, you will see the unfailing light, and from Calvary you will go on to Tabor.

Meanwhile, always pronounce the *fiat* of trusting resignation, and take advantage of this period of divine testing for your great sanctification and the salvation of souls.... Don't forget the reassurances of he who speaks to you in the name of God. Believe and hope. With faith and hope you will arm yourself in order to sustain the struggle in which the heavenly Father's goodness has involved you. With faith and hope, you will not be without the sweet nectar of love, which unites you more and more to the Supreme Good.

Letters, Vol. 3, 327

Help me not to waste sufferings in rebellion and self-pity. Today, Lord, I offer you all the pains, toil, and anxieties I experience, (as well as the joys and the beauty of this lovely day) in order that, united to your work of redemption, they may benefit souls, including my own, and hasten the coming of your kingdom.

~ 303. Upholding Each Other by Prayer ~

I appeal to you, brethren, by our Lord Jesus Christ and by the love of the Spirit, to strive together with me in your prayers to God on my behalf.

ROMANS 15:30

May Jesus always be in the midst of your heart, to fill it and make it abound with his holy love. This ... is the assiduous wish for you on the part of he who greatly desires to see you ascend to the heights of Christian perfection. I have no suitable words with which to thank you for your prayers during those days of trial [of military service], and therefore I beg the good God that he may make up for my deficiency by repaying you a thousand times. I will not tell you how much I suffered physically and spiritually during those days, because the good Jesus and your angel guardian partly manifest this to you. However, more than ever, long live the lovable will of the divine Father, who arranges everything with admirable wisdom for his glory and our sanctification.

Letters, Vol. 3, 485–86

Lord, it is your will that we uphold each other by prayer. Help me, Lord, to pray without ceasing for those in need. Teach me, Lord, how to pray.

~ 304. Keep Talking to God ~

Let me have silence, and I will speak.... Then call, and I will answer; or let me speak, and do thou reply to me.

JOB 13:13, 22

During the course of the day, when you are unable to do anything else, call on Jesus even in the midst of all your occupations, with resigned groanings of the soul. He will come to stay united to your soul always, through his grace and holy love. Fly in spirit before the tabernacle when you cannot go there with the body, and there express your ardent desires. Speak to, pray to, and embrace the Beloved of souls.

Letters, Vol. 3, 452

Lord, I am often speaking to you, night and day. I surely have no trouble venting my feelings. But how bad I am at listening to you! Teach me to listen!

～ 305. The Surest Sign of Love ～

And he called to him the multitude with his disciples, and said to them, "If any man would come after me, let him deny himself and take up his cross and follow me."

MARK 8:34

Dear Father, may Jesus fill your soul with all his choicest graces and enable you to experience more and more the happiness of the cross when carried with a Christian spirit. Father, how sweet is the word "cross"! Here at the foot of Jesus' cross souls are clothed in light and inflamed with love; here they acquire wings to bear them upward in loftiest flight. May the same cross always be our bed of rest, our school of perfection, our beloved heritage.

For this reason we must never separate the cross from Jesus' love; otherwise it would become a weight which in our weakness we could not carry. May the Sorrowful Virgin obtain for us from her most holy

Son the grace to penetrate more deeply into the mystery of the cross and like her to become inebriated with Jesus' sufferings. The surest sign of love is the capacity to suffer for the beloved, and since the Son of God endured many sufferings for pure love, there is no doubt that the cross carried for him becomes as lovable as love itself.

Letters, Vol. 1, 672

Lord, how far I am from seeing suffering as the saints do! How right they are about love: It is only fluffy words if there is no willingness to suffer for the one loved. Help me, Lord, to learn to love with deeds not just words.

~ 306. The Soul Freed From Death ~

Then I called on the name of the Lord: "O Lord, I beseech thee, save my life!"... The Lord preserves the simple; when I was brought low, he saved me. Return, O my soul, to your rest; for the Lord has dealt bountifully with you. For thou hast delivered my soul from death,... I walk before the Lord in the land of the living.

PSALM 116:4, 6-9

Despite everything that is taking place within me, I feel alive in me the hope to not despair. Is this hope vain? Whatever, I feel I must say to Jesus with Job: "I will hope in you even in desperation." This state [of spiritual anguish], which has always been increasing, lasted until this morning, the day of the Assumption of the Most Holy Virgin. I was at the altar for the celebration of Mass when there happened what I am about to say.

I must say in advance that I do not know how I ascended the holy altar this morning. Physical suffering and interior pain competed in torturing my whole poor being. I felt these mortal agonies so vividly that I am unable to describe them. I only say that as I approached the moment of consuming the sacred species, this state of torture increased always more. I felt myself dying. A mortal sadness pervaded me through and through, and I felt that all was finished for me: my life in time and eternity. The dominant thought that saddened me the most was of never being able to demonstrate again my reverence and love to divine Goodness. It was not hell so much that terrorized me as the clear knowledge that down there, there is no more love. And this ... made me feel ... an infinity of deaths together.

I had reached the limit. I had arrived at the culmination of my agony, and where I believed I would find death, I found the consolation of life. In the act of consuming the sacred species of the holy Eucharist, a sudden light pervaded me within, and I saw clearly the heavenly Mother with the Child Jesus in her arms, who both said to me, "Be calm! We are with you, you belong to us, and we are yours."

With that said, I saw no more. Then calm and peace and all my sufferings at once disappeared. I felt myself for the whole day drowned in an ocean of sweetness and indescribable love for God and souls.

From Pio's diary,
kept under obedience for less than a month,
Summer 1929

How true and wonderful it is, Lord, that sometimes when I seem helpless and without means to escape disaster, you suddenly change everything in either my life or my perceptions. Praise to you, Master of the Universe and Master of my heart and soul!

∼ 307. A Paradox of Suffering ∼

The kingdom of God is within you.

LUKE 17:21, Douay-Rheims

You suffer, but be resigned so that you can say with the prophet: "Lo, it was for my welfare that I had great bitterness." Suffer with resignation, because there is good reason for this, and it is wanted by the one who wants to make you similar to his only Son....

Do not be afraid, because he who has placed you in this suffering is pleased with you. You must know also that Jesus himself suffers in you, for you, and with you, so as to join you to his passion for the sake of your brothers' health. God has not abandoned you, and he will not abandon you. It is not justice but love crucified that is crucifying you and wants you united to his most bitter suffering, without any consolation or support other than desolation.

Your fear for your past life is futile, because our Lord has already cancelled these defects from your soul. Equally futile is your anxiety for the future, since the present is a crucifixion of love. And I say "love" because this is not retributive nor preventive justice....

Do not be anxious to seek God outside of you. He is in you and with you, in your sighs and in your seeking, like a mother who incites her child to seek her while she hides behind him. Unfortunately I know only too well the agony of your state....

But you must not worry nor be afraid. He "kills one to bring one to life," he "brings one down to Sheol to raise one up," and with a garland added on.

Letter of August, 12, 1918, to a spiritual son
reprinted in *The Voice of Padre Pio*,
Vol. 26, Summer, 1996, 29

Lord, give me the faith to look at all my troubles as gifts from you.

∼ 308. A Beautiful Heart Trumps Fine Dress ∼

But many that are first will be last, and the last first.

MATTHEW 19:30

Anna Maria D'Orazi was a young boarding school student when she came with her mother to visit Padre Pio shortly after World War II. It was May 5, a day at San Giovanni Rotondo when Padre Pio presided over children's First Communions. Maria had not yet made her First Communion because her mother, a dress designer, had not yet found time to make a splendid white dress and organize the traditional party. Now Anna Maria experienced a burning desire to make her First Communion this day.

Her mother disapproved, saying she would be like an orphan with no party, no presents, and no dress. Finally she told her child to ask Padre Pio, thinking he would say no. But when Anna Maria asked the Padre after he heard her confession, he agreed that the absence of the white dress meant nothing.

However, the world did not agree with Anna Maria and Padre Pio. When the children were lined up, Anna Maria, in her simple green dress, was not allowed to go with the other girls, who looked like little brides in their white dresses. She was pushed aside until the last of the boys, also dressed in their smartest, had received Jesus. Finally, last of all, she was permitted to kneel at the communion rail.

Anna Maria recalls, "I saw Padre Pio coming toward me, radiant and smiling, while he held the Sacred Host in his fingers above the ciborium, and when he was directly in front of me I heard him say: 'Get up and come here.' I got up and followed him.... He made me climb the altar steps, and he gave me Communion in front of the tabernacle. A hushed murmur of voices filled the whole church, everyone ... greatly moved.... All this was explained to me afterward by my mother, more moved and overwhelmed than myself, because I did not understand the significance of Padre Pio's gesture. I was only enraptured ... because I was making my First Communion.... The sweetness of this memory accompanies me in the most difficult moments in my life."

The Voice of Padre Pio,
Vol. 27, No. 12, 1997, 16–17

Lord, how often I mistake the trappings for the substance of things. Help me, like Pio and Anna Maria, to cut to the heart of the matter, especially in the spiritual.

∼ 309. Thy Will Be Done ∼

Thy kingdom come, Thy will be done, on earth as it is in heaven.

MATTHEW 6:10

My very dear Father, may Jesus be always in our hearts and transform us entirely into himself! I received your letter, which was like sweet balm to my poor heart, so sorely tried by misfortune. I did as you ordered me, but there was no reply this time either. May God's will be done!

I am still in this prison [hospital], afflicted but resigned. I am now quite sure that Jesus wants me to undergo this trial, that is to say—dear God!—he wants me to share the lot of so many of our brothers. It's necessary that I too become a soldier. I would like to be mistaken this time, but it isn't possible. Recommend me to God, that he may enable me to do his holy will in this also.

For the moment I don't need any money, because I have no way of spending it. Continue to bless me.

Letter from Padre Pio
to his spiritual father, Padre Benedetto,
September 2, 1917

Lord, give me the grace to have no will but your will.

～ 310. Love and the Sick ～

Love is patient and kind.

1 CORINTHIANS 13:4

Padre Pio founded a hospital called the Home for the Relief of Suffering, which today sits directly across from the friary. On May 6, 1956, the day the hospital was officially opened, Padre Pio exhorted the doctors who work there:

You have the mission of curing the sick; but if you don't bring love to the sickbed, I don't think the medicines will be of much use. I have experienced this:... When I was ill in 1916-17, my doctor, when curing me, first of all gave me a word of comfort. Love cannot manage without words. How can you express it if not with words that relieve the sick person spiritually? Bring God to the patients; it will be of more worth than any other cure.

The Voice of Padre Pio, Vol. 27, No. 12, 1997, 7

Lord, when I help someone who is ill, let me never forget that love is the most important medicine. And when I am ill, Lord, please send me medical men and women who are not only wise and skilled but filled with love.

∾ 311. Count It All Joy ∾

Do you not know that in a race all the runners compete, but only one receives the prize? So run that you may obtain it. Every athlete exercises self-control in all things. They do it to receive a perishable wreath, but we an imperishable.

1 CORINTHIANS 9:24-25

I should be less happy if I did not see you so downcast, because I should then see the Lord bestowing less jewels upon you. Hence, in the holy charity of Jesus, while earnestly desiring your spiritual profit and your progress toward perfection, I rejoice more and more to see you in your present state. My joy is by no means foolish, for in the combat there is a crown to be won, and the better the fight put up by the soul, the more numerous the palms of victory.

Don't you know how the apostle St. James exhorted his brethren to rejoice when they were harassed by various storms and numerous reverses? *Count it all joy, my brethren, when you meet various trials* (Jas 1:2). Moreover, how can we fail to rejoice when we find ourselves involved in many combats, knowing as we do that every victory achieved has a corresponding degree of glory? May the thought of eternal bliss with Jesus and of being made similar to the Son of God encourage you and prevent you from yielding to the enemy's temptations.

Letters, Vol. 2, 68

Lord, help me to keep my eyes on you as I struggle toward the finish line.

∼ 312. Do Good to Your Enemies ∼

But love your enemies, and do good, and lend, expecting nothing
in return; and your reward will be great, and you will be sons of
the Most High; for he is kind to the ungrateful and the selfish.

LUKE 6:35

You do well to desire the reconciliation between those two people [and
yourself], and you will do even better if you make efforts to bring it
about. Let us pray confidently to the Lord that he may bring them to
a better frame of mind by enlightening them and touching their
hearts. Don't be unduly distressed about the matter, for the Lord,
according to the great Doctor, St. Augustine, *allows the wicked to live*
on, either that they may change their ways or else that through him the
good may have a chance to practice patience.

Letters, Vol. 2, 77–78

Lord, this is the heart of religion: to forgive and to do good to ALL. It is
also darn hard sometimes. But I count on your grace to help me love those
who do not love me, by which I mean to desire the same good things—
above all, heaven—for them as I do for myself.

∼ 313. This Wretched House ∼

And he said to his disciples, "Therefore I tell you, do not be anxious
about your life, what you shall eat, nor about your body, what you
shall put on. For life is more than food, and the body more than
clothing. Consider the ravens: they neither sow nor reap, they have
neither storehouse nor barn, and yet God feeds them. Of how much

more value are you than the birds! And which of you by being anxious can add a cubit to his span of life? If then you are not able to do as small a thing as that, why are you anxious about the rest? Consider the lilies, how they grow; they neither toil nor spin; yet I tell you, even Solomon in all his glory was not arrayed like one of these. But if God so clothes the grass which is alive in the field today and tomorrow is thrown into the oven, how much more will he clothe you, O men of little faith! And do not seek what you are to eat and what you are to drink, nor be of anxious mind. For all the nations of the world seek these things; and your Father knows that you need them. Instead, seek his kingdom, and these things shall be yours as well."

LUKE 12:22-31

As regards the question of the house, Jesus would be just as glad if you were to continue to live where you are at present. I believe I am not going against Jesus' will when I suggest that it would be better for you to find, if possible, a house closer to a parish church or to a convent. At all events, if this is not feasible, don't let it worry you. I tell you quite frankly that your anxiety about this wretched house is a bit excessive, and I don't approve of it. May I ask you, then, to curb your anxiety about it unless you want to displease Jesus. It would be advisable for you to let the head of the family take care of the matter.

Letters, Vol. 2, 78

Lord, help me to be ever more detached from material things and ever more trustful that you will supply all my needs.

∼ 314. The Game of Love ∼

It is for discipline that you have to endure. God is treating you as sons; for what son is there whom his father does not discipline?... Besides this, we have had earthly fathers to discipline us and we respected them. Shall we not much more be subject to the Father of spirits and live? For they disciplined us for a short time at their pleasure, but he disciplines us for our good, that we may share his holiness. For the moment all discipline seems painful rather than pleasant; later it yields the peaceful fruit of righteousness to those who have been trained by it.

HEBREWS 12:7, 9-11

Don't be daunted by the cross. The surest test of love consists in suffering for the loved one, and if God suffered so much for love, the pain we suffer for him becomes as lovable as love itself. In the troubles which the Lord bestows on you, be patient and conform yourself gladly to the divine Heart in the knowledge that all is a continual game on the part of your Lover.

Tribulations and trials have always been the heritage and the portion of chosen souls. The more Jesus intends to raise a soul up to perfection, the more he tries it by suffering. Rejoice, I say to you, in seeing yourself so privileged, in spite of your own unworthiness. The more you are afflicted, the more you ought to rejoice, because in the fire of tribulation the soul will become pure gold, worthy to be placed and to shine in the heavenly palace.

Letters, Vol. 2, 140

Lord, I could do without trials and tribulations, but I will trust that all you permit is for my growth and eternal joy.

∼ 315. On Spiritual Roses ∼

Listen to me, O you holy sons, and bud like a rose growing by a stream of water; send forth fragrance like frankincense, and put forth blossoms like a lily. Scatter the fragrance, and sing a hymn of praise; bless the Lord for all his works.

SIRACH 39:13-14

Take heart ... even though you are not free from interior suffering; even I know that, because you are what you are in our Lord, your sadness will be in peace. And may love mitigate your suffering, as I truly have the heart of a father [toward you], which is also partly that of a mother. I am extremely pleased with your progress in piety, and that progress always necessitates difficulties with which to exercise itself at the school of the cross, the only school where our souls can be perfected.

Be courageous, my daughter. There are both spiritual and bodily rose bushes. In the latter the thorns are constantly present and the roses wither, but in the former, the thorns pass but the roses persist.

A letter of December 27, 1917,
quoted in *The Voice of Padre Pio*, Vol. 28, No. 3, 1988, 7

Dear Lord, today let me open like a bud to the sunshine of your love.

∼ 316. Bilocation: Sent As God's Messenger ∼

And he dreamed that there was a ladder set up on the earth, and the top of it reached to heaven; and behold, the angels of God were ascending and descending on it!

GENESIS 28:12

Sr. Maria Geltrude of the Sacred Heart of Jesus was a Capuchin nun in the Convent of San Giovanni Battista at Bagnacavallo. A great woman of prayer, God permitted her some terrible temptations as well as incredible graces. During a period of the terrible temptations, a fellow Capuchin, a priest, advised her to seek help from Padre Pio. She did not believe he could do anything for her, but she prayed and asked the archangel St. Raphael to intercede for her.

On January 20, 1950, she had the shock of seeing in her cell Padre Pio. Standing by the window, he upbraided her severely for her discouragement. Sr. Geltrude began to weep, and Padre Pio sat down, the nun on her knees at his feet. Now he spoke to her in a fatherly way and put his hands on her head. At his touch, the temptations left her completely, never to return.

The Voice of Padre Pio, Vol. 30, No. 2, 2000, 9

Lord, your messengers come to us in so many ways. Help me to sense through events like Padre Pio's visit to the cloistered nun the incredible magnitude both of the spiritual world and of your loving mercy.

∼ 317. Nature Reveals God's Beauty ∼

My beloved has gone down to his garden, to the beds of spices, to pasture his flock in the gardens, and to gather lilies.

SONG OF SONGS 6:2

I went down to the nut orchard, to look at the blossoms of the valley, to see whether the vines had budded, whether the pomegranates were in bloom.

SONG OF SONGS 6:11

Spring was beginning again; the bare earth flourished in different greens and, where it had flowered, [was] painted in bright vermilion, yellow, and other colors.... The shepherds with their reed pipes challenged the nightingales, who, silent so long, now softly chirped in the woods as if remembering forgotten notes.

From a school essay, "The Sunflower,"
quoted in *The Voice of Padre Pio,* Vol. 28, No. 7, 1998, 15

Lord, there is something about a garden of flowers, about the beauties of pastures, and about a bird's song after winter that saturates my soul with freshness and joy. As Pio did, I see something of your face in nature, Lord, and it is beautiful! Today, Lord, whatever the season, open my eyes to see more of you in your creation.

～ 318. Filled With the Fullness of Good: Growing in Charity ～

For this reason I bow my knees before the Father, from whom every family in heaven and on earth is named, that according to the riches of his glory he may grant you to be strengthened with might through his Spirit in the inner man, and that Christ may dwell in your hearts through faith; that you, being rooted and grounded in love, may have power to comprehend with all the saints what is the breadth and length and height and depth, and to know the love of Christ which surpasses knowledge, that you may be filled with all the fulness of God.

EPHESIANS 3:14-19

[From a letter to his spiritual director.] Why are you so anxious about your soul? Are you not aware that Jesus is content with you and that you are very dear to his divine heart? Don't worry in the least about this; you should be busy about one thing only—namely, continual progress in holy charity. Although Jesus is pleased with you, he wishes you to grow more and more in charity by perfecting your own soul, by bringing new souls to him all the time, and also by leading on to perfection those souls who are already in his sanctifying grace.

Letters, Vol. 1, 706

Lord, how I long to be rooted and grounded in love, that I too may grow in charity until I reflect you wherever I go.

～ 319. Suffering and Rapture "of the Blessed" ～

Therefore we ourselves boast of you in the churches of God for your steadfastness and faith in all your persecutions and in the afflictions which you are enduring.

2 THESSALONIANS 1:4

I am suffering and suffering very much, but thanks to our good Jesus, I still feel a little strength; and when aided by Jesus, what is the creature not capable of doing? I don't desire by any means to have my cross lightened, since I am happy to suffer with Jesus. In contemplating the cross on his shoulders, I feel more and more fortified, and I exult with a holy joy. However, I feel within me the great need to cry out louder and louder to Jesus with the doctor of grace: "Give me what you command and command what you will" (St. Augustine).

Hence, my dear Father, do not allow the idea of my sufferings to cast a shadow on your spirits or to sadden your heart. So let us not weep, my dear Father; we must hide our tears from the One who sends them, from the One who has shed tears himself and continues to shed them every day because of man's ingratitude. He chooses souls, and despite my unworthiness, he has chosen mine to help him in the tremendous task of men's salvation.... This is the whole reason why I desire to suffer more and more without the slightest consolation. In this consists all my joy.

Unfortunately, I am in need of courage, but Jesus will not refuse anything. I can testify to this from long experience, as long as we do not stop asking him for what we need.... All I want you to do is to ask our most sweet Jesus insistently to keep me far from sin. The heavenly beings continue to visit me and to give me a foretaste of the rapture of the blessed.

Letters, Vol. 1, 342–43

Lord, no wonder there are levels of heaven, as the saints tell us. Padre Pio and St. Paul are in a completely different league than this wimp. I'm embarrassed to say it, Lord, but you know everything anyway: You know I have no desire to suffer with you. I'm so sorry about that—and so grateful to you for suffering for me. If I do have to suffer, give me the grace to take it. Meantime, if I can have my druthers, let me serve you in joy and peace and leave the heavy-duty suffering to the big league boys.

∼ 320. The Marvel of a Faithful Friend ∼

A faithful friend is a sturdy shelter: he that has found one has found a treasure. There is nothing so precious as a faithful friend, and no scales can measure his excellence. A faithful friend is an elixir of life; and those who fear the Lord will find him.

SIRACH 6:14-16

May Jesus always be the peaceful King of your heart, and may he grant you all the spiritual benefits you desire and earnestly wish for the souls of others. Amen.

At the approach of your beautiful name day I feel welling up in my heart more than ever a sense of most lively gratitude to you, the one who has been concerned more than anyone else about my spiritual progress. I give praise to God for all this, and to you I return my infinite thanks, while I solemnly promise to repay you, as far as this is in my power, by grateful prayer to God for all the good you have done me.

For your feast day please accept my most sincere and earnest good wishes, which come from the bottom of my heart, especially for your progress in the spiritual life. May God be pleased to grant my earnest wishes, which are always that you may be preserved in holy love. May he grant me the happiness of seeing you advance more and more in the ways of the Lord.

Letters, Vol. 1, 705

Lord, I am struck by how grateful Pio was to his friend, particularly for that friend's concern for Pio's spiritual progress, and how his own desires for good things for his friend were also completely spiritual. I have been blessed with many friends, Lord, and I thank you for every one of them. Help my friendship never to lead anyone away from you, Lord. May those I love who do not know you find in me an invitation to make your acquaintance. And for those who have led me closer to you or mirrored something of your beauty and love, I thank you, Lord, with all my heart.

～ 321. Sacrificial Service to Souls ～

For the Son of man ... came not to be served but to serve.

MARK 10:45

You must know that I do not have a free moment: A crowd of souls thirsting for Jesus fall upon me, so that I don't know which way to turn. Before such an abundant harvest, on one hand I rejoice in the Lord, because I see the ranks of elect souls always increasing and Jesus loved more; and on the other hand I feel broken by such a weight. There have been periods when I heard confessions without interruption for eighteen hours consecutively.

From two letters of the post-stigmata ministry
of the early 1920s,
quoted in *The Voice of Padre Pio*, Vol. 27, No. 12, 1997, 9

Lord, help me to add my mite to the coming of your kingdom alongside the great souls, like Padre Pio, who brought you such an abundant harvest of souls by sacrificing simply everything.

~ 322. Count on God ~

We know that in everything God works for good with those who love him, who are called according to his purpose.

ROMANS 8:28

May the heavenly Child always be at the center of your heart; may he sustain it, enlighten it, inspire it, and transform it to his eternal love! This is the most ardent prayer I say for you in these days before the stable of Bethlehem. Oh, how dearly I hope the divine Infant will grant you this prayer! May Jesus continue to grant his graces to all, especially to you, giving you courage and resignation up to the last day of your pilgrimage!

As regards your usual trials of the spirit, I recommend calm and resignation always to the divine will, being certain that, as it is Jesus' will that your soul should experience these terrible trials, in the end all will work out for the glory of God and your salvation. Rest assured that this is precisely the case. O my good daughter, if you have neither sufficient gold nor incense to offer our Lord, you will at least have the myrrh of bitterness. And I perceive that he willingly accepts this....

Finally, Jesus glorified is beautiful; but even though he is so in that state, he seems to me to be even more beautiful crucified.

Letter of December 27, 1917,
quoted in *The Voice of Padre Pio*, Vol. 28, No. 3, 1998, 6

Lord, Padre Pio's prayer for his spiritual daughter is what I ask for myself, especially that you may give me courage and perseverance up to the day of my death here and birth into new life with you.

∼ 323. Heavenly Confusion ∼

When my soul was embittered, when I was pricked in heart, I was stupid and ignorant, I was like a beast toward thee. Nevertheless I am continually with thee; thou dost hold my right hand. Thou dost guide me with thy counsel, and afterward thou wilt receive me to glory. Whom have I in heaven but thee? And there is nothing upon earth that I desire besides thee. My flesh and my heart may fail, but God is the strength of my heart and my portion for ever.

PSALM 73:21-26

Dear Father [Padre Agostino], in what sore straits does God place the soul that loves him ardently without ever growing weary! The fact of being unable to explain all that this loving God is doing in my soul is for me the source of atrocious torment. This is the reason for all those storms that upset me. I do not understand this. I have no reason to doubt that it is the Lord who is acting in me, and even though I have forced myself to begin to doubt, I have never been able to persuade myself that these inestimable favors which I receive from God are the devil's work.

Yet the thought, which crosses my mind especially at certain times, the thought that I may be deceived, is heartrending. I say to myself, perhaps it is possible that as a punishment for my grievous and innumerable infidelities the Lord can permit me to deceive both myself and my directors unawares. How am I to overcome this atrocious doubt if by a clear light in my soul I am fully aware of the many faults into which I involuntarily fall continually, in spite of the many heavenly favors with which my soul is filled? I realize my wretchedness and am filled with confusion.

Letters, Vol. 1, 468–69

Lord, I hope I am not deceived in believing that I am your child and that you love me in spite of the many faults and weaknesses which stud my days. If I am in an illusion about the state of my soul, please enlighten me. And if my discernment is true, bring me further into your light, and strengthen me to become all you want me to be.

～ 324. The Heart May Love More Than Mind Perceives ～

He brought me to the banqueting house, and his banner over me was love. Sustain me with raisins, refresh me with apples; for I am sick with love.

SONG OF SONGS 2:4-5

What I understand most truly and clearly is that my heart loves to a much greater extent than my intellect perceives. Of this alone I am certain, and I have never had the slightest doubt about it. Moreover, I do not believe I am telling an untruth when I say that I have never been tempted in this respect. I am so perfectly sure that my will loves this most tender Spouse that, apart from Holy Scripture, I am certain of nothing else to the same degree to which I am certain of this.

Letters, Vol. 1, 469

What a great thought, Lord: that perhaps my heart loves steadfastly as my will desires in spite of my intellect's doubts and restlessness. Surely to know you, Lord, is to love you. I love you now but not nearly as much as you deserve to be loved. Give me more love, Lord, to love you with!

∼ 325. Searching for God ∼

With my whole heart I seek thee.

PSALM 119:10

Upon my bed by night I sought him whom my soul loves; I sought him, but found him not.... "I will rise now and go about the city, in the streets and in the squares; I will seek him whom my soul loves."

SONG OF SONGS 3:1-2

I seem to be searching continually for something I cannot find, and even I myself do not know what I seek. I love and suffer very little, and I wish I could love much more this thing I am seeking. I would like to suffer much more for the ideal I am pursuing.

But, my dear Father, although I don't know what this good is that my heart of its own accord seeks so avidly, I seem to know one thing for certain: that this good is inexhaustible and not circumscribed by limits. I seem to understand, moreover, that my heart will never be able to contain it entirely, for in my ignorance I feel that this is a very great good, an immense good, an infinite good. Is this Jesus? If not, then who is it?

Letters, Vol. I, 403,
quoted in *The Voice of Padre Pio*, Vol. 26, Summer 1996, 31

You are the great good, Lord, that all seek who desire happiness, joy, beauty, wisdom, or truth, whether they know it or not. Padre Pio understood that you are "not circumscribed by limits" but are "an infinite good." Stretch my heart, Lord, to take in more of your goodness, your truth, your beauty.

∼ 326. The Dark Night of the Soul ∼

My God, my God, why hast thou forsaken me? Why art thou so far from helping me, from the words of my groaning? O my God, I cry by day, but thou dost not answer; and by night, but find no rest.
PSALM 22:1-2

Farewell to the delights with which the Lord had inebriated my soul! Where is that enjoyment of the adorable divine presence? Everything has disappeared from intellect and spirit. It is a continual desert of darkness, dejection, apathy; this is the native land of death, the night of abandonment, the cavern of desolation. Here the soul is far from its God and left to itself.

My soul continues to groan beneath the weight of this night.... It is incapable of thinking of supernatural things.... My will seems to make an effort to love, but in a flash, dear Father, it becomes hard and motionless as a stone. My memory tries to take hold of something to console it, but all in vain....

What increases my torment more than anything is the occasional vague remembrance of having previously known and loved this same Lord whom I now feel I neither know nor love.... I then try to find at least in creatures the traces of the One for whom my soul longs, but I no longer recognize the usual image of him who has abandoned me. It is precisely at this point that my soul is overcome by terror, and no longer knowing what to do to find its God, it wails bitterly to the Lord: *My God, my God, why have you abandoned me?*

Letters, Vol. 1, 804

Father, how terror stricken I have felt when it seemed you were completely gone and deaf to my prayers. Padre Pio experienced this, and so did your only begotten Son. Why not me then, Lord? But you know my weakness. Do not put me to the test again, Lord, but have mercy on me.

∼ 327. God Is Never Really Absent ∼

Therefore he never withdraws his mercy from us. Though he disciplines us with calamities, he does not forsake his own people.

2 MACCABEES 6:16

Do not say you are all alone in climbing Calvary and that you are all alone as you struggle and weep, for Jesus is with you and will never abandon you.

Letters, Vol. 2, 479

Lord, whether I feel it or not, never let me doubt that you are with me and will only my good.

∼ 328. Be Helpful to All—For Jesus' Sake ∼

For though I am free from all men, I have made myself a slave to all, that I might win the more.... I have become all things to all men, that I might by all means save some. I do it all for the sake of the gospel, that I may share in its blessings.

1 CORINTHIANS 9:19, 22-23

[Pio writes to Padre Agostino, his spiritual director, who was a chaplain in the army:]

Can you doubt that such a good Father as is our God has appointed you to be the spiritual father of those poor brothers of ours, without giving you a superabundance of honey by which to alleviate their sufferings? It isn't lawful to entertain such a doubt, but pay attention to the few words my heart speaks to yours. Nothing can dry up and actually does dry up the milk and honey of charity like regrets, affliction, and melancholy. Live, then, in holy joy among those sons of our land. Give them spiritual comfort kindly and graciously, so that they may seek it gladly.

I am not telling you to fawn upon them, my dear Father, but be tender, mild, and amiable. In a word, love with a cordial, fatherly, and pastoral love these poor unfortunates of our times, and you will have done all; you will be all things to all men, a father to each one and helpful to all. This attitude alone is sufficient.

I hope that the Lord who has intended you to work for the benefit of many will give you the help, strength, courage, and love you require. To him alone be honor, glory, and blessing at all times. Live completely in Jesus, for he loves your soul very much.

Letters, Vol. 1, 1086–87

Lord, help me to have a sweet and amiable disposition with everyone—even if this requires a miracle at times! May what you have done in me lead people to desire to know you.

~ 329. Confide and Hope in God ~

O God, from my youth thou hast taught me, and I still proclaim thy wondrous deeds.... O God, who is like thee? Thou who hast made me see many sore troubles wilt revive me again; from the depths of the earth thou wilt bring me up again. Thou wilt ... comfort me again. I will also praise thee with the harp for thy faithfulness, O my God; I will sing praises to thee with the lyre, O Holy One of Israel.

PSALM 71:17, 19-22

May Jesus continue to be always totally yours; may he comfort you in your every affliction and render you always more worthy of his divine embraces! This is the synthesis of all the prayers which I assiduously say for you before Jesus. May he be pleased to grant them all. I exhort you not to doubt divine pleasure in your regard. Confide, therefore, and humble yourself always more under the hand of the divine craftsman, and let yourself be guided as he pleases.

Letters, Vol. 3, 1050

Lord, I am yours. Do with me as you will.

~ 330. Heaven ~

Then I saw a new heaven and a new earth; for the first heaven and the first earth had passed away, and the sea was no more. And I saw the holy city, new Jerusalem, coming down out of heaven from God, prepared as a bride adorned for her husband; and I heard a great voice from the throne saying, "Behold, the dwelling of God is with men. He will dwell with them, and they shall be his people, and God himself will be with them; he will wipe away every tear from their eyes, and death shall be no more, neither shall there be mourning nor crying nor pain any more, for the former things have passed away." And he who sat upon the throne said, "Behold, I make all things new."

REVELATION 21:1-5

What else can we desire than God's will? What other wish can a soul have when it is consecrated to him? What else do you desire, then, if not that God's plan may be fulfilled in you?

Take courage, therefore, and go forward on the path of divine love, with the firm conviction that the more fully your own will becomes united and conformed to God's will, the more you will advance toward perfection.... Let us keep our thoughts, I say, continually fixed on heaven, our true homeland, of which this earth is merely an image.

Letters, Vol. 2, 469–70

Thank you, Lord, for showing St. John some of the glories and loveliness to come. May we all merrily meet with you in heaven, our Father, our Savior, and the Spirit, our Comforter and Guide. Lord, may your kingdom come soon!

∽ 331. God Does Not Abandon His Children ∽

Fear not, be not dismayed; for the Lord God, even my God, is with you. He will not fail you or forsake you.

1 CHRONICLES 28:20

I received your letter, and even though I understand the complaints you make, I must not let a point that struck me strongly pass without comment. You say that everybody has abandoned you, including myself. Apart from the abandonment of others, I say that you are wrong in complaining about my having abandoned you. Unfortunately, you anticipated my reprimand for you. We have changed places. Do you remember? You have become so indifferent toward your old [spiritual] director, that you even neglect certain rules, I don't say of Christian obedience, but of common politeness. As regards everything else, God knows if I have ever failed to care for your spiritual good. God knows how much I groaned and sighed, feared and prayed continually for you to Jesus.

The supposed abandonment on the part of God is a pure invention on the part of Satan. Jesus is and will always be yours. Don't abstain from working for the good of others, but neither should you neglect your own spiritual betterment. Jesus will always sustain you in everything.

Letters, Vol. 3, 379

Lord, sometimes I feel very alone. But I know you will no more abandon me than I would abandon one of my children. I do not sense your presence, but I will believe you are with me anyway.

∼ 332. To Rest by Jesus ∼

The apostles returned to Jesus and told him all that they had done and taught. And he said to them, "Come away by yourselves to a lonely place, and rest a while."

MARK 6:30-31

Oh my dauther! How beautiful is his face, how sweet his eyes and what a good thing it is to stay close to him!… We must place all our desires and affections there.…

Letters Vol. 3, 409–410

Lord, even if I am working for you like the apostles, I must still make time to rest and replenish my energies by being with you "in a lonely place" whether through retreats, prayer groups, keeping the Sabbath for church and recreation, or daily prayer time, perhaps with a book like this.

∼ 333. On Confession ∼

He who conceals his transgressions will not prosper, but he who confesses and forsakes them will obtain mercy.

PROVERBS 28:13

Raise your heart always to those heavenly heights, and do all you can to attain that eternal beatitude which awaits us. The children of the world usually only confess their sins on their deathbeds, even though this present life should be lived in the light of eternal life. The children of God, however, touch this truth with their very hands their whole lives.

Letters, Vol. 4, unidentified page

quoted in *The Voice of Padre Pio* magazine Vol. 28, No. 11, 1998, 9

Lord, I thank you for the opportunity to unburden myself in confession and know the joy of your forgiveness.

~ 334. God's Healing Through His Saints ~

The prayer of a righteous man has great power in its effects. Elijah was a man of like nature with ourselves and he prayed fervently that it might not rain, and for three years and six months it did not rain on the earth. Then he prayed again and the heaven gave rain, and the earth brought forth its fruit.

JAMES 5:16-18

Not long after World War II a Polish woman physician, a survivor of a Nazi concentration camp, came down with terminal cancer. Her friend Cardinal Wojtyla in Rome sent a message to Padre Pio, to whom he had once confessed on a visit to San Giovanni Rotondo. Padre Pio, receiving the little note, remarked, "I cannot say no to this."

Shortly thereafter, the doctors decided they had been mistaken. The woman was not terminal: It was an inflammation, not a cancerous growth. Wanda Poltawska went on with her life as a mother, wife, and doctor. She knew nothing of her friend's intervention nor of Padre Pio. Even when she eventually learned of the Cardinal's letter and his subsequent one of thanks, she says she didn't want to reflect on what might have happened. But in 1967 she had an opportunity to go to Rome and that May went to San Giovanni Rotondo. She attended Padre Pio's Mass and later wrote, "It is impossible to find adequate words to describe this Mass."

After [the Mass], on his way to [the] sacristy, [Pio] stopped, looked about him, and then found Wanda in the crowd. She says: "I shall never forget his glance. Smiling, he came even closer to me, patted me on the head, and said, 'Adesso, va bene?' ('Now you are OK?') I did not answer; I had no time. What could I say? But ... I knew he recognized me. In this moment I also knew that it wasn't because of a wrong diagnosis that I had found myself suddenly well several years earlier."

> Wanda Poltawska's testimony is found in
> *The Voice of Padre Pio*, Vol. 32, No. 1, 2002, 19;
> the letters from Cardinal Wojtyla, now Pope John Paul II,
> are in the friary archives

Dear Lord, you honored the cardinal's faith in Pio's intercessory prayer with a complete cure.

Padre Pio, now closer to God than ever, pray for me and for all those I hold in my heart who need healing.

～ 335. Life Is Short: Do Good While You Can ～

Man ... lives the few days of his vain life, which he passes like a shadow.

ECCLESIASTES 6:12

May the heavenly Child always be at the center of your heart; may he govern it, enlighten it, vivify it, and transform it to his eternal love! This is my sincere and affectionate wish, which I sent you from far away on Christmas Day. This is also the most cordial prayer I said for you on that day, and which I will continue to say always and assiduously before Jesus. Therefore, accept this prayer and good wish of mine, as the most beautiful expression of the heart of he who sincerely loves you with paternal tenderness before Jesus.

And then, I must not let the first month of the year pass, my dearest daughter, without sending your soul greetings from mine, and to assure you more and more of the affection my heart nurtures for yours, never ceasing to desire for both all sorts of blessings and spiritual happiness. But, my good daughter, I warmly recommend that poor [heart] of yours to you. Take care to render it, daily, more and more pleasing to our most sweet Savior, and see to it that the present year is more fertile in good works than the last, as, with the same speed with which the years pass by and eternity becomes closer, we must redouble our courage and raise our spirit to God, serving him with greater diligence in everything that our vocation and Christian profession require of us.

Letters, Vol. 3, 490–91

Lord, as the days of my life dwindle, help me to live each one joyfully and in a way that adds my mite to the coming of your kingdom.

∼ 336. The Laughter of Happy Men ∼

Thus says the Lord: Behold, I will restore the fortunes of the tents of Jacob, and have compassion on his dwellings; the city shall be rebuilt upon its mound, and the palace shall stand where it used to be. Out of them shall come songs of thanksgiving, and the voices of those who make merry.

JEREMIAH 30:18-19

[Padre Aurelio knew Padre Pio for over fifty years. Between 1916 and 1918, when Aurelio was a seminarian, Padre Pio was the director. Padre Aurelio recalls:]

He was very paternal and understanding. There was ... one exception: He was very strict when we boys would talk in church.... But he would close his eyes to everything else, always....

We were impressed by his humanity, even more than by his holiness. He understood us, he had compassion, and he was especially sympathetic. After we were ordained and lived with him as priests, he was holy, yes,... but we would go to him because in him we found sympathy, charity, and understanding.... During World War I we had nothing to eat, so the boys used to steal bread and other things [from the kitchen].... Padre Pio knew of it; he didn't condone it but he let it go....

He also had a fine sense of humor. One day in 1917 we played a practical joke.... We had something like a kite, but it was very, very big. Underneath it we put a little bomb and a little lamp attached to it.... We had a long rope tied to the end of the kite. For about an hour we flew the kite all around the sky. The people saw it and were terrified. Padre Pio and the chief of police knew all about it, but they let us enjoy the joke.

A Padre Pio Profile, 112–14

Lord, in World War II you protected the home of your saint, San Giovanni Rotondo, from bombing, even though nearby towns were left as rubble. Yet this great mystic had a wondrous ability to laugh at himself and to appreciate other people's attempts to lighten life with humor, including practical jokes. Help me too, Lord, to never take myself too seriously and to keep my sense of humor.

∼ 337. Peace ∼

Peace I leave with you; my peace I give to you; not as the world gives do I give to you. Let not your hearts be troubled, neither let them be afraid.

JOHN 14:27

We should always keep before our mental gaze our priestly state and not stop advancing in this beautiful virtue [of simplicity], until we are able to say with St. Paul to every class of people in all sincerity: *Be imitators of me as I am of Christ.* But we will never advance even a single step in this virtue if we do not strive to live in a holy and immutable peace. Jesus' yoke is easy and his burden light, so we should not allow the enemy to creep into our hearts and rob us of this peace.

Peace is simplicity of heart, serenity of mind, tranquility of soul, the bond of love. Peace means order, harmony in our whole being; it means continual contentment springing from the knowledge of a good conscience; it is the holy joy of a heart in which God reigns. Peace is the way to perfection; indeed, in peace is perfection to be found.

The devil, who is well aware of all this, makes every effort to have us lose our peace. We should be on the alert for every slightest sign of agitation, and as soon as we realize we have fallen into dejection, we must turn to God with filial confidence and abandon ourselves completely to him. All agitation on our part is very displeasing to Jesus, since such uneasiness is never unaccompanied by imperfection and can always be traced to egoism and self-love.

Letters, Vol. 1, 678–79

Lord, give me your peace, which does not depend upon things going well but can exist at the bottom of the heart that is all yours, no matter what hurricanes roar on life's surface.

~ 338. Where God Is, There Is No Room for Fear ~

And behold, Jesus met them and said, "Hail!" And they came up and took hold of his feet and worshiped him. Then Jesus said to them, "Do not be afraid."

MATTHEW 28:9-10

The soul must be saddened by one thing alone, offending God, and even in this we must be very cautious. We must be sorry, it is true, for our failings, but with a calm sorrow while we continue to trust in the divine mercy. We should also guard against certain reproaches and remorseful feelings in our own regard, for more often than not these come from the devil with a view to disturbing the peace we enjoy in God.

If similar reproaches and remorse serve to humble us and make us careful to act well, without depriving us of our trust in God, we may be sure they come from God. But if they cause us confusion and make us fearful, diffident, slothful, and remiss in doing good, we may be certain they come from the devil, and as such we must drive them away and take refuge in confidence in God. If we keep our souls calm and peaceful in every difficult situation, we will gain much ground in the ways of God; on the other hand, if we lose this peace, everything we do with a view to eternal life will yield little or no fruit.

From what I have said ... you will already understand how far I am from sharing ... some of your secret anxieties about your spiritual state. I beg you ... to set aside these excessive and useless anxieties. The Lord is with you, and there is no room for fear.

Letters, Vol. 1, 679

Help me remember, Lord, that you want me to not be afraid but to simply have confidence in your care of me in every situation.

∼ 339. Simplicity ∼

Now they were bringing even infants to him that he might touch them; and when the disciples saw it, they rebuked them. But Jesus called them to him, saying, "Let the children come to me, and do not hinder them; for to such belongs the kingdom of God. Truly, I say to you, whoever does not receive the kingdom of God like a child shall not enter it."

LUKE 18:15-17

Jesus likes to give himself to simple souls; we must make an effort to acquire this beautiful virtue of simplicity and to hold it in great esteem. Jesus said: *Unless you turn and become like children, you will never enter the kingdom of heaven.* But before he taught us this by his words, he had already put it into practice. He became a child and gave us the example of that simplicity he was to teach us later also by his words.

Let us empty our hearts and keep far from us all human prudence. We must try to keep our thoughts pure, our ideas upright and honest, and our intentions holy. We should also endeavor to have a will that seeks nothing but God and his glory. If we make every effort to advance in this beautiful virtue, he who teaches it will enrich us continually with new light and new heavenly favors.

Letters, Vol. 1, 677–78

Lord, I have seen a child leap off a high wall into his father's arms. Help me to leap into your arms with the same confidence.

∼ 340. The Greatness of God ∼

My soul magnifies the Lord, and my spirit rejoices in God my Savior.
LUKE 1:46-47

As the days pass, I see ever more clearly the greatness of God, and in this light, which grows brighter and brighter, my soul burns with the desire to be united to him by indissoluble bonds. By this light I see how deserving this adorable Lord is of our love and feel more and more inflamed with love for him. But, dear God! This very desire to be united with him, to love him as much as a creature can, causes in me the keenest suffering, since I see more and more clearly how far I am from the certain possession of him without fear of losing him.

Letters, Vol. 1, 412

Lord, do not ever let me be separated from you, and give me an ever clearer understanding of your greatness and glory.

∼ 341. The Transcendence of God ∼

There is a God in heaven who reveals mysteries.
DANIEL 2:28

On ... occasions, although I am not thinking of such a thing at all, my soul goes on fire with the most keen desire to possess Jesus entirely. Then with an indescribable vividness communicated to my soul by the Lord, I am shown as in a mirror my whole future life as nothing but a martyrdom. Without knowing why, and with unspeakable love, I yearn for death. Despite all my efforts I am driven to ask God with tears in my eyes to let me be taken from this exile. I feel inflamed with such a lively and ardent desire to please God and am gripped by such a fear of falling into the slightest imperfection that I would like to flee from all dealings with creatures.

Simultaneously, however, another desire rises up like a giant in my heart, the longing to be in the midst of all peoples, to proclaim at the top of my voice who this great God of mercy is. Now and then ... the Lord [also] grants me certain pleasures that even I myself do not understand. The happiness I experience is so extreme that I would like to share it with others so that they might help me to thank the Lord.

Again, when I am busy about even indifferent things, a mere word about God or the sudden thought of some such word affects me so deeply that I am carried out of myself. Then the Lord usually grants me the grace of revealing to me some secrets, which remain indelibly impressed on my soul. I am unable, however, to describe [them],... for ... I have no adequate words for the purpose. Even the secrets which I succeed to some extent in putting into words lose so much of their splendor that I regard myself with compassion and disgust.

Letters, Vol. 1, 413–14

Lord, no one knows you as do the saints, and even they cannot plumb your depths and heights. You are both gloriously above us and within us. Help me to know you as much as this little brain and heart can.

⁓ 342. A Hymn of Praise ⁓

Sing a hymn of praise; bless the Lord for all his works.

SIRACH 39:14

Beloved daughter of the heavenly Father and betrothed of his Son: May the divine Spirit come down into your heart and fill it entirely with heavenly charisms. How good our God is, who lavished so many graces upon us and loves us so dearly although we do not deserve it. May he be forever blessed by all creatures.

At the opening of the sacred novena in honor of the holy Child Jesus, I felt my soul being born, as it were, to a new life. My heart felt too small to contain the heavenly favors, and my soul seemed to disintegrate in the presence of this God, who took human flesh for our sake. How can we help loving him more and more ardently? Oh, let us draw near to the Child Jesus with hearts free from sin, that we may discover how sweet and delightful it is to love him.

I will never fail to pray to this divine Child for all men, and much more will I pray during these holy days. I will pray especially for you and for all those whom you have so much at heart. I will ask him to give you a share of those charisms he has poured out and continues to pour all the time into my own soul.

Letters, Vol. 2, 288–89

Lord, today I will praise and bless you for all the good you do me. May your holy name always incite me to praise you and give thanks.

∼ 343. Jesus Holds You Tightly in the Dark ∼

I adjure you, O daughters of Jerusalem, if you find my beloved, that you tell him I am sick with love.

SONG OF SONGS 5:8

You ... complain about your being in darkness and aridity. You seek your God, you sigh for him, you call him, and you cannot find him.

Does it appear to you that God has hidden himself, that he has abandoned you?

But I repeat, do not fear: Jesus is with you, and you are with him! In darkness, tribulation, anxiety of spirit, Jesus is with you. You see nothing but darkness in your spirit, and I assure you on behalf of God that the light of the Lord fills and totally surrounds your spirit. It is a defect of the eye, which cannot yet bear this most pure light. But wait until the eye recovers completely, and then you will certainly see this light. You see yourself in tribulation, and God repeats to you through the mouth of authority: *I will be with him in trouble* (Ps 91 [90]:15). You believe you are abandoned, and I assure you that Jesus is holding you more tightly than ever to his divine heart.

Letters, Vol. 3, 978–79

My soul is dry today. I feel no joy in you, Lord, nor any sense of your presence. Yet Padre Pio assures me that this is all a game of love, that you absent yourself, Lord, so that I may increase in desire for you. I pray this is so. I pray that you aren't leaving me because of my spiritual sloth!

∽ 344. In God's Arms ∽

He who keeps his commandment abides in God, and God in him.
1 JOHN 3:24, Challoner-Rheims

You are afraid of being lost and of having already lost God, and you ask me where he is to be found! He is within you, and you are in him! You are like the passenger shut up in his cabin on the ship, who doesn't see the ship or notice that it is moving! He is merely upset by its vibration, and he fears he will be shipwrecked and that the ship will plunge to the bottom of the ocean. However, although he doesn't see it, he is on the ship, and although it seems to him that the ship is standing still, it is actually moving and traveling several knots an hour. He is afraid it will sink, that the vibrations due to its movement are signs of imminent disaster, whereas the ship is afloat and vibrates precisely because it is breasting the waves and forging ahead.

To this passenger who complains that he is at a standstill and looks for a ship to rescue him, we can answer: If you go out of your cabin for a moment into the open air, you will see that you are on the ship, that it is afloat and forging ahead at a great speed, and that it is vibrating by reason of the force with which it breasts and cleaves the waves. Have no fear, then, of shipwreck, and don't even ask where the Lord is, because in him and in his arms no misfortune of any kind can befall us.

Letters, Vol. 3, 981–82,
in much of which Pio is quoting his spiritual director,
Padre Benedetto

Lord, how I wish I could know that you are within me and I within you. But what I do not know experientially I will cling to by faith and hope.

∼ 345. A New Behavior of Love ∼

"Drink deeply, O Lovers!"

SONG OF SONGS 5:1

The bitterness of love is still sweet and its weight suave. Therefore, why do you continually say, when feeling its great transports, that you are unable to contain it? Your heart is small, but it is expandable, and when it can no longer contain the grandeur of the Beloved and resist its immense pressure, do not fear, because he is both inside and out; by pouring himself into the interior, he will surround the walls. Like an open shell in the ocean, you will drink your fill, and exuberantly you will be surrounded and carried along by his power.

In a short while you will no longer be new to this new behavior of love, and its assaults will no longer be unbearable for you. Accustomed to the usual flames, you will call it into competition, and you will struggle like Jacob with the angel [Genesis 32:22ff], without falling. Do not complain if you are still unable to definitively embrace the Supreme Good. The time will come when you will possess it definitively and totally.

Letters, Vol. 3, 1040–41

Lord, help me to love you as your saints do.

∼ 346. Worry: A Sign of Little Trust in the Lord ∼

Therefore I tell you, do not be anxious.... Which of you by being anxious can add one cubit to his span of life?

MATTHEW 6:25, 27

I see in a bad light your feverish anxiety about the poor sufferer [your sick sister]. It seems to me that the time has come to put an end to this once and for all. Your attitude toward her illness is a sign that you have little trust in the Lord, and this seriously wounds the heart of the one who has taken it upon himself to look after you and direct you. May the good God enlighten you with regard to my rightful dissatisfaction on this score.

You are also worried about your sister's enemies, who laugh behind her back because of her sufferings. But tell me, please, what more can you expect from them, if they are enemies? Let us remember that if they are her enemies, they are also God's enemies. Well, then, the enemies of God insult the cross and all those who are crucified upon it with the Son of God. For you this ought to be a source of gladness, as it is for many souls.

Letters, Vol. 2, 411–12

Lord, I thank you that I worry less today than years ago. It heartens me, dear God, to see that my soul has made some progress.

~ 347. The Company of Those Who Believe ~

They devoted themselves to the apostles' teaching and fellowship, to the breaking of bread [the Eucharist] and the prayers.... Now the company of those who believed were of one heart and soul.

ACTS 2:42; 4:32

The Third Order of St. Francis [see page 213] has always been, and is still, even more so today, an important factor in seeing that humanity returns to the light of faith, to the healthy principles of Christian morals.... However, a well-organized and assiduous propagation is necessary, enabling all to understand the great and noble goal, which is the sanctification of one's own soul, the reformation of society, the reformation of the family, [and] spiritual graces ... connected to this.

Letters, Vol. 3, 1100–1

Lord, I thank you for the Third Order of St. Francis and for all the groups in the Church and in Christianity where people band together to serve you. I thank you too, Lord, for my own spiritual companions, who inspire and encourage me.

~ 348. Which Master Do I Serve? ~

No servant can serve two masters; for either he will hate the one and love the other, or he will be devoted to the one and despise the other. You cannot serve God and mammon.

LUKE 16:13

Let us also ask our good Jesus for the humility, trust, and faith of our dear saint [St. Clare, foundress with St. Francis of Assisi of the Poor Clares, the first women's branch of the Franciscans]; let us pray fervently to Jesus like her. Let us abandon ourselves to him, detaching ourselves from this lying world, where everything is folly and vanity. Everything passes; only God remains for the soul, if it knows how to love him well.

Letters, Vol. 3, 1104–5

Lord, there are so many things in the world I love—things beautiful, bright, and true—from roses and sunshine to good people who love you. Help me to love them all in you and for you, so that you and the kingdom always have first place in my heart.

∼ 349. The Know-It-All ∼

Let no one deceive himself. If any one among you thinks that he is wise in this age, let him become a fool that he may become wise. For the wisdom of this world is folly with God. For it is written, "He catches the wise in their craftiness."

1 CORINTHIANS 3:18-19

[Padre Pellegrino, who lived with Padre Pio for years, recalls:]

The sun had already set behind the dark mountain. In the friary orchard, Padre Pio, sitting on a little wall, was surrounded by new and old friends. These were spread out, some sitting, some standing, in the farmyard, [where they threshed] ... the grain gathered by the mendicant friars. The subject under discussion that evening was the obligation to study ethics, Christian morality, and, in particular, Catholic morality. [When the bell rang for prayers] one person who, in my opinion, gave himself too many airs, and who, at times, interpreted even Padre Pio's advice for his own personal use, hurried to have the last word: "Only he who has studied morality in depth will save his soul." Padre Pio, who, after having made a move to rise, sat down again in order to listen to the friend's remark, as if he desired to take it in, finally rose to his feet, stretched out his arm toward the ... [speaker], and with a radiant smile said to him: "Don't play the know-it-all."

The Voice of Padre Pio, Vol. 28, No. 6, 1988, 11

Lord, help me to always know how little I know about your judgments and your ways.

∼ 350. Human Aversion to Suffering ∼

He withdrew from them about a stone's throw, and knelt down and prayed, "Father, if thou art willing, remove this cup from me; nevertheless not my will, but thine, be done."

LUKE 22:41-42

You asked me to throw some light on your attitude toward suffering and told me that you often go in search of comfort, that nature cries out to be spared, and hence it seems to you that your love for God is not sincere and perfect. But be consoled on this score, because your suffering is as God wills. If nature suffers and demands its rights, this is a condition of man's life as a wayfarer. Secretly and tacitly he feels the pain of suffering and naturally wants to escape from it, for man was created to enjoy happiness, and trials are a consequence of sin. As long as we remain in this world we shall always feel a natural aversion for suffering. This is a chain that will accompany us everywhere.

You may be quite sure that if in the higher part, at the apex of our spirit, we desire the cross and therefore embrace and submit to it for love of God, this will not prevent us from feeling in the lower part of the soul the demands of nature, which objects to suffering. In point of fact, who more than our divine Master loved the cross? Well, then, his most holy humanity prayed during his voluntary agony that the chalice might pass from him if possible.

You must agree with me that your spirit is always willing to do God's will and makes every effort to do it. It is the flesh ... that is weak, but God wants the spirit.... Let nature object, then,... for this feeling does not depend on the will, and therefore it does not make us guilty before God. Rather does it become a cause of merit for us if we hold it in check and subdue it.

Letters, Vol. 2, 437

If Padre Pio never said anything else, this is enough. So many times, Lord, I have felt like such a wimp because, while offering up pain or suffering, I was also praying frantically for you to take it away. My aversion to all the bad stuff of life and my desire to be healthy and happy made me feel as if I had no chance to ever become holy or even truly to love you. But I see now that my being made, as Pio says, for happiness is always going to make me feel as I do. You will be satisfied that in my will I desire to have no will but yours, whatever happens to me. Thank you, God, and thank you, Padre Pio!

～ 351. The Trial of Abandonment ～

And at the ninth hour Jesus cried with a loud voice,... "My God, my God, why hast thou forsaken me?"

MARK 15:34

Persevere in your vocation that our Lord calls you to, and do not be afraid, because in this perseverance you will sanctify yourself. I know, my beloved son, that you suffer, but resign yourself, because suffering borne in a Christian manner will sanctify you. You suffer, but you must rejoice too, because one day your suffering will change into joy. You suffer, but have no fear, because Jesus repeats to you with the prophet: "I will be with him in trouble." You suffer, but you must know that Jesus himself suffers in you, for you, and with you.

Jesus has not abandoned you, and he will not abandon you. Exclaim with him on the cross: "My God, my God, why have you abandoned me?" But consider, my son, that the suffering humanity of our Lord was never really abandoned by the divinity. Yes, you suffer all the effects of divine abandonment, but you were never abandoned.

This is so for souls that are enamored of the cross of Jesus and that have chosen him as their portion. They suffer everything—the trial of abandonment too—but God is always with them. Therefore, rest assured that Jesus is with you.

Letter to Frater Samuel, a spiritual son, November 15, 1918

Lord, sometimes you truly seem to have abandoned me. But I will cling by faith to the belief that you are simply so close that my eyes cannot focus on you. Come, Lord Jesus; deliver me and heal me.

∼ 352. Bringing the Gospel to Others ∼

I did not shrink from declaring to you anything that was profitable, and teaching you in public and from house to house, testifying both to Jews and to Greeks of repentance to God and of faith in our Lord Jesus Christ.... But I do not account my life of any value nor as precious to myself, if only I may accomplish my course and the ministry which I received from the Lord Jesus, to testify to the gospel of the grace of God.

ACTS 20:20-21, 24

The clock is striking midnight and, worn out by the immense amount of work which kept me busy all day, I am taking up my pen [because ordered to do so] to write you something about my soul. Woe is me! I can find no rest, weary as I am and immersed in extreme grief. In the most hopeless desolation, in the most agonizing affliction, not because I fail to find my God but because I am not winning over all my brothers to God.... I am seeking their salvation from God, but I don't know whether God accepts any of my groanings. Indeed, I may add that I doubt at times whether I myself even possess the grace of God....

I am in the dark as to whether the Lord accepts what I am striving to do to relieve the misery of others and by observing the continual aridity of my own heart, its restlessness and anxiety at the sight of so many suffering souls and my inability to help them ... at certain moments, if I were not sustained by divine grace, I should be on the point of dying.... Nothing but submission to the divine will brings me some little peace. But then my gaze falls once more on my brothers, by whom I am surrounded, and I am plunged again in deep distress. Exceeding sweetness as the soul turns its gaze on God, extreme distress as it turns on the neighbor. Between these two extremes ... I see myself in continual agony without ever dying.

Letters, Vol. 1, 1284–85

Padre Pio, pray for me that the Lord will give me something of your completely unselfish love for all people. Lord, I thank you for calling people like St. Paul and St. Pio to war with the world, the flesh, and the devil on behalf of others' salvation. May their prayerful intercession bring your kingdom nearer.

∼ 353. Chosen for a Mission ∼

You did not choose me, but I chose you and appointed you that you should go and bear fruit.

JOHN 15:16

Where better could I serve you, O Lord, if not ... under the banner of the Poor One of Assisi?... [Jesus], seeing my embarrassment, smiled at length, and that smile left an ineffable sweetness in my heart, so that sometimes I truly felt it so near that I thought I saw his shadow. And my flesh, my entire being, rejoiced in the Savior, in my God. O my God, may infinite praise and thanks be rendered to you.... You ... confided a very great mission to your son, a mission which is known to you and me alone. Dear God! My Father! How have I corresponded to that mission?! I don't know. I only know that perhaps I should have done more, and [this] is the reason for my present uneasiness of heart....

Therefore, arise once again, O Lord, and free me first and foremost from myself; do not allow he whom you called ... to be lost. Therefore, arise once again, O Lord, and confirm in your grace those whom you confided to me, and don't permit any of them to be lost.

Written on Pio's November 1922 retreat

Lord, call me to be your own eternally, as you called Pio. Let me praise you forever. Padre Pio, pray for me.

～ 354. The Virtue That Triumphs Over God Himself ～

Take my yoke upon you, and learn from me; for I am gentle and lowly in heart, and you will find rest for your souls.

MATTHEW 11:29

Be vigilant, and fortify yourself more and more with prayer and the beautiful virtue of humility. You will find that you will not be submerged in the stormy sea. May the little ship of your spirit have the strong anchor of trust in divine goodness, and keep before the eyes of your soul God's promise: Whoever confides in him will not be confused, and he "opposes the proud but gives grace to the humble," that we should "watch and pray that we might not enter into temptation."

So when you feel oppressed by temptation, the means to oblige God to come to your aid is through humility of spirit, contrition of heart, and confident prayer. It is impossible for God to be displeased with this demonstration, impossible for him not to come to our aid and give in. It is true that God's power triumphs over everything; but humble and suffering prayer triumphs over God himself!...

By constantly using these methods, you will always succeed in rendering yourself pleasing to God. You will envelop his justice in loving pity, to the point of obtaining everything you wish from him: forgiveness for your sins, the grace to overcome all your enemies, holiness, and eternal health.

> August 27, 1915, letter to a spiritual daughter,
> quoted in *The Voice of Padre Pio*, Vol. 30, No. 7, 2000, 7

Lord, help me make up for all my faults and failings by the gift of humility. St. Pio, pray for me to receive this grace.

~ 355. The Lord's Peace ~

May the Lord bless his people with peace!

PSALM 29:11

We must take care never to be upset by any disaster whatsoever which may befall us, for perturbation is never free from imperfection, originating as it does in egoism and self-love. When we are perturbed, the enemy's attacks are more frequent and direct, for he takes advantage of our natural weakness, which prevents us from following the straight path of virtue. The enemy of our salvation knows only too well that peace of heart is a sure sign of the divine assistance, and hence he lets slip no opportunity to make us lose this peace. We must therefore always be on our guard in this respect. Jesus will help us.

Letters, Vol. 1, 109–10

Lord, give your peace to me and to all those I love and pray for.

～ 356. For the Good of Souls ～

And he said to them, "Go into all the world and preach the gospel to the whole creation."

MARK 16:15

Lift up your heart all the time, and let us pray with a pure heart, a contrite and humble heart, so that the enemy may be quite unable to touch your soul in this extreme trial by fire, to which God in his mercy has been pleased to subject you. For my own part I cannot but share with you willingly the suffering that weighs upon you, while praying more diligently to the good God for you and wishing you from our most sweet Jesus the spiritual and material strength to pass through the final trial of his fatherly love for you. This trial, moreover, will turn out to be for God's glory, your own merit, and the good of many souls.

Letters, Vol. 2, 527–28

Lord, may your kingdom come in me and in every soul. May every beat of my heart repeat this prayer as long as I live.

~ 357. Easing Burdens ~

Therefore confess your sins to one another, and pray for one another, that you may be healed.

JAMES 5:16

A person whose heart is brimming over with sorrow can never speak too much, can never sufficiently disclose his wounds to the one appointed by God to direct him.

Letters, Vol. 1, 727

What consolation to see that God allows us to ease our burdens by talking about them. Help me, Lord, to tread the fine line between sharing with those who are my prayer partners, spiritual directors, or confessors and keeping quiet when sharing would be gossip or would lower someone's esteem for a third party.

~ 358. A Guiding Hand ~

Where there is no guidance, a people falls; but in an abundance of counselors there is safety.

PROVERBS 11:14

I am still tormented continually by the snares of the enemy. However, I have noticed in myself for several days now an inexplicable spiritual happiness. I am unaware of the cause of this. I no longer experience the great difficulty I had formerly in resigning myself to God's will. In fact, I drive away the tempter's slanderous attacks with such ease that I feel neither annoyed nor wearied.

But is this a good or a bad sign? It crosses my mind that the reason for this is a cooling off in my love for God. I leave it to you to imagine how bitter this thought is for me. In the meantime, nobody but you can rid my mind of these doubts.

Letters, Vol. 1, 260–61

Lord, even saints are not omnipotent. The young Padre Pio needed advising from Padre Benedetto and Padre Agostino, his two spiritual directors. Give me the humility always to seek advice and not set myself up as "spiritually wise."

∼ 359. Daily Prayer ∼

I will meditate on thy precepts, and fix my eyes on thy ways.
PSALM 119:15

As regards ... meditation, I exhort you to establish at least two periods a day for this purpose. Try to spend not less than half an hour for each period. Try to see that those periods of meditation are possibly in the morning, in order to prepare yourself for the battle, and in the evening, in order to purify your soul from any earthly affections which have become attached to it during the day. Try to take up once again the practice of the holy hour [prayer before the Blessed Sacrament], which you used to do before—always, however, within the limits of possibility, without causing yourself serious discomfort.

Letters, Vol. 3, 257

Lord, help me to pray regularly and before I begin each day. Help me also to more regularly spend a little time with you before bed.

∼ 360. God's Peace ∼

...through the tender mercy of our God, when the day shall dawn upon us from on high to give light to those who sit in darkness and in the shadow of death, to guide our feet into the way of peace.

LUKE 1:78-79

Remember ... that spiritual peace can be maintained even in the midst of all the storms of this life. As you know very well, it consists essentially in peaceful relations with those around us, wishing them well in all things. It also consists in being on good terms with God through sanctifying grace. The proof that we are united to God is our moral certainty of not having any mortal sin on our conscience.

To sum up, peace consists in having achieved victory over the world, the devil, and our own passions. Tell me now if it is not true that this peace, which Jesus has brought us, can continue quite well to be ours not merely when we enjoy abundant spiritual consolations but when the howling and shrieking of the enemy fills our hearts with pain and grief.

Letters, Vol. 2, 202

Lord, grant me the peace you alone can give.

∼ 361. Loving My Own Soul ∼

You shall love your neighbor as yourself.

LEVITICUS 19:18

May it please Jesus soon to reunite our scattered brethren [due to World War I service] for the good of his chosen ones. God knows how much I am praying for the end of this trial, but I have no words to tell you how much I pray God to comfort you and sanctify you more and more. I can only say that I truly love your soul; I love it incomparably, just as I love my own, and I desire for you the height of Christian perfection for which you yourself ardently long. Every sacrifice which your soul makes, every good it does, is directed to God for the sanctification of all.

Letters, Vol. 1, 983

Lord, thank you for the reminder that I must love my own soul as well as that of my neighbor.

～ 362. Thankfulness ～

Sing psalms and hymns and spiritual songs with thankfulness in your hearts to God.

COLOSSIANS 3:16

My soul is full of gratitude to God for the many victories it obtains at every instant, and I cannot refrain from uttering endless hymns of blessing to this great and munificent God. Blessed be the Lord for this great goodness! Blessed be his great mercy! Eternal praise be to such tender and loving compassion.

Letters, Vol. 1, 730

Lord, I am grateful for all you have done for me. Give me the grace of being ever more grateful.

∼ 363. Struggling Against Myself ∼

We know that the law is spiritual; but I am carnal.... But if Christ is in you, although your bodies are dead because of sin, your spirits are alive because of righteousness.... We ourselves, who have the first fruits of the Spirit, groan inwardly as we wait for adoption as sons.... Likewise the Spirit helps us in our weakness.

ROMANS 7:14; 8:10, 23, 26

Life is nothing but a continual struggle against one's self, and it does not open to beauty without the price of suffering.

Have a Good Day, 139
quoting *Notizie su Padre Pio,* Angela Serritelli's Italian manuscript

Lord, may the sufferings I and all I care about have endured open us to the beauty of your kingdom.

∼ 364. Trust ∼

Blessed be the Lord! for he has heard the voice of my supplications. The Lord is my strength and my shield; in him my heart trusts; so I am helped, and my heart exults, and with my song I give thanks to him.

PSALM 28:6-7

Oh, how good God is, my dearest Lauretta! It is true that he is good to all, but he is particularly good to those who place all their trust in him.

Letters, Vol. 3, 917

I trust you, Jesus. Increase my trust!

∼ 365. Loving God and All Creation ∼

And God saw everything that he had made, and behold, it was very good.

GENESIS 1:31

Padre Pio is the real poet of life who knows how to praise and thank God. He once said: "Whoever wants to love can. It is enough to remove what is disorder. Entering into order we love God!"

A friar exclaimed: "Yes, yes, stripping ourselves of the affection of all creatures!"

"No," [Pio responded,] "loving God and all creation."

Padre Alessandro of Ripabottoni,
recalling his confrere in *Voice of Padre Pio*, Vol. 27,
Summer 1997, 7

Dear Pio, true son of St. Francis, pray for us, that we may joyfully use the good things God has made for us in order to serve him and to help our needy and suffering brothers, whatever form their distress takes. Above all, may we love God with a generosity approaching your own total self-donation, until we come at last to mingle merrily at the eternal banquet with you and all the saints. Amen.

Further Reading

Alessandro of Ripabottoni. *Padre Pio of Pietrelcina: Everybody's Cyrenean.* Italy: Our Lady of Grace Capuchin Friary, 2nd edition, 1996.

Ruffin, Bernard C. *Padre Pio: The True Story.* Huntington, Ind.: Our Sunday Visitor, 1991.

Schug, John A. *A Padre Pio Profile.* Petersham, Mass.: St. Bede's, 1988.

Treece, Patricia. *Apparitions of Modern Saints: Appearances of Thérèse of Lisieux, Padre Pio, Don Bosco, and Others.* Ann Arbor, Mich.: Servant, 2001.

Treece, Patricia. *Meet Padre Pio: Beloved Mystic, Miracle Worker, and Spiritual Guide.* Ann Arbor, Mich.: Servant, 2001.

Treece, Patricia. *Nothing Short of a Miracle.* Huntington, Ind.: Our Sunday Visitor, 1994.

Treece, Patricia. *Quiet Moments With Padre Pio: 120 Daily Readings.* Ann Arbor, Mich.: Servant, 1999.

Treece, Patricia. *The Sanctified Body.* New York: Doubleday, 1989. Currently out of print.

To purchase books, you may contact the following sources:

Our Lady of Grace Capuchin Friary
71013 San Giovanni Rotondo, FG, Italy

National Centre for Padre Pio, Inc.
Mrs. Vera Calandra
2213 Old Route 100
Barto, PA 19504
Telephone: 610-845-3000

Books from Servant and OSV may be found at your local bookstore
or may be ordered direct from the publisher:
Servant 1-800-458-8505 and OSV 1-800-348-2440